LINGUISTICS AND THE FORMAL SCIENCES

The formal sciences, particularly mathematics, have had a profound influence on the development of linguistics. This insightful overview looks at techniques that were introduced in the fields of mathematics, logic, and philosophy during the twentieth century, and explores their effect on the work of various linguists. In particular, it discusses the foundations crisis that destabilised mathematics at the start of the twentieth century, the numerous related movements which sought to respond to this crisis, and how they influenced the development of syntactic theory in the 1950s. This book provides a ground-breaking and detailed reassessment of Chomsky's early work, and concludes by discussing the resulting major consequences for current syntactic theory. Informative and revealing, this book will be invaluable to all those working in formal linguistics, in particular those interested in its history and development.

MARCUS TOMALIN is a Fellow of Downing College, University of Cambridge. His academic interests are wide-ranging and include syntactic theory, the history of linguistics, mathematical models of linguistic theory development, and the modelling of syntactic structure in large vocabulary speech recognition systems. He publishes regularly on these diverse topics in various international journals.

CAMBRIDGE STUDIES IN LINGUISTICS

General Editors: P. AUSTIN, J. BRESNAN, B. COMRIE,
S. CRAIN, W. DRESSLER, C. J. EWEN, R. LASS,
D. LIGHTFOOT, K. RICE, I. ROBERTS, S. ROMAINE,
N. V. SMITH

Linguistics and the Formal Sciences

The Origins of Generative Grammar

In this series

71 KNUD LAMBRECHT: *Information structure and sentence form: topic, focus, and the mental representation of discourse referents*
72 LUIGI BURZIO: *Principles of English stress*
73 JOHN A. HAWKINS: *A performance theory of order and constituency*
74 ALICE C. HARRIS and LYLE CAMPBELL: *Historical syntax in cross-linguistic perspective*
75 LILIANE HAEGEMAN: *The syntax of negation*
76 PAUL GORREL: *Syntax and parsing*
77 GUGLIELMO CINQUE: *Italian syntax and universal grammar*
78 HENRY SMITH: *Restrictiveness in case theory*
79 D. ROBERT LADD: *Intonational morphology*
80 ANDREA MORO: *The raising of predicates: predicative noun phrases and the theory of clause structure*
81 ROGER LASS: *Historical linguistics and language change*
82 JOHN M. ANDERSON: *A notional theory of syntactic categories*
83 BERND HEINE: *Possession: cognitive sources, forces and grammaticalization*
84 NOMI ERTESCHIK-SHIR: *The dynamics of focus structure*
85 JOHN COLEMAN: *Phonological representations: their names, forms and powers*
86 CHRISTINA Y. BETHIN: *Slavic prosody: language change and phonological theory*
87 BARBARA DANCYGIER: *Conditionals and prediction*
88 CLAIRE LEFEBVRE: *Creole genesis and the acquisition of grammar: the case of Haitian creole*
89 HEINZ GIEGERICH: *Lexical strata in English*
90 KEREN RICE: *Morpheme order and semantic scope*
91 APRIL MCMAHON: *Lexical phonology and the history of English*
92 MATTHEW Y. CHEN: *Tone Sandhi: patterns across Chinese dialects*
93 GREGORY T. STUMP: *Inflectional morphology: a theory of paradigm structure*
94 JOAN BYBEE: *Phonology and language use*
95 LAURIE BAUER: *Morphological productivity*
96 THOMAS ERNST: *The syntax of adjuncts*
97 ELIZABETH CLOSS TRAUGOTT and RICHARD B. DASHER: *Regularity in semantic change*
98 MAYA HICKMANN: *Children's discourse: Person, space and time across languages*
99 DIANE BLAKEMORE: *Relevance and linguistic meaning: The semantics and pragmatics of discourse markers*
100 IAN ROBERTS and ANNA ROUSSOU: *Syntactic change: a minimalist approach to grammaticalization*
101 DONKA MINKOVA: *Alliteration and sound change in early English*
102 MARK C. BAKER: *Lexical categories: verbs, nouns and adjectives*
103 CARLOTA S. SMITH: *Modes of discourse: the local structure of texts*
104 ROCHELLE LIEBER: *Morphology and lexical semantics*
105 HOLGER DIESSEL: *The acquisition of complex sentences*
106 SHARON INKELAS and CHERYL ZOLL: *Reduplication: doubling in morphology*
107 SUSAN EDWARDS: *Fluent aphasia*
108 BARBARA DANCYGIER and EVE SWEETSER: *Mental spaces in grammar: conditional constructions*
109 MATTHEW BAERMAN, DUNSTAN BROWN and GREVILLE G. CORBETT: *The syntaxmorphology interface: a study of syncretism*
110 MARCUS TOMALIN: *Linguistics and the formal sciences: The origins of generative grammar*

Earlier issues not listed are also available

LINGUISTICS AND THE FORMAL SCIENCES

THE ORIGINS OF GENERATIVE GRAMMAR

MARCUS TOMALIN
Downing College, Cambridge

CAMBRIDGE UNIVERSITY PRESS
Cambridge, New York, Melbourne, Madrid, Cape Town, Singapore, São Paulo

Cambridge University Press
The Edinburgh Building, Cambridge CB2 8RU, UK

Published in the United States of America by Cambridge University Press, New York

www.cambridge.org
Information on this title: www.cambridge.org/9780521854818

© Marcus Tomalin 2006

This publication is in copyright. Subject to statutory exception
and to the provisions of relevant collective licensing agreements,
no reproduction of any part may take place without the written
permission of Cambridge University Press.

First published 2006
This digitally printed version 2008

A catalogue record for this publication is available from the British Library

ISBN 978-0-521-85481-8 hardback
ISBN 978-0-521-06648-8 paperback

Cambridge University Press has no responsibility for the persistence or accuracy of URLs for external or third-party Internet websites referred to in this publication, and does not guarantee that any content on such websites is, or will remain, accurate or appropriate.

since feeling is first
who pays any attention
to the syntax of things
will never wholly kiss you;

e. e. cummings

Contents

	Acknowledgments	*page* xi
	List of mathematical symbols	xii
	List of abbreviations	xiii
1	**Introduction**	1
2	**The consequences of analysis**	21
2.1	Chapter overview	21
2.2	Calculus: doubts and disputes	22
2.3	Rigour, arithmetic, and axioms	26
2.4	Set theory and paradoxes	29
2.5	Logicism	32
2.6	Formalism	38
2.7	Intuitionism	45
2.8	Evangelism and pedagogy	47
3	**Mathematical linguistics**	54
3.1	Chapter overview	54
3.2	Axiomatics	55
3.3	Recursive definitions	60
3.4	Logical systems	67
3.5	Constructional system theory	73
3.6	Constructive nominalism	84
3.7	Formal linguistic theory	88
3.8	New directions	106
4	**Systems of syntax: 1951–1955**	108
4.1	Chapter overview	108
4.2	Biography and influences	109
4.3	Simplicity and grammar	112
4.4	Constructive nominalist syntax	121
4.5	Logic and linguistic theory	125

5	**Transforming generative grammar: 1955–1957**	140
5.1	Chapter overview	140
5.2	Stochastic processes and autonomous grammar	140
5.3	From discovery to evaluation	149
5.4	Constructional levels	156
5.5	Transforming transformations	159
5.6	Recursive rules	168
5.7	Formal syntax	174
6	**Conclusion**	183
	Notes	201
	Bibliography	209
	Index	220

Acknowledgments

I began tentatively to explore some of the topics presented here in November 1995, and, over the intervening years, the central issues have become increasingly distinct. As usual, this process of gradual clarification has involved numerous people, many of whom cannot be mentioned here. Explicit thanks, though, are due to Peter Matthews and Ian Roberts, who encouraged me to pursue this research at an early stage. For similar reasons, I owe a debt of gratitude to Neil Smith and Ted Briscoe, whose comments and advice were of significant value. More recently, I have benefited greatly from discussions with Theresa Biberauer and Fiorien Bonthuis: over the past two years I have repeatedly subjected them both to countless ill-formed questions and incoherent musings, and they have invariably responded with humour, intelligence, and acuity. Less obviously, perhaps, the disparate members of the Cambridge Syntax Reading Group should also be mentioned, since they have contributed to this project considerably, without necessarily realising that they were assisting. In addition, I have been enriched by my connections with various members of Downing College, especially Cathy Phillips, who has watched over me for many years now, and Will Poole, whose restless polymathic brilliance always leads me towards deeper insight.

Obviously, I am indebted to Cambridge University Press for agreeing to publish this book. In particular, Andrew Winnard has been involved in the process of manuscript preparation from the very beginning; he has been my guide throughout.

Heterogeneously, I acknowledge Phil Woodland, for offering me so many opportunities; Gary Thorne, for inexpressible friendship and inspiration; and members of my various families, both the living and the dead, for laughter, confusion, and love. Finally, though, last and most, my accomplice, Sarah, for everything.

While it is hoped that all solecisms, inexactitudes, and stupidities have been unremittingly excised from this text, the remaining errors exist to remind us of our impefections.

This book is dedicated to Arbutus Cove, Victoria B.C., where, turning the corner, I glimpsed the sea.

Mathematical symbols

'∀' indicates universal quantification: '$\forall x[\phi(x)]$' means 'for all x it is the case that $\phi(x)$ holds'.

'∃' indicates existential quantification: '$\exists x[\phi(x)]$' means 'there exists an x for which $\phi(x)$ holds'.

'¬' indicates negation: '$\neg \phi(x)$' means 'it is not the case that $\phi(x)$ holds'.

'→' indicates implication: '$p \to q$' means 'if p, then q'.

'∧' indicates conjunction: '$p \wedge q$' means 'p and q'.

'∨' indicates disjunction: '$p \vee q$' means 'p or q'.

'ℕ' indicates the set of natural numbers: $\mathbb{N} = \{1, 2, 3, ...\}$.

'∈' indicates 'is a member of': '$x \in A$' means 'x is a member of set A'.

'∉' indicates 'is not a member of': '$x \notin A$' means 'x is not a member of set A'.

Abbreviations

Books/Book-length Manuscripts/Theses

LCW	Carnap, R. (1928), *Der logische Aufbau der Welt* [*The Logical Construction of the World*]
LPV	Quine, W. V. O. (1953), *From a Logical Point of View*
LSL	Carnap, R. (1937[1934]), *The Logical Syntax of Language*
LSLT	Chomsky, N. (1975[1955]), *The Logical Structure of Linguistic Theory*
MMH	Chomsky, N. (1979b[1951]), *Morphophonemics of Modern Hebrew*
MP	Chomsky, N. (1995), *The Minimalist Program*
MSL	Harris, Z. S. (1951), *Methods in Structural Linguistics*
PM	Whitehead, A. N. and Russell, B. A. W. (1925[1910]), *Principia Mathematica* [*The Principles of Mathematics*]
SA	Goodman, N. (1951), *The Structure of Appearance*
SS	Chomsky, N. (1957), *Syntactic Structures*

Papers

'LSS'	Chomsky, N. (1955a), 'Logical Syntax and Semantics: Their Linguistic Relevance'
'SCN'	Goodman, N. and Quine, W. V. O. (1947), 'Steps Towards a Constructive Nominalism'
'SSA'	Chomsky, N. (1953), 'Systems of Syntactic Analysis'
'TMDL'	Chomsky, N. (1956), 'Three Models for the Description of Language'

1 *Introduction*

The emergence of Transformational Generative Grammar (TGG) in the 1950s is an event in the history of linguistics that has been recounted many times, in many different ways, by many different people, and since this book is primarily concerned with the development of TGG, some sort of *apologia* is required in order to justify retelling the same story yet again. Accordingly, it is hoped that this introduction will provide the requisite justification, and, in summary explanation, it can be stated at the outset that the main motivation for the particular narration offered here is dissatisfaction – specifically, dissatisfaction stemming from the conviction that none of the existing versions of the TGG narrative provide sufficient information concerning the influence of contemporaneous advances in the formal sciences upon the development of linguistic theory in the twentieth century. If indeed it is the case that this aspect of TGG history has been neglected in the past, then this neglect is certainly surprising, since the earliest proponents of TGG have never disguised the fact that the theory derived considerable inspiration from the formal sciences. For instance, in 1995 (to consider just one example) Chomsky stated explicitly that '[g]enerative grammar can be regarded as a kind of confluence of long-forgotten concerns of the study of language and mind, and new understanding provided by the formal sciences' (Chomsky 1995: 4), and the scientific nature of TGG itself has often been noted over the years. Indeed, it has sometimes been claimed that TGG was a superior linguistic theory primarily because it was more 'scientific' (whatever that means) than the syntactic theories that preceded it. For instance, this was the basic claim made by Robert Lees in his influential 1957 review of *Syntactic Structures*, the text that was partly responsible for inculcating a widespread interest in TGG in the late 1950s. Although Lees' review is well known, it is worth quoting the relevant passage in full:

> Chomsky's book on syntactic structures is one of the first serious attempts on the part of a linguist to construct within the tradition of scientific theory-construction a comprehensive theory of language which may be understood in the same sense that a chemical, biological theory is ordinarily understood

by experts in those fields. It is not a mere reorganisation of the data into a new kind of library catalogue, nor another speculative philosophy about the nature of Man and Language, but rather a rigorous explication of our intuitions about our language in terms of an overt axiom system, the theorems derivable from it, explicit results which may be compared with new data and other intuitions, all based plainly on an overt theory of the internal structure of languages; and it may well provide an opportunity for the application of explicit measures of simplicity to decide preference of one form over another form of grammar. (Lees 1957: 377–378)

It is significant that Lees' assessment of TGG's status as a scientific theory concentrates upon its use of 'an overt axiom system', suggesting that it is this aspect of the approach that enables the linguistic theory developed to be 'rigorous'. The implication here is that, before TGG, linguistic theories did not use this kind of methodology (or at least not so extensively), and that they provided instead either 'a mere reorganization of the data', or else a 'speculative philosophy' which (presumably) could not be validated empirically. Clearly, then, TGG was perceived by some of its first adherents to be a more scientific theory than its predecessors partly because it employed the axiomatic-deductive method and so obtained 'explicit results', and, given this perception, it is curious that the relationship between TGG and the formal sciences that influenced it has not been explored more fully.

Before assessing the existing historiographical studies of TGG, though, it is necessary to clarify some of the terminology used above. For instance, the phrase 'formal sciences' has already been deployed several times without comment and, since it will haunt the ensuing discussion, an initial consideration of its meaning is already overdue. In particular, it should be confessed from the outset that, in the following chapters, this phrase will be used in a rather broad sense. As expected, it will be understood to include various branches of pure mathematics and symbolic logic, but, in addition, it will also be stretched to include various kinds of applied mathematics and logic – an extension that is not free from controversy.[1] For example, specific attempts to use the methodology of classical logic to analyse processes of knowledge acquisition (e.g., logical empiricism) will be considered as instances of 'formal science', as will efforts to explore the logical relationship between language and the real world (e.g., truth-theoretical semantics). Consequently, the phrase will come to denote a rather heterogeneous collection of related theories drawn mainly from mathematics and philosophy, and, at times, it may seem as if it denotes so much that ultimately it denotes nothing at all. However, it is important to recognise that the theories grouped together beneath this umbrella term all utilise some form of the axiomatic-deductive method and that, therefore, despite their many differences, they all involve the deduction of consequences (i.e., theorems) from a small set of intuitively obvious axioms or assumptions, and, as a result, they can be viewed as being unified by the same basic scientific method. In the light of this observation, it should be remembered that not all intellectual enterprises (specifically, not even all sciences) can be pursued by means of this method. In order for an axiomatic-deductive system to be constructed at all, it is necessary to be able to state initial assumptions, to identify primary elements of some kind, and to make valid deductive inferences from these assumptions and elements. There are many areas of research that are not understood with sufficient precision to permit an axiomatic-deductive analysis. However, the 'formal sciences' all attempt to utilise this methodology, and it is one of their characteristic features. Other similarities will be mentioned as and when they become relevant to the discussion sustained in the rest of this book, but, from henceforth, the cautionary quotation marks will be dropped, enabling the 'formal sciences' to become merely the formal sciences.

Another terminological problem that was avoided in the first couple of paragraphs concerns the phrase 'Transformational Generative Grammar', and since this phrase appears frequently in this book, it is imperative that its meaning is clear. It is already the case (in the foregoing discussion of Lees' review) that 'TGG' has been referred to as if it were a single, identifiable, unchanging, monolithic entity. However, if the work presented in the following chapters demonstrates anything, it demonstrates that it is alarmingly anachronistic to use the term 'TGG' broadly to refer to the various theoretical stances and projects associated with Noam Chomsky (b. 1928) during the years *c*. 1951–*c*. 1956, since, although the various lines of research eventually fused into an identifiable theory, a coherent picture did not begin to emerge until *c*. 1957, when Chomsky began to draw together his ideas concerning the structure of linguistic theory, the validity (or otherwise) of statistical models in syntactic research, the benefits (or otherwise) of logical syntax and semantics, and so on. However, this convergence of ideas was of ephemeral duration, and by the early 1960s the theory had begun to change once more. Perhaps, instead of 'TGG', the term 'Transformational Analysis' should be used to refer to the theory presented in Chomsky's 1955 text *The Logical Structure of Linguistic Theory*, since this was the title he gave to his 1955 Ph.D. thesis? Unfortunately, though, the range of work that Chomsky accomplished in his earliest publications and manuscripts is sufficiently wide that any single term would cause difficulties and eventually demonstrate its own inadequacy. Consequently, for the purposes of the following discussion, the term 'TGG' will be understood to refer to the syntactic theory that Chomsky expounded in *The Logical Structure of Linguistic Theory* (c. 1955) and, less formally (but in a broader context), in *Syntactic Structures* (1957). As a result, 'TGG' can become TGG again. It should be added, though, that since the intention is to show how the formal sciences gradually began to influence syntactic theory in general, ultimately resulting in the creation of TGG, the focus of the discussion will often be upon various papers, theses, and manuscripts concerning linguistic theory that appeared during the years 1900–1957 and not just on Chomsky's work from the 1950s. The task is to situate TGG more securely (if possible) in the scientific context of the time.

Accordingly, having provided at least an initial discussion of some of the difficulties, terminological and otherwise, that are inevitably encountered in a study of this kind, it is necessary to assess existing publications concerning the genesis of TGG in order to motivate more particularly the need for a serious consideration of the influence exerted by the formal sciences upon the development of TGG. The following discussion of the existing historiographical literature makes no claim to be exhaustively comprehensive. Indeed, the body of secondary literature concerning the development of TGG has started to accumulate at such a rate that a detailed summary of all the posited interpretations, assessments, revisions, and disagreements would leave little time or space for a discussion of primary sources. Instead, the overview offered here is intended generally to indicate how historiographical studies of TGG have developed since the 1960s, with the perceived deficiencies in the existing studies being highlighted. One final word of warning, though. As is usually the case, this introduction was written after the rest of the book was complete. Therefore, some of the topics mentioned in passing here may seem richer, deeper, less arbitrary, and less idiosyncratic after the main chapters of the following text have been perused. Consequently, although the rest of this introduction effectively constitutes a survey of related literature, like all such surveys it should be re-evaluated after the rest of the book has been read.

The earliest historical studies of the development of TGG can be found in the first textbooks devoted to the theory, and these began to appear in the early 1960s. Although these books often contained some sort of overview of the development of the theory, the summaries offered were usually brief and generally gave the impression that the origins of TGG could be traced back to *Syntactic Structures*, and no further. A fine example of this kind of pedagogic text is Emmon Bach's *An Introduction to Transformational Grammars* (1964). The plural of the title is revealing: the syntactic theory Bach presented had not yet developed into the study of a single, genetically embedded Universal Grammar, consequently, there could still be lots of TGGs. In his more historically inclined passages,

Bach gives particular emphasis to the influence of the formal sciences upon the development of TGG. For instance, he states explicitly that the theory 'has taken its inspiration from modern logic' (Bach 1964: 9), and he goes on to suggest that mathematics, logic, and linguistics have moved closer together during the last one hundred years (i.e., 1864–1964):

> In the last century a great deal has been learned about the structure of deductive systems (systems of logic, mathematics, axiom systems for various sciences). Logicians and mathematicians have been concerned more and more with studying various 'language systems' or 'calculi' from an abstract point of view. At the same time, modern linguistics has tended towards describing languages as abstract formalised systems. In many ways, the theory of language presented here may be considered the result of a convergence between these two currents. The grammars that we shall study are attempts to state the principles by which sentences of a language may be constructed, in much the same way that a formalised mathematical theory may be used to construct theorems. (Bach 1964: 9–10)

Like Lees before him, therefore, Bach states clearly that TGG makes use of the same kind of axiomatic-deductive systems utilised by various branches of mathematics, and, in addition, he suggests that linguistics and mathematics have been converging for at least a century. Later, he observes more specifically that the use of techniques derived from 'modern logic and mathematics' in TGG may constitute 'the most lasting result of the linguistic research of the last decade' (Bach 1964: 143). Unfortunately, though, Bach feels that 'to document this bit of cultural history in detail would take us well beyond the bounds of this introduction' (Bach 1964: 144). Consequently, he leaves this topic largely undeveloped and does not return to it later in the book.

As the 1960s progressed it became increasingly obvious to the international linguistics community that TGG was significantly more than an ephemeral fad, and consequently the issue of the historical roots of the theory began to inspire more interest. Chomsky himself contributed to this general trend when he published *Cartesian Linguistics: A Chapter in the History of Rationalist Thought* (1966), a somewhat disingenuous attempt to demonstrate that historical precedents existed for concepts such as deep structure and surface structure – concepts he was then in the process of elaborating. Specifically, Chomsky declared that TGG could be viewed as 'a reawakening of interest in questions that were, in fact, studied in a serious and fruitful way during the seventeenth, eighteenth and early nineteenth centuries' (Chomsky 1966: 1), and he sought to argue his case by focusing on such works as the *Port-Royal Grammar* (1660) and by reassessing the work of linguists such as Wilhelm von Humboldt. Although (much to his

6 *Introduction*

annoyance) Chomsky's book has never really been taken seriously by linguistic historiographers, who tend to classify it as a work of ideological propaganda rather than as an objective historical assessment of the development of syntactic theory, it certainly seems to have inspired an interest in the task of situating TGG securely within the history of ideas.[2] However, since Chomsky was primarily concerned with linguistic research that had been completed before the mid-nineteenth century, he did not consider the actual development of TGG itself, and therefore *Cartesian Linguistics* offers few insights into the emergence of generative grammar. Curiously, a more revealing contemporaneous insight into the nature of this development can be gleaned from the writings of the post-Bloomfieldian Charles Hockett (1916–2000), who, by the late 1960s, had become a rather lonely figure in the world of international linguistics. During the previous decade Hockett had been generally recognised as one of the dominant linguists of his generation, but, as the years passed, linguistic theory started to take a distinctly Chomskyan turn, and Hockett found himself marginalised; a prematurely redundant relic of a bygone era. His response was to publish *The State of the Art* (1968), a book in which he expressed his dissatisfaction with Chomsky's general approach to syntactic theory, and it was while he was preparing the ground for his robust critique of Chomskyan syntax that Hockett recalled the circumstances surrounding the development of TGG in the 1950s:

> Lacking any explicit guidance as to where to turn for a broadened basis for linguistic theory, Chomsky was forced on his own resources and tastes, and turned towards the abstract fields of logic, mathematics, and philosophy, rather than to science. If Harris' work suggested either of these directions, it was the former. Indeed, a number of us at the time, in our search for 'rigor', were gazing longingly towards mathematics . . . the move was reasonable, since linguistics (or language) surely has interconnections of various sorts with these scholarly endeavours just as it has with anthropology, psychology and biology. (Hockett 1968: 36)

Certainly Hockett cannot be presented as an impartial historian of syntactic theory, mainly because he himself was an active participant in the various debates of the 1950s, and was specifically interested in utilising techniques derived from mathematics in linguistic research. Nevertheless, his comments are perhaps of some significance.[3] It is revealing, for instance, that, while recalling the heady days of the previous decade, when linguists (and not just those closely associated with TGG) were 'gazing longingly' towards mathematics, Hockett uses a first-person plural pronoun, suggesting that a number of linguists were turning to mathematics as a possible source of analytical techniques because they felt that particular methodologies employed by the formal sciences (i.e., for Hockett, 'abstract' sciences such as logic and mathematics) could enable linguistic theory to be endowed with greater rigour. As will be shown in section 2.3, the use of the term 'rigour' in this context is replete with significance. Unfortunately, though, like Bach before him, Hockett does not provide a detailed account of precisely which branches of mathematics he considered to have been especially influential, nor does he indicate how the linguists managed to acquire a working knowledge of contemporaneous developments in mathematics.

During the 1970s, as it became increasingly clear that Chomsky's place in the history of linguistics was secure, his early work began to be scrutinised more closely by linguistic historiographers. For instance, John Lyons discussed various aspects of TGG in his relatively non-technical book *Chomsky* (Lyons 1970), and while he certainly argues in this text that Chomsky's work had ushered in a new period of linguistic research (describing *Syntactic Structures* as a 'short but epoch-making book' (Lyons 1970: 36)), Lyons is keen also to emphasise the similarities between TGG and the type of grammatical research conducted by the post-Bloomfieldians. For example, at one point he remarks that

> Chomsky's general views on linguistic theory as presented in *Syntactic Structures* are in most respects the same as those held by other members of the Bloomfieldians school, and notably by Zellig Harris. In particular, it may be noted that there is no hint, at this period, of the 'rationalism' that is so characteristic a feature of Chomsky's more recent writing. His acknowledgement of the influence of the 'empiricist' philosophers, Nelson Goodman and Willard Van Orman Quine, would suggest that he shared their views; but there is no general discussion, in *Syntactic Structures*, of the philosophical and psychological implications of grammar. (Lyons 1970: 36)

It is striking that Lyons should emphasise the apparent absence of rationalism in Chomsky's early work, and that he should associate this absence with the influence of the 'empiricist' philosophers Nelson Goodman (1906–1998) and Willard Van Orman Quine (1908–2000). However, although Lyons returns to the topic of 'the evolution of Chomsky's thought from empiricism to rationalism' (Lyons 1970: 38) later in the book, he does not discuss the influence of Goodman and Quine's constructive nominalism upon Chomsky's early work, nor does he assess Chomsky's later rejection of nominalistic techniques. Instead, the focus of Lyons' discussion is exclusively upon Chomsky's better-known 1959 critique of behaviourism.[4]

Another authoritative (and now sadly neglected) study of Chomsky's work, which appeared in the early 1970s, was Finngeir Hiorth's *Noam Chomsky: Linguistics and Philosophy* (1974). As the title suggests, Hiorth was as interested

8   *Introduction*

in the philosophical implications of Chomsky's research as he was in its consequences for linguistics, and, as a result, his book discusses the origins of TGG in greater detail than most previous (and subsequent) studies. For instance, Chomsky's frequently ignored 1953 paper is discussed in (comparatively) considerable detail, and Hiorth concludes that it 'does not necessarily show that Chomsky ever had great faith in the importance of formal, purely symbolic, analyses for the purpose of empirical linguistic research' (Hiorth 1974: 35). In this context Hiorth goes on to consider the influence of constructive nominalism upon the young Chomsky, observing that

> In 1952–1953 Chomsky not only had a firm belief in the power of formal methods; he also believed in an 'inscriptional nominalistic'... approach. The trend in his thinking at that time was due to the influence of Nelson Goodman and W. V. Quine. The occurrence of the term 'nominalistic' here did not reflect any mature belief in philosophical nominalism. To my knowledge in Chomsky's later work there is no trace of nominalism. (Hiorth 1974: 37)

This (brief) mention of Goodman and Quine is unusual in the historiographical literature devoted to TGG, where virtual silence is the norm. Regrettably, though, Hiorth does not trace the precise nature of the influence of constructive nominalism, and it is suggested that after 1953 Chomsky rejected nominalistic methods altogether – a rather misleading claim, as the discussion in chapters 4 and 5 of this book seeks to demonstrate. Hiorth's interest in the influence of mathematics and logic upon TGG is also manifest, though, when he considers Chomsky's complex attitude towards logical syntax and semantics and the nature of their relationship to syntactic theory. The focus of his discussion is upon the exchange between Yehoshua Bar-Hillel (1915–1975) and Chomsky in the mid-1950s, but there is a brief mention of Rudolf Carnap (1891–1970), particularly his influence upon Bar-Hillel. After this the bulk of Hiorth's text concentrates upon *Syntactic Structures* and Chomsky's publications from the 1960s.

The year after Hiorth's text appeared, Chomsky himself published his own account of the genesis of TGG. His overview was contained in his introduction to *The Logical Structure of Linguistic Theory*, a truncated version of which was published for the first time in 1975. Chomsky's discussion is detailed, and the section that concerns his own intellectual development during the late 1940s and 1950s contains the following passage:

> At Harris's suggestion I had begun to study logic, philosophy, and foundations of mathematics more seriously as a graduate student at the University of Pennsylvania, and later at Harvard. I was particularly impressed by Nelson Goodman's work on constructional systems. In its general character, this work was in some ways similar to Harris's, and seemed to me to provide the

> appropriate intellectual background for the investigation of taxonomic procedures that I then regarded as central to linguistic theory. But Goodman's ongoing critique of induction seemed to point in a rather different direction, suggesting the inadequacy in principle of inductive approaches. Goodman's investigation of the simplicity of systems also suggested (to me at least) possibilities for nontaxonomic approaches to linguistic theory. Quine's critique of logical empiricism also gave some reason to believe that this line of enquiry might be a plausible one. Quine argued that the principles of scientific theory are confronted with experience as a systematic complex, with adjustments possible at various points, governed by such factors as general simplicity. (Chomsky 1975[1955]: 33)

This revealing summary suggests that during the early 1950s Chomsky perceived a close association between the methodology of constructional system theory and the techniques employed by the post-Bloomfieldians, especially Harris. Unfortunately, as will be shown below, Chomsky's reference to 'Goodman's ongoing critique of induction' seems to have convinced certain linguistic historiographers that Goodman was a rationalist who rejected empirical procedures when, actually, the opposite was in fact the case. Indeed, as is shown in section 5.3 below, Goodman's apparent critique of induction was merely the prelude to a robust defence of the same, and Chomsky himself was well aware of this. Quine, who started out as an adherent of Carnapian logical empiricism, shifted his position more than Goodman, so that by the 1950s he was certainly disillusioned with Carnap's approach, and, as indicated in the above passage, his writing from this period influenced Chomsky directly. Chomsky's recollections also indicate the direct association between Goodman's ideas concerning the simplicity of constructional systems and his own early preoccupation with the concept of grammatical simplicity. It should be noted, though, that, while it is illuminating to read Chomsky's own reflections upon these aspects of his early work, his reminiscences do not really reveal anything that was not already implied by certain comments and footnotes in his original papers and manuscripts.

Another significant passage in Chomsky's 1975 recollections occurs when he considers some of the particular branches of mathematics that influenced his thinking during the formative years in the early 1950s.

> Perhaps a word might be usefully added on the general intellectual climate in Cambridge at the time when [*The Logical Structure of Linguistic Theory*] was written. Interdisciplinary approaches to language communication and human behaviour were much in vogue... Oxford ordinary language analysis and Wittgenstein's later work were attracting great interest. The problem of reconciling these approaches (if possible) with Quine's provocative ideas on

language and knowledge troubled many students. Mathematical logic, in particular recursive function theory and metamathematics, were becoming more generally accessible, and developments in these areas seemed to provide tools for a more precise study of natural language as well. All of this I personally found most stimulating. (Chomsky 1975[1955]: 39)

This passage supports Hockett's description of linguists 'gazing longingly' towards mathematics in the 1950s. Recursive function theory and metamathematics are specifically highlighted, but, since no details are given, questions remain. Which aspects of recursive function theory and metamathematics interested linguists at this time? Where was information concerning these subjects obtained? Who was making these ideas accessible? Precisely which linguists were interested in these topics? There are many unresolved issues. Indeed, although the above passage helpfully confirms the nature of the influences that are detectable in Chomsky's early publications and manuscripts, it also frustrates since it raises numerous further queries without providing answers.

In the same year that Chomsky published his authoritative account of the development of TGG, detailing the manner in which he had reformulated linguistic theory by rejecting the 'taxonomic' approaches of the post-Bloomfieldians, another text appeared that seemed to question this interpretation of linguistic history. This text, *American Structuralism*, was written by Dell Hymes and John Fought, and their detailed re-evaluation of structuralist research in the 1940s and 1950s undermined the (then) generally accepted view that Chomsky's work had inspired a complete revolution in syntactic theory. Hymes and Fought's main argument was that the post-Bloomfieldians could not usefully be grouped together as a single group that pursued a coherent research programme, since, in truth, they constituted a disparate collection of individuals who were responsible for 'a variety of alternative conceptions, and individual directions of interest' (Hymes and Fought 1981[1975]: 156). Therefore, Hymes and Fought argued that it was misleading to view Chomsky's work as a reaction against a homogeneous generation of linguists, and, in a passage reminiscent of Lyons, they provocatively suggest that 'in 1957 Chomsky's work might appear to be to a great extent a victory for one Bloomfieldian approach to syntax (that of Harris) as against another (that of Trager, Smith, et al.)' (Hymes and Fought 1981[1975]: 155). However, with specific reference to the origins of TGG, Hymes and Fought do not explore the influence of the formal sciences upon the work of the post-Bloomfieldians in any great detail, and they largely neglect the gradual mathematisation of syntactic theory that occurred during the 1940s and 1950s, with the result that their account of the genesis of TGG, though impressive, is, in this respect, incomplete.

As indicated above, Hymes and Fought's work was certainly provocative, and by 1980 Frederick Newmeyer was sufficiently provoked to publish his *Linguistic Theory in America: the First Quarter-Century of Transformational Generative Grammar*. This work is still generally considered to be the first major historical study of the whole development of (pre-1980) generative grammar. Indeed, Newmeyer himself claimed (rather grandly) that 'what I have written is, to my knowledge, the only work that combines a comprehensive account of the forging of modern linguistic theory with a detailed elaboration and explanation of its development' (Newmeyer 1980: xi). However, Newmeyer devotes most of his attention to the post-1957 development of TGG, with only two out of eight chapters considering research into syntactic theory published during the 1940s and early to mid-1950s; and his approach to this research is strikingly robust. For instance, he entirely rejects Hymes and Fought's suggestion that the so-called 'structuralists' never really constituted a coherent group, arguing instead that structural linguistics provided an homogeneous context for the 'Chomskyan Revolution' that was inaugurated by the publication of *Syntactic Structures*. For instance, we are told that *The Logical Structure of Linguistic Theory* 'completely shattered the prevailing structuralist conceptions of linguistic theory' (Newmeyer 1980: 35), although these conceptions are never exhaustively described in their full complexity. In this context, Newmeyer discusses behavioural psychology in a rather cursory manner, suggesting that the sort of 'empiricist assumptions' (Newmeyer 1980: 11) associated with it were also a characteristic feature of structural linguistics. However, no attempt is made to associate the 'empiricist assumptions' of structural linguistics with the type of logical empiricism that was championed by Carnap and Goodman, and which exerted such a profound influence over Chomsky's earliest work. Indeed, although Goodman is mentioned in his capacity as one of Chomsky's teachers, and as a person who was influential in enabling Chomsky to obtain a Junior Fellowship at Harvard in 1951, there is no discussion of the nature of his intellectual influence upon Chomsky. Similarly, although statistical methods for modelling of language are briefly discussed with reference to Hockett (i.e., Newmeyer 1980: 2), no attempt is made to explore the connections that existed between various sub-branches of mathematics, logic, and syntactic theory during the 1940s and 1950s.

Unfortunately, Newmeyer's discussion of Chomsky's early work is as selective as his discussion of the structuralists. Perhaps it is not surprising that the main emphasis falls upon *Syntactic Structures*, even though Newmeyer acknowledges that most of the text was 'excerpted' from *The Logical Structure of Linguistic Theory* (Newmeyer 1980: 30). Also, though a brief consideration of the notion of simplicity in relation to the task of grammar evaluation is offered, Newmeyer inexplicably neglects to mention the influence of Goodman's work concerning the basal simplicity of constructional systems upon the young Chomsky; and the influence of Goodman and Quine is further scanted when Chomsky's first published paper, which appeared in 1953, fails to receive detailed consideration. It is almost as if Chomsky's flirtation with constructive nominalism (which inevitably came with considerable empirical/empiricist baggage) is being intentionally excised from the history of TGG. In a similar fashion, Newmeyer does not discuss Chomsky's ideas concerning the relationship between linguistic theory and logic, ideas which were expressed in two papers during the years 1954–1955; and further opacities in Newmeyer's version of events include the lack of a detailed consideration of the gradual appropriation of transformation rules from Carnapian logical syntax and the neglect of Bar-Hillel's influence upon Chomsky during the mid-1950s, particularly in his exploration of recursive rules in syntactic analysis. A revised edition of Newmeyer's text appeared in 1986, but the main changes were to chapters 6–8, which were rewritten in order to provide an insight into the most recent developments in syntactic theory (i.e., Principles and Parameters, Generalised Phrase Structure Grammar, Lexical-Functional Grammar, and the like), and no attempt was made substantially to alter the account of TGG's early development.

It is ironic that in the very same year the first protracted statement of the 'Chomskyan Revolution' interpretation of TGG history appeared, the validity of this very interpretation was questioned again when Stephen Murray suggested in his article 'Gatekeepers and the Chomskian Revolution' (Murray 1980) that the popular notion of Chomsky fighting to have his radical new ideas accepted by a discouraging and dismissive dominant linguistic establishment was in need of fairly drastic revision. Rather than merely asserting a different interpretation, though, Murray managed to obtain contemporaneous documents, including correspondence from Bernard Bloch (1907–1965), who was the editor of the influential journal *Language* during the 1950s. The correspondence Murray unearthed indicated that, rather than persecuting Chomsky, Bloch had actively encouraged him to publish his work, and (not surprisingly) this evidence generated considerable interest since it seemed at odds with Chomsky's own account of events, which he had provided in his 1975 recollections, as discussed above. Consequently, Murray's paper suggested that TGG was more closely connected to post-Bloomfieldian syntactic theory than was generally acknowledged at the time, and therefore his research contributed to the gathering revisionist movement, which sought to explore the development of TGG with greater accuracy. Nevertheless, despite Murray's provocative research, the main focus in the 1980s was often upon post-1957 developments of the theory. For instance, in a 1989 paper 'Philosophical Speculation and Cognitive Science', George Lakoff explored the different assumptions that underlie interpretivist interpretations of TGG and the offshoot of the theory that became known as Generative Semantics. As shown below, research into this subject blossomed in the 1990s when the topic became something of an obsession among certain historians of linguistics.

The various historiographical controversies mentioned above inspired a flurry of research into the development of TGG in the 1990s, and one of the most significant studies of this period was Peter Matthews' book *Grammatical Theory in the United States from Bloomfield to Chomsky* (1993). As is clear from Matthews' humorous introduction, his basic intention was to question the validity of the caricatured history of TGG that had become commonplace by the early 1990s, largely due to the influence of Newmeyer's widely read account. Indeed, Matthews refers to Newmeyer's 1980 book as 'the official history of transformational-generative grammar' (Matthews 1993: 208), and, if it is indeed the case that Newmeyer's version of events is generally accepted as the standard interpretation, then Matthews' own text can be viewed as an insightful alternative history of TGG. While Newmeyer had been keen to (over)emphasise the difference between Chomsky's work and that of his predecessors, Matthews was equally keen to redress the balance by stressing some of the similarities and connections that existed between post-Bloomfieldian research and TGG. As a result, TGG is often presented as if it were the logical consequence of certain research traditions pursued by leading post-Bloomfieldian linguists, and, in this sense, Matthews' work can be classified as belonging to the revisionist Lyons–Hymes–Fought–Murray tradition. To take but one example, Matthews draws particular attention to the fact that Hockett was discussing the predictive nature of syntactic theory as early as 1948, and demonstrates that TGG largely fulfilled this particular research goal.[5] However, despite this emphasis on continuity, Matthews, like Newmeyer before him, still focuses primarily upon the relationship between TGG and the other linguistic theories that preceded it. Consequently, the full complexity of the intellectual environment out of which TGG emerged is not fully portrayed. For example, there is a detailed discussion of the relationship between linguistic form and meaning in the work of both Leonard Bloomfield (1887–1949) and Chomsky, yet there is no attempt to consider these issues with reference to Hilbertian Formalism, the metamathematical movement that dominated large areas of scientific discourse during the 1930s, 1940s, and 1950s, and which fascinated many linguists, including

14 *Introduction*

Bloomfield and Chomsky (as discussed at length in chapters 3 and 4 below). Also, although such topics as grammatical simplicity are considered, there is no mention of constructional system theory, and Matthews does not trace the influence of Goodman (and/or Quine) upon the young Chomsky. Without such assessments, though, any discussion of the topic of simplicity criteria in TGG is inevitably impoverished.

As already implied above, during the first half of the 1990s various researchers began to focus on later developments within the TGG tradition rather than upon the question of origins, and the fragmentation of the 'generativists' camp in the 1960s received considerable attention. For instance, Randy Harris' *Linguistic Wars* appeared in 1993, closely followed by Geoffrey Huck and John Goldsmith's *Ideology and Linguistic Theory: Noam Chomsky and the Deep Structure Debates* (1995), and both texts considered the rise and fall of Generative Semantics in the 1960s and 1970s. However, despite this focus on later events, the development of the initial TGG formalism is discussed in both publications. Unfortunately, Harris' book, which is self-professedly written in the 'popular science' (Harris 1993: vii) tradition, is rather too swift and glib in its treatment of the origins of TGG to be taken seriously. There is an attempt to consider the implications of the term 'formal', but no mention either of David Hilbert (1862–1943) or of metamathematics, and therefore no real exploration of the consequences of formalising syntactic theory. By contrast, Huck and Goldsmith's assessment of TGG's origins is more convincing, and it includes the following evaluation of Goodman's influence upon Chomsky:

> Another of Chomsky's teachers [i.e., in addition to Harris] who had a significant influence on him was the philosopher Nelson Goodman. Having taken several courses with Goodman at the University of Pennsylvania, Chomsky was struck by the similarity between Harris's perspective on language and Goodman's perspective on philosophical systems generally, what Goodman called 'constructional systems'. The important feature of constructional systems in this regard is that there exist objective criteria for evaluating how simple or complex they are. Thus, if a theory of language were a constructional system, then that theory would be subject to the principles that govern such systems; that is, it could be evaluated according to criteria of simplicity and economy. Furthermore, as a constructional system, the theory of language should be formalizable; in fact, if language is to be evaluated as a constructional system, it must be formalized, because only in that way can its simplicity relative to other theories be measured. (Huck and Goldsmith 1995: 13)

Although it is always refreshing to encounter even a brief discussion of the influence of constructional system theory in an historiographical study of TGG, the above account is inadequate in a number of respects. For instance, it does not consider the implications of the empiricist assumptions of the constructional systems that Chomsky explored in his earliest work. Also, there is no mention of Chomsky's direct use of one of Goodman's own constructional systems in his 1953 paper. Consequently, Huck and Goldsmith's discussion tantalises rather than satisfies, though, in their defence, it should be remembered that their main concern was with the ideological linguistic wars of the 1960s and 1970s rather than with the philosophical foundations of pre-1957 syntactic theories.

The year 1994 saw the publication of the collection of articles and papers *Noam Chomsky: Critical Assessments*, edited by Carlos Otero. This publication fully acknowledges the influence of Chomsky upon contemporary society and culture, and constitutes a significant step towards his official canonisation as one of the great intellectuals of the twentieth century. Various papers in the collection touch upon aspects of the origins of TGG, but perhaps the most comprehensive overview is contained in Otero's introduction to volume I, 'Chomsky and the Cognitive Revolution of the 1950s: The Emergence of Transformational Generative Grammar', the stated purpose of which is to place Chomsky's work in 'a more general context' (Otero 1994a: 1). Consequently, a wide range of scientific topics is discussed, including relativity theory, quantum mechanics, computer science, and others. However, Otero's discussion is often so brief that misleading statements intrude. For instance, he claims that Whitehead and Russell's exploration of the logical foundations of mathematics 'led directly to the research programme of the formalists' (Otero 1994a: 10), when, in fact, the first of Hilbert's papers concerning the metamathematical approach to foundations problems (the methodology that would later be referred to as Formalism) appeared in 1904, six years before the first volume of Whitehead and Russell's *Principia Mathematica* was published. While it is certainly true that Hilbert's *later* work was directly influenced by *Principia Mathematica*, Otero's statement clearly gives a false impression of the chronology of events. Another problem is that, since Otero seeks to provide 'a preliminary' (Otero 1994a: 1) discussion of some of the topics considered by the papers in volume I, he does not himself make direct connections between the advances in the formal sciences that he recounts and the development of TGG. For instance, although the work of Kurt Gödel (1906–1978), Alonzo Church (1903–1995), Stephen Kleene (1909–1994), Emil Post (1897–1954), and others is (briefly) discussed, no attempt is made to consider the way in which aspects of this work were knowingly used by linguists working in the 1940s and 1950s. Indeed, discussion of the post-Bloomfieldians in general is kept to a minimum, giving the false impression that Chomsky was one of the first linguists to concern himself with mathematical techniques; and since these issues are not addressed in any of the papers and essays contained in the volume, this false impression is never corrected.

Another 1994 publication that contains a detailed consideration of the genesis of TGG is Stephen Murray's *Theory Groups and the Study of Language in North America: A Social History*. While primarily a work of anthropology rather than a straightforward historiographical study, Murray's book extends his research into the development of syntactic theory in the twentieth century that he had begun in the early 1980s. With specific reference to the sections of the book that deal with the period 1951–1957, Murray's research once again involves digging up forgotten letters and documents that provide insights into the actual reception of TGG in the 1950s. However, although he robustly renews his attack on Newmeyeresque interpretations of linguistic history, he does not provide an account of the relationship between linguistics and the formal sciences during the 1950s, though the book does emphasise the closeness of the connections that existed between the post-Bloomfieldians and the proto-generativists, reinforcing the idea that TGG was largely a continuation of existing research concerns. Indeed, perhaps Murray's most stimulating and thought-provoking contribution in his book stems from his interest in generative grammar as a scientific theory. Influenced by the well-known work of Thomas Kuhn (1922–1996), particularly *The Structure of Scientific Revolutions* (1962), Murray discusses the status of generative grammar as a scientific theory, and while happy to acknowledge that TGG does appear to meet some of the criteria for an authentic scientific revolution, he suggests that later versions of the theory fall alarmingly short. Indeed, the sketch that Murray provides of MIT-based research into generative grammar in the post-1980 period is remarkable for its condemnatory tone. Describing Chomsky as 'an ageing dictator', Murray summarises the way in which sycophantic 'cohorts' compete for favour and seek to emulate 'Chomsky's contemptuous rhetoric', and he condemns the general 'MIT ethos of imperviousness to criticism' (Murray 1994: 445). In Murray's opinion, the main consequence of this is that linguistics at MIT is more akin to a dictatorship than a scientific research centre, and, since the influences of the formal sciences upon syntactic theory is a central theme of this book, some of these issues are of relevance and will be discussed again later.

Partly prompted by the new revisionist accounts of linguistic history, such as those by Matthews and Murray, that had appeared in the early 1990s, Newmeyer collected together a number of his most recent essays and reviews and published them in 1996 as *Generative Linguistics: A Historical Perspective*. Clearly, general academic interest in linguistic historiography had increased since 1980, for, in 1996, Newmeyer felt able to claim (somewhat solecistically) that 'the origin and development of generative grammar are now a hot topic' (Newmeyer 1996: 1). However, the chapter of Newmeyer's new book that dealt primarily with the question of origins largely restated his well-known interpretation of the history of TGG in terms of a Chomskyan revolution, and his main purpose appears to have been to refute the recent criticism of his earlier work. Compared to the studies due to Matthews, Huck, Goldsmith, and Murray, Newmeyer's arguments are often disappointingly assertive and superficial. In chapter 2, for instance, he attempts to provide a thorough account of the development of TGG, but the discussion contains numerous obscurities and errors. For instance, he claims that Chomsky's 1951 Master's thesis was 'the first to point out that the procedures of American descriptivist linguists can be likened to the programme of Carnap's *Der logische Aufbau der Welt*' (Newmeyer 1996: 15), yet Carnap's work is not explicitly mentioned in either the submitted or published version of Chomsky's thesis. Consequently, Newmeyer's claims are misleading, and they sometimes seem designed to support a simplistic, pre-existing interpretation of linguistic history rather than to constitute an intense investigation of the bewildering complexity of actual events.

As the 1990s approached their conclusion, a number of significant contributions to TGG historiography appeared. For instance, in 1999 a two-volume collection of papers by various scholars was collected together and published in honour of E. F. K. Koerner as *The Emergence of the Modern Language Sciences*. This selection contains a number of papers that specifically discuss the development of TGG. One of the most stimulating is Danny Steinberg's elaborately entitled 'How the Anti-Mentalist Skeletons in Chomsky's Closet Make Psychological Fiction of his Grammars'. As the title leads one to expect, Steinberg's basic argument is that during the 1950s Chomsky was 'a fervent formalist and anti-mentalist' (Steinberg 1999: 267), who, although he began to shift towards a rationalist stance after 1959 (the basic shift that Lyons had observed in 1970), never managed entirely to relinquish the ideological vestiges of his early empiricism. Astonishingly, although Steinberg is keen to argue that the pre-1959 Chomsky favoured an anti-mentalist approach to syntactic theory, he does not even mention the influence of Goodman and Quine's empiricism upon Chomsky's early work, nor does he discuss Chomsky's use of constructional systems and the empirical assumptions inherent in such an approach to syntactic analysis.

Since the start of the new millennium a number of studies have been published that are concerned either entirely or in part with the origins of TGG. For instance, Giorgio Graffi's 2001 publication *200 Years of Syntax: A Critical Survey* contains a whole section (specifically, section 8.4) that considers 'The

Emergence of Generative Syntax'. Graffi emphasises the 'scientific formation' of the young Chomsky, and although an attempt is made to assess the influence of Harris, Goodman, Quine, and Bar-Hillel, the treatment is all too brief. For instance, Goodman and Quine are disposed of in a single sentence in which it is remarked that 'their criticism of induction (Goodman) and of the "dogmas of empiricism" (Quine)' (Graffi 2001: 331) were the main aspects of their influence upon the young Chomsky. Clearly this is little more than a rather timid paraphrase of Chomsky's own 1975 account (quoted above), and contributes nothing to a detailed exploration of these issues. In particular, there is no mention of Goodman's preoccupation with simplicity criteria and the influence this had (and continues to have) upon Chomsky. Further, although there is a discussion of the Chomsky versus Bar-Hillel debate concerning the relationship between linguistic theory and logical syntax and semantics, the analysis essentially consists of a brief summary of the main arguments, and there is no exploration of the relationship between the views expressed in that debate and other contemporaneous attitudes towards mathematics, logic, and the formal sciences in general. In addition to Graffi's account, Peter Matthews returned to the topic of the origins of TGG in his 2001 publication *A Short History of Structural Linguistics*, and though this text continues the process of exploring the relationship between the young Chomsky and the post-Bloomfieldians that was begun in Matthews' 1993 book, it does not contribute anything of significance to the discussion of the influence of the formal sciences upon the genesis of TGG.

As the above summary of the existing historiographical studies demonstrates, previous work has not paid sufficient attention to the influence of the formal sciences upon the development of TGG, providing only occasional, cursory overviews at best. Accordingly, the discussion sustained in the following chapters is intended to rectify this situation, and the basic structure of the book can be summarised as follows. Chapter 2 provides an overview of the developments within mathematics that resulted in the so-called 'foundations crisis' of the early twentieth century. After a brief consideration of the illogicalities associated with early forms of the calculus, the rigorisation movement of the nineteenth century is described, along with the emergence of Cantorian set theory. The paradoxes of set theory are assessed, and the crisis in the foundations of mathematics is discussed. Each of the three main foundational schools – Formalism, Logicism, and Intuitionism – are considered in some detail; and, finally, several influential textbooks that spread the gospels of Logicism and Formalism are described. With the intellectual context securely established, chapter 3 traces the gradual influence of the formal sciences upon syntactic theory during the first half of the twentieth century. The main purpose is to set the stage for the detailed consideration of TGG that is contained in chapters 4 and 5. A number of separate but related strands are followed. The main topics considered are the interest of pre-TGG linguists in the axiomatic-deductive method, the use of recursive definitions in logic and pre-TGG linguistics, the development of constructional system theory, the advent of constructive nominalism, the increasing preoccupation of linguists with logical syntax and logical semantics, and the gradual perception that, during the 1940s and 1950s, linguistics had become more mathematical. By contrast, chapters 4 and 5 constitute a sustained assessment of the influence of the formal sciences specifically upon the development of TGG. Initially, the focus is upon Chomsky's pre-1956 work, and the main issues considered are his preoccupation with simplicity criteria, his early belief in the utility of a constructive nominalist approach to syntactic theory, and his complex attitude towards the use of techniques derived from logic in linguistic analysis. The discussion then shifts to Chomsky's work from the years 1955–1957, and numerous topics are considered, including his negative appraisal of stochastic techniques, his advocacy of evaluation procedures over discovery procedures, his rejection of the empiricist implications of constructional system theory, his use of constructional techniques in his own work, his early notion of transformation rules, his deployment of recursive rules, and the axiomatic-deductive character of 1957-style TGG.

Although this introduction has now reached its natural conclusion, it is necessary to make one final point. While such words as 'historiography', 'post-Bloomfieldians', and phrases like 'the 1950s' have figured prominently in the preceding paragraphs, just as they will feature conspicuously in the ensuing chapters, it would be entirely incorrect to assume that this book only deals with issues that have become quaint and intriguing exhibits in a dusty museum that seeks to preserve now extinct linguistic theories. On the contrary, the implications of the issues addressed in this book for contemporary generative grammar are potentially profound. Ever since the advent of the Minimalist Program (MP) in the early 1990s, most leading researchers within the field have attempted, in various ways, to reduce the theory of generative grammar to its essential elements, rejecting all theoretical constructs that can be reinterpreted in terms of more fundamental components; and, intriguingly, many of the elements that have now come to be viewed as essential and irreducible were originally incorporated into TGG when they were adapted from the formal sciences in the 1950s. For instance, such techniques as the axiomatic-deductive method and formal recursion, as well as general concerns with theory-internal simplicity, were all associated, in different guises, with the earliest versions of generative grammar, and therefore their continued presence within contemporary versions of the theory is of considerable interest. While these issues are discussed at greater length in the conclusion, it is important here simply to stress the current relevance of the topics considered in this book. Indeed, perhaps it could be claimed that to consider the aims and goals of contemporary generative grammar, without first attempting to comprehend something of the intellectual context out of which the theory developed, is to labour in a penumbra of ineffectual superficiality.

These words of caution complete this introduction; the requisite *apologia* for yet another retelling of an old story has been offered, and a detailed exploration of the complex relationship between linguistic theory and the formal sciences can now commence.

2   *The consequences of analysis*

2.1   Chapter overview

The purpose of this chapter is to summarise some of the movements within the formal sciences that occurred during the nineteenth and twentieth centuries, and which were ultimately to exert a profound influence over the development of TGG. Since the origins of TGG are the main focus of the following chapters, and since any search for origins necessarily entails an infinite regress if taken to an extreme, an arbitrary beginning is required, and the starting point chosen for this discussion is the emergence of the calculus as an identifiable set of algorithmic procedures in the late seventeenth century. Accordingly, the advent of the calculus is discussed in section 2.2 and some of the disputes associated with its appearance are reviewed, along with the main subsequent advances that led to the creation of the branch of mathematics known as 'analysis'.[1] In section 2.3 various attempts to provide a more secure foundation for analysis are briefly assessed, with particular attention being given to the endeavour to derive the calculus from the rudiments of number theory. The development of set theory, which grew out of the need to secure the basis of arithmetic, is summarised in section 2.4, and some of the resultant paradoxes are explored. The remaining sections of the chapter discuss the three main theories that emerged at the end of the nineteenth century and the beginning of the twentieth century in direct response to the foundations crisis prompted by set theory. These are standardly known as Logicism (section 2.5), Formalism (section 2.6), and Intuitionism (section 2.7). As a postlude to this chapter (and a prelude to the next), section 2.8 considers some of the main textbooks which appeared during years 1911–1955, and which made many of the topics considered in this chapter available for the first time to a wider audience. In particular, the texts considered in this section were instrumental in enabling ideas developed in various sub-fields of the formal sciences to be utilised within the context of linguistics. It is crucial to recognise throughout that the topics considered here all point directly towards the discussion of syntactic theory that is developed in chapters 3, 4, and 5. While it may not always be immediately obvious how some of the topics assessed in the following sections relate to syntactic theory, the many associations will eventually emerge.

2.2 Calculus: doubts and disputes

Although the mathematical techniques associated with the calculus have their roots in the work of René Descartes, Buonaventura Cavalieri, Pierre de Fermat, Blaise Pascal, Isaac Barrow, and many others, a significant date that can be used (somewhat arbitrarily) to denote the commencement of the public history of the calculus is 1684, the year in which Gottfried Wilhelm Leibniz (1646–1716) published his paper 'A New Method for Maxima and Minima'. The significance of this paper lies in the fact that (i) it contains a clear statement of the basic procedure of differentiation, (ii) it introduces the product rule, the quotient rule, and the power rule, and (iii), as the title of the paper suggests, it provides a new practical operation for obtaining maxima and minima. Consequently, by introducing his 'remarkable type of calculus'[2] (Leibniz 1863c[1684]: 467) to the wider mathematical community, Leibniz's 1684 paper inaugurated a new stage in the development of modern mathematics. Two years later, he published 'Concerning a Deeply Hidden Geometry', which introduced the process of integration, and demonstrated that it was the inverse of differentiation; an observation of such importance that it is now usually referred to as 'the fundamental theorem of the calculus'. As is well known, while these papers constituted a significant contribution to the advancement of mathematics, Leibniz's conclusions had been largely anticipated by Isaac Newton (1643–1727). In particular, in several unpublished papers written during the years 1664–1671, Newton had also formulated the processes of differentiation and integration, using his own notational system, and he went on to employ these techniques extensively in *The Mathematical Principles of Natural Philosophy* (1687), his seminal work of mathematical physics. Despite the fact that both Newton and Leibniz obtained similar basic results in their respective versions of the calculus, a plethora of unforeseen consequences eventually resulted from the fact that they both provided different conceptual justifications for the procedures they introduced. Revealingly, though, neither man was able to construct a convincing foundation for the calculus. For instance, in his 1665 paper 'A Method for Finding Theorems', Newton used the symbol 'o' to indicate 'an infinitely little distance', adding (in parenthesis!) that this manoeuvre 'cannot in this case bee understood to bee good unlesse infinite littleness may bee considered geometrically' (Newton 1967[1665]: 282). Newton required numbers such as 'o'

because, when calculating certain kinds of derivatives, he obtained formulae such as³

$$v = o + \frac{a}{2} + x \tag{2.1}$$

in which the term containing 'o' 'must be blotted out' leaving the reduced equation

$$v = \frac{a}{2} + x \tag{2.2}$$

In order to accomplish this, Newton argued (dubiously) that, in equations such as (2.1), the 'o's became infinitely small and could therefore simply be ignored (Newton 1967[1665]: 273). However, as the initial quotation from his 1665 paper demonstrates, Newton himself had profound doubts about the validity of such reasoning, since he was not convinced that the notion of 'infinite littleness' had any validity in an algebraic context that was entirely removed from geometric presentations.

Newton never managed to eradicate his early uncertainties concerning infinitely small numbers, and, in the 1670s, he started to approach the problem in a different way by claiming that differentiation actually involved quantities that were continuously flowing rather than static, infinitesimally small numbers of the sort he had used in his earlier work. In his 1670 paper 'Concerning the Method of Series and Fluxions', for example, Newton presented the infinitesimal increments as being in a state of flux, describing them as 'quantities [that] increase during each infinitely small instant of time'[4] (Newton 1969[1670]: 80), and such passages suggest that Newton was starting to think of his infinitely small quantities as constantly varying, hence his use of the term 'fluxions'. However, the definitions and explanations that he offered in order to clarify his notion of a 'fluxion' were no less opaque than his remarks concerning infinitesimals, and, needless to say, such vague statements did little to elucidate this crucial aspect of the new calculus.[5] However, Newton appears not to have been satisfied with his use of fluxions since several years later, in *The Mathematical Principles of Natural Philosophy*, he adopted yet another approach to the calculus and, instead of referring to infinitely small quantities or fluxions, he spoke instead of ultimate ratios and limits, observing that

> these ultimate ratios [ultimae rationes] in which quantities disappear are not actually the ratios of ultimate quantities, but limits [limites] towards which the ratios of quantities decreasing without limit [sine limite] always converge, and to which they approach nearer than by any given difference, but actually never go beyond [nunquam vero transgredi], nor in effect reach until

the quantities are infinitely diminished [diminuatur in infinitorum]. (Newton 1972[1687/1726]: 88)

Although Newton's inchoate notion of a limit would eventually be developed by a later generation of mathematicians, and would ultimately provide a secure basis for the calculus, Newton himself did not manage to clarify the vagueness inherent in the approach, as outlined in the above quotation. As a result, his definitions of the techniques he proposed remained imprecise, and he continued to justify his use of these poorly defined mathematical procedures primarily by means of geometric (rather than purely algebraic) arguments, and by emphasising the undoubted utility of the experimental results he obtained.

If Newton's vague definitions were inadequate, Leibniz's attempts at explanation and justification for his version of the calculus were no more convincing. In 'A New Method for Maxima and Minima', for instance, Leibniz had simply avoided the issue by asserting that his work would be understood by those familiar with such topics:

> The demonstration of all this will be easy to one who is experienced in these matters and who considers the fact, until now not sufficiently emphasised, that dx, dy, dv, dw and dz can be taken as proportional to the momentary differences [differentiis... momentaneis proportionales haberi posse], either increments or decrements, of the corresponding x, y, v, w, z. (Leibniz 1863c[1684]: 223)

No explanation of these 'momentary differences' was forthcoming, though, and, without pausing for further discussion or clarification, Leibniz immediately began to introduce the basic theory of differentiation. Not surprisingly, this kind of optimistic appeal to sympathetic specialists in tacit possession of shared knowledge did not exactly convince the sceptics, and Leibniz's methods swiftly came under probing attack. For instance, in a 1695 paper, Bernhard Nieuwentijdt criticised the use of infinitesimal numbers, and Leibniz responded (rather inadequately) simply by rebuking his overly scrupulous critics.[6]

Predictably, given the parallel development of the calculus and the inevitable priority debates that ensued, distinct traditions began to establish themselves during the late seventeenth century, and these were broadly associated either with the Newtonian or with the Leibnizian version of the calculus. Essentially, the divisions were national, with leading British mathematicians such as John Landen, Brook Taylor and Colin Maclaurin developing Newton's fluxional treatment, while continental mathematicians such as Jakob Bernoulli, Johann Bernoulli and Leonhard Euler steadily extended Leibniz's work.[7]

However, despite the various divisions and disagreements, the calculus swiftly became the dominant research topic in certain mathematical circles, and it was during the eighteenth century that the branch of mathematics known as analysis began to emerge, largely as a result of significant advances made in the theories of differential equations, power series, and the calculus of variations. These advances were often associated with impressive experimental results, which were frequently taken as sufficient evidence of the validity of the underlying methods, though the basic theory still lacked clear foundations. Although the more pragmatic practitioners of the new analytical techniques seemed content with this situation, many leading intellectuals were understandably dismayed by the fact that analysis was based upon such insecure foundations, and the attacks upon its credibility, which had started in the late seventeenth century, increased in intensity. Perhaps the most vehement critique was delivered by George Berkeley (1685–1753). In his magisterially polemical discourse *The Analyst* (1734), Berkeley incisively lampooned those mathematicians who uncritically availed themselves of the procedures provided by the calculus, accusing them of being too willing to accept the sort of logical absurdities that they were swift to ridicule in Christianity. He concentrated his attack upon the poorly defined infinitesimals, memorably referring to them as 'Ghosts of departed Quantities' (Berkeley 1992[1734]: 199). Although Berkeley's criticism may have been the most trenchant, and possibly the most influential, it was certainly not unique, and similar negative assessments were articulated by Pierre Gassendi and Pierre Bayle, amongst others.

Gradually, as the criticisms increased in potency and number, it became obvious that the intellectual credibility of the most admired branch of modern mathematics was at stake. Not surprisingly, the leading mathematicians of the age were dissatisfied with this situation, and they responded by attempting (yet again) to demonstrate the validity of analysis. Various approaches were adopted. In his *Foundations of Differential Calculus* (1755), for instance, Leonhard Euler (1707–1783) endeavoured to remove the geometric basis of the calculus (which was part of the Newtonian legacy) by founding it instead upon the theory of functions. As a result, his approach was more systematic than that of his predecessors, since he undertook a thorough study of all the elementary functions and their respective derivatives and integrals. Unfortunately, though, he was still unable to deal adequately with infinitesimals, referring to them as the ratio of 'infinitely small quantities [quantitates infinite parva]' (Euler 1912[1755]: 69), without being able to state clearly what this meant. Infinitesimals continued to pose non-trivial problems throughout the second half of the eighteenth century, but a significant advance was largely anticipated by Jean le Rond D'Alembert

(1717–1783), who revived Newton's vague notion of a limit and argued in a 1754 article 'Differential' that the use of such limits, when clearly defined, could provide a more secure foundation for the whole of analysis. While this idea would eventually inspire a whole generation of mathematicians in the nineteenth century, it was not recognised as especially significant by D'Alembert's contemporaries, and indeed Joseph Louis Lagrange (1736–1813) rejected both Leibnizian infinitesimals and D'Alembertian limits when presenting his version of the calculus. Lagrange articulated his approach most coherently in his 'Essay Concerning a New Method' (1760), a work in which he attempted to present the calculus of variations (introduced by Euler) in a purely algebraic framework. The final years of the eighteenth century were characterised by a flurry of alternative proposals, all seeking to situate analysis upon a stable, logical basis; but the existence of so many different proposals only served to increase the general sense of disquiet.

2.3 Rigour, arithmetic, and axioms

As indicated in section 2.2, the various disagreements and disputes associated with the development of analysis in the eighteenth century were directly inspired by the dubious logical status of its conceptual foundation. Consequently, at the start of the nineteenth century, a number of mathematicians renewed the attempt to establish the validity of analysis in an unambiguous fashion. Of these, Augustin-Louis Cauchy (1789–1857) proved to be the most influential reformer. His general approach to the problem was first outlined in his *Algebraic Analysis* (1821) before being elaborated in his *Lesson Concerning the Infinitesimal Calculus* (1823) and other publications. According to Birkhoff, this work 'marked the dawn of a new era' (Birkhoff 1973: 1) in the development of the calculus, and Cauchy's proposals certainly proved to be extremely influential. In essence, Cauchy believed that analysis could be rendered secure by constructing it upon the foundation provided by number theory, and a characteristic feature of his work was the repeated desire for rigour. For instance, in the preface to his *Lesson Concerning the Infinitesimal Calculus*, Cauchy stated that his main aim was 'to reconcile rigour [rigueur]... with the simplicity which results from the direct consideration of infinitesimals [quantité infiniment petite]' (quoted in Birkhoff 1973: 1). In this context, as Grabiner has shown, in the early nineteenth century mathematical 'rigour' generally required a tripartite methodology:

> First, every concept of the subject had to be explicitly defined in terms of concepts whose nature was held to be already known... Second, theorems had

to be proved, with every step in the proof justified by a previously proved theorem, by a definition, or by an explicitly stated axiom... Third, the definitions chosen and the theorems proved, had to be sufficiently broad to support the entire structure of valid results belonging to the subject. (Grabiner 1981: 5)

In essence, this indicates that one of Cauchy's most significant contributions was to focus attention upon the the axiomatic-deductive method, and, as will be discussed in later sections, it was this concern with deduction and valid proof techniques that resulted in the late nineteenth-century preoccupation with axiomatics, which, in turn, would influence the development of linguistics in the twentieth century.

In brief, then, Cauchy's basic strategy was to guarantee the security of analysis by basing it upon number theory, and to provide rigorous proofs for the basic theorems. A number of consequences were to follow from this general approach. For instance, since Cauchy emphasised the role of proofs in mathematical arguments, he appeared to undermine the long-standing yet dubious tradition of justifying the use of specific theoretical techniques by emphasising the obvious utility of the experimental results obtained: in the Cauchian framework, analysis had to be justified without reference to practical utility. Another consequence concerned the perceived relationship between analysis and logic. Given the increased rigour demanded by Cauchy's project, he frequently had to seek sufficient and necessary conditions for the theorems he was endeavouring to prove, and, since the task of determining such conditions was primarily accomplished by means of logical deduction, it is not surprising that his work suggested a relationship between logic and calculus, indirectly encouraging mathematical rather than purely philosophical research into logical systems (although these disciplines clearly overlap).[8] In passing it should be noted that although Cauchy's emphasis on rigour was (to some extent) new, he nevertheless drew heavily upon the work of his most illustrious predecessors. For instance, following D'Alembert he used the concept of a limit in order to construct definitions of differentiation and integration, and this in turn enabled him to unite the theory of functions, advocated by Euler, with theories concerning the convergence of infinite series that had been explored by Taylor and others.[9] In other words, Cauchy largely succeeded in synthesising various approaches to analysis that had been presented as rival alternatives during the eighteenth century, thus paving the way for greater agreement amongst the members of the international mathematical community.

As mentioned above, Cauchy's work proved to be extremely influential throughout the nineteenth century, and his most able successors included Karl

Weierstrass (1815–1892), Richard Dedekind (1831–1916), and Georg Cantor (1845–1918). These men were all involved in the movement that is sometimes referred to as 'the arithmetisation of analysis'; that is, the research programme (begun by Cauchy) that attempted to ensure the security of the foundations of analysis by basing it upon the rudiments of number theory. Weierstrass, in particular, was instrumental in achieving Cauchy's ambition to remove illogicality and vagueness from the core of the calculus, and in a series of lectures delivered during the academic year 1858/1859 at the University of Berlin he began his exploration of the foundations of analysis that would ultimately provide the basic $\epsilon - \delta$ definition of a limit, and the corresponding definitions of differentiation and integration that are essentially those still used today.[10] However, as Weierstrass was well aware, the task of founding analysis upon number theory obviously presupposed the security of the latter, and, as a result, a considerable amount of research in the mid- to late nineteenth century was devoted to the task of exploring the foundations of arithmetic. Often during this period it was assumed (somewhat dangerously) that the real numbers were well defined and that it was the irrational and complex numbers that required coherent specification. Accordingly, in 1872, Dedekind published a booklet entitled *Continuity and Irrational Numbers* in which he undertook to provide an exhaustive definition of the irrational numbers. The method he employed required the creation of a technical procedure he called a 'cut' ('*Schnitt*'), which was used to divide the continuous number line into two classes, a method that would eventually became a standard procedure in number theory.[11]

During the 1870s and 1880s Dedekind continued his probing exploration of various aspects of number theory, focusing increasingly on the rational numbers, and in 1888 he published what was to become his best-known paper, 'What are Numbers and What Should they Be?' In this work Dedekind outlined an axiomatic approach to the task of defining the rational numbers, and this kind of methodology was entirely in keeping with the movement towards greater rigour that had been initiated by Cauchy, since, as mentioned earlier, during the nineteenth century axiomatic systems were used increasingly by mathematicians concerned with foundational questions. Dedekind's research into number theory was extended by Giuseppe Peano (1858–1932), who, in his *Principles of Arithmetic* (1889), derived the rational numbers from axioms concerning the positive whole numbers. With Peano's work it seemed as if the foundations of number theory were close to being rendered secure.

Given the preoccupations of his contemporaries as summarised above, it is not surprising that Cantor was interested in the foundations of number theory at the start of his career. Indeed, his first papers were entirely devoted to the task of exploring and extending work in this area already largely accomplished by Dedekind and others.[12] However, during the 1870s he began to develop new ideas, inspired by his number-theoretical investigations, and so began the intellectual odyssey that led him to formulate the rudiments of modern set theory. Since set theory was largely responsible for triggering the crisis of foundations which shook mathematics to its core in the early twentieth century, it is necessary briefly to summarise the basics of the conceptual scheme Cantor introduced.

2.4 Set theory and paradoxes

As implied above, Cantor's *Mengenlehre* (his name for the collection of definitions and operations that eventually developed into modern set theory) was initially inspired by research into trigonometric series that was accomplished by Dedekind, Bernhard Riemann (1826–1866), and Eduard Heine (1821–1881). In particular, as part of a research endeavour the results of which were published in 1867, Riemann had examined functions that possessed an infinity of turning values (i.e., maxima and minima) and/or discontinuities (Riemann 1990[1867]), and this work raised many unresolved issues. In a similar manner, in 1870 Heine considered various problems associated with the convergence of trigonometric functions, and his work required the notion of an infinite number of points on the real number line (Heine 1870). Cantor was intrigued by these number-theoretical concerns, and in his pre-1872 papers he extended and refined some of these ideas. However, he swiftly realised that the notion of an infinite collection of mathematical objects, which was required if the real number line was to be adequately defined, had been treated rather informally by number theorists in the past; even by those associated with the Cauchy–Weierstrass rigorisation programme. Therefore, in a series of papers published between the years 1872 and 1895 Cantor gradually developed an approach to number theory that was grounded in the concept of a set (*'Menge'*). His ideas evolved gradually, and there were a number of significant moments when his thinking coalesced. For instance, the publication of the first paper primarily devoted to set theory in 1874 was a significant occurrence, as was the appearance of his monumental *Foundations of a General Theory of Manifolds* (i.e., for 'manifolds' read 'sets') in 1883, which summarised the main aspects of the theory to date. However, perhaps his most influential paper was 'Contributions to the Foundations of Transfinite Set Theory', which was published in 1895, and which was subsequently dispersed widely throughout the international mathematical community. Since an exhaustive discussion of the gradual development of set theory is neither feasible nor desirable here, the following summary is intended to introduce only those aspects of the theory that relate to topics considered at length in later sections.[13]

In the Cantorian tradition a set is viewed as a collection of objects; a given set constitutes a single entity, and the elements it contains are referred to as the 'members' of that set. For instance, using modern notation, the statement '$A = \{\alpha, \beta\}$' indicates that A is a set that contains two members, the elements α and β. Sometimes sets can be defined by specifying properties of their members. For example, the statement '$C = \{x \mid x \text{ is an even number}\}$' indicates that C is the set of even numbers, with the symbol '$\mid$' being understood to mean 'such that'. Set membership is indicated using the symbol '$\in$' (i.e., '$\alpha \in A$' indicates that α is a member of the set A), while the symbol '$\notin$' is defined as the inverse of '$\in$' (i.e., '$\gamma \notin A$' indicates that γ is not a member of the set A). Cantor introduced the basic operations of set theory that are now referred to as union ('$\cup$'), intersection ('$\cap$') and difference (a.k.a. complement) ('$\setminus$'). In addition, he defined the notion of a subset: if A and C are both sets, then A is a proper subset of C if every member of A is also a member of C but it is not the case that every member of C is also a member of A (i.e., in symbols, '$A \subset C$'). Cantor also introduced the notion of a power set: given a set, A, the power set of A contains all possible subsets of A and is is denoted symbolically as '$P(A)$'. Although these various definitions and operations seem innocuous in the finite realm, one of Cantor's motivations for developing his theory was to devise a method of dealing with the infinite sets of points on the real number line. Since he considered a set to be a self-contained whole (i.e., a collection of individuals that could be treated as an individual entity itself), he was able to explore the notion of an infinite set simply by extending the concept of a finite set. For instance, if $A = \{x \mid x \text{ is an even number}\}$, then clearly the set A contains an infinite number of elements, since it contains all the even numbers. Eventually, following this kind of reasoning, Cantor reached the startling conclusion that infinite sets are not all the same size. In order to illustrate this idea he used the notion of one-to-one correspondence. For instance, to give an example of the correspondence principle being used to indicate that two sets are the same size, since the elements in the set of whole numbers, $I = \{1, 2, 3, \ldots\}$, can be put into one-to-one correspondence with the elements in the set of even numbers, $E = \{2, 4, 6, \ldots\}$, these sets can be considered to be the same size, which is clearly counter-intuitive since $E \subset I$. This result suggests that, in set theory at least, a part can be equal to the whole.

Cantor's research into infinite sets created the branch of number theory known as 'transfinite arithmetic'. As indicated above, his exploration of the basic set-theoretical formalism caused him to consider the possibility that there were infinite sets of different sizes, and, in order to examine this more fully, he introduced transfinite cardinal and ordinal numbers. Given a finite set A, where $A = \{\alpha, \beta\}$, the cardinality of A is 2 (in modern notation, '$|A| = 2$'), since A contains two members. The same ideas can be extended to infinite sets and Cantor introduced the symbol '$\aleph_0$' (aleph-null) to represent the cardinal number associated with the set of whole numbers (i.e., if $I = \{1, 2, 3, \ldots\}$, then $|I| = \aleph_0$). By the mid-1890s Cantor had explored various properties of the transfinite cardinals and, in particular, he was able to demonstrate that the power set of a given set must have a larger cardinal number than the original set itself, and this seemingly harmless theorem was to have unforeseen consequences during the early years of the twentieth century. The transfinite ordinal numbers (which Cantor also introduced) are similar in principle to transfinite cardinals, the difference being that they can only be obtained for sets the elements of which have been organised in a pre-defined sequence. Accordingly, Cantor used the symbol 'ω' to represent the transfinite ordinal associated with the set of whole numbers. Since, in Cantorian arithmetic, numbers are created by a generative procedure that involves adding '1' to an existing number, Cantor realised that an infinity of ordinal numbers could be obtained simply by applying the same procedure to ω. In this fashion, the infinite sequence

$$1, 1+1, \ldots, \omega, \omega+1, \ldots, \omega^2, \ldots, \omega^\omega, \ldots \qquad (2.3)$$

can be produced. Since these ordinals denote the size of corresponding sets, it follows that an infinity of differently sized infinite sets could be constructed.

Cantor's *Mengenlehre* was an undeniably provocative theory, and it quickly inspired controversy. Nevertheless, it appealed to those mathematicians concerned with the task of arithmetising analysis, since it seemed to offer a plausible framework that could be used to secure the foundations of number theory once and for all. Consequently, Cantor's work was elaborated by other researchers, and it began to be used as a theoretical basis in many different sub-branches of mathematics. Without doubt, the most important post-Cantorian extension of the theory was due to Ernst Zermelo (1871–1953) and Adolf Fraenkel (1891–1965), who managed to provide an axiomatic foundation for set-theoretic concepts. Indeed, the so-called 'ZF' axiom set they provided is still standardly used as the basis for modern classical set theory, and it has enabled the discipline to blossom into a highly sophisticated branch of twentieth-century mathematics.[14] However, despite the prevalent enthusiasm for set theory that characterised the mid-1890s, Cantor himself soon began to identify apparent weaknesses in his work, and the problems seemed to cluster around the transfinite aspects of the theory. For instance, in a series of letters to Dedekind written in 1899, Cantor considered the logical validity of the set of all sets and argued that, since this set contains all other sets, its transfinite cardinal must be larger than any other transfinite cardinal. However, since the set of all subsets of a given set must have a larger cardinal than the set itself (as he had previously demonstrated), it follows that there is a larger cardinal number than the largest cardinal number (Cantor 1937[1899]). This paradox caused him to recommend that the set of all sets and its associated cardinal number should not be included in discussions of the subject since the concept was not coherent. Accordingly, he began to speak (somewhat vaguely) of consistent and inconsistent sets, the latter including those that result in paradoxes.

Alarming as the discovery of this paradox was, Cantor later realised that the problems were not confined to transfinite cardinals, and he began to discover unexpected inconsistencies in the theory of transfinite ordinal numbers. As mentioned above, a basic theorem of transfinite arithmetic states that the ordinal number of the set of all ordinal numbers up to and including n is larger than n, and the ordinal number associated with the set of ordinal numbers $\{1, 2, 3, \ldots, \omega\}$ is $\omega + 1$. Therefore the set of *all* ordinals should be associated with an ordinal that is larger than the largest in the set. But this is a contradiction, since the set contains *all* ordinals. Cantor communicated this concern to Hilbert in c. 1896, and it later became known as the Burali-Forti Paradox after Cesare Burali-Forti (1861–1931), who discussed the problem in a later paper. These problems, perhaps 'paradoxes', were a cause of real unease when they became known to the mathematical community: how could set theory possibly provide a secure foundation for number theory if it clearly contained inherent illogicalities itself? Indeed, the difficulties resulting from transfinite arithmetic largely inspired the various proposals for securing the foundations of mathematics that coalesced into the three dominant ideologies that came to be known (rather too simplistically perhaps) as Logicism, Formalism, and Intuitionism. Since these philosophical-mathematical movements ultimately influenced the development of linguistics in the twentieth century, it is necessary to consider them separately in some detail.

2.5 Logicism

Although logic has its roots in antiquity, the development of modern symbolic logic was given significant impetus in the seventeenth century when Leibniz began to consider the possibility of a universal symbolic language that could be used to clarify all arguments and resolve all disputes, as proposed in his *Dissertation Concerning the Art of Combinations* (1666). Leibniz's ideas were extended only spasmodically by his immediate successors, and it was not until the start of the nineteenth century that more focused and ambitious treatises concerning logic began to appear. In England, Augustus De Morgan (1806–1871), George Boole (1815–1865), and Francis (F. H.) Bradley (1846–1924) made significant contributions to the logic of relations and explored the connections between logic, algebra, and probability theory; in Germany, Hermann Grassmann (1809–1877) and Ernst Schröder (1841–1902) advanced the theory of logical operators and clarified the nature of the identity relation; while, in America, Charles Peirce (1839–1914) fused the work of Boole and De Morgan, thus creating a Boolean logic of relations which required him to adopt the basic principles of the propositional calculus.[15] However, while these various research trends served to augment the range and power of symbolic logic, it was Gottlob Frege (1848–1925) who first proposed that logic could provide a secure foundation for arithmetic and (by extension) mathematics in general. In his first work devoted entirely to logic, *Concept-Script* (i.e., *Begriffsschrift*), which was published in 1879, Frege presented a sophisticated logical system that included the truth-functional propositional calculus, the analysis of propositions as functions and arguments (rather than the traditional subject-predicate decomposition), the basic theory of existential and universal quantification, the use of derivations based entirely on the expression-form of statements, and numerous other procedures and techniques that have since become a standard part of classical logic. However, it was not until his next major work, *The Foundations of Arithmetic*, that Frege explicitly suggested that the type of logical system he had outlined in his *Concept-Script* could be used as a basis for arithmetic. This bold claim, which he went on to explore more thoroughly in *The Fundamentals of Arithmetic* (1893), effectively initiated the Logicism movement that was to dominate research into symbolic logic during the early twentieth century.[16]

While Frege was developing his logico-mathematical philosophy during the 1880s, Peano was busy in Italy extending the work of Boole, Grassmann, and Schröder, thereby establishing his own school of symbolic logic. In his ambitious *Principles of Arithmetic* (mentioned in section 2.3 above) he argued (like Frege) that arithmetic could be constructed upon the foundation provided by logic. To this end, he set about devising a consistent notational system that would enable him to axiomatise mathematics using a logical symbolic language. In addition, one of Peano's most significant contributions was to move logic away from the purely algebraic tradition that had dominated in the mid-nineteenth century, and he achieved this (in part) by examining the relationship between logic and Cantorian set theory.[17] Gradually Peano's work became known to a wider international audience, helped by his involvement in the creation of the journal *Rivista di matematica* (i.e., *Mathematical Review*) in 1891, which enabled his ideas (and that of his growing number of students) to be disseminated with greater ease.

The movement to derive the whole of arithmetic (and therefore mathematics) from the parsimonious essentials of symbolic logic culminated in the work of Alfred Whitehead (1861–1947) and Bertrand Russell (1872–1970). Whitehead had been awarded a fellowship at Trinity College, Cambridge in 1884 after submitting a (now lost) dissertation on James Clerk Maxwell's theory of electromagnetism, and his interest in symbolic logic developed during the 1890s while he was working on his book *A Treatise on Universal Algebra with Applications*, which eventually appeared in 1898. During this time he was involved in examining a dissertation by Russell on the foundations of geometry, so the two future collaborators first met as fellow and student. Russell's early interest in the philosophy of mathematics was inspired by his initial attempt to axiomatise the rudiments of geometry, and he did not begin seriously to devote himself to the study of symbolic logic until 1897.[18] His interest in the subject had been stimulated by his study of Bradley's *The Principles of Logic* (1883), and after 1897 he made swift and purposeful progress in the task of turning himself into a fully-fledged logician. During the years 1897–1910, working in conjunction with Whitehead, he began to synthesise the work of Cantor, Frege, and Peano (amongst others) in an ambitious attempt to derive the whole of mathematics from a small collection of self-evident logical axioms, in direct pursuance of what came to be known as the Logicist programme, and, crucially, many of Whitehead and Russell's contributions to the theory of symbolic logic were motivated by the various paradoxes associated with set theory.

Russell had first encountered Cantor's set theory in 1895, when he obtained a pamphlet copy of the *Foundations of a General Theory of Manifolds*; he studied Cantor's work intensely from 1896 to 1897, and, by 1899, was largely persuaded of the validity of his basic approach. But problems began to emerge. In November 1900 Russell discovered a 'fallacy' in Cantor's work (now generally known as 'Russell's Paradox'), which can be succinctly expressed as the following question: given the set, S, which is the set of all sets that are not members of themselves, is S a member of itself or not? The answer to this question is paradoxical since, if S is a member of itself, then (obviously) it follows that it is not a member of itself – and vice versa. Disturbed by this illogicality, Russell began assiduously to collect similar paradoxes during the early 1900s, often giving them names (i.e., 'The Liar's Paradox', 'Berry's Paradox', 'The Burali-Forti Paradox', and so on), and part of the task he set for the research programme that he and Whitehead were pursuing was to extirpate fully these paradoxes from set theory. The first clear statement of Russell's intent was contained in his *Principles of Mathematics*, which appeared in 1903. In the introduction to this text, Russell articulated his 'general doctrine' (which he associated with Leibniz) that 'all mathematics is deduction by logical principles from logical principles' (Russell 1938[1903]: 5), and, in the ensuing text, he went on to articulate his convictions more precisely:

> The connection of mathematics with logic...is exceedingly close. The fact that all mathematical constants are logical constants, and that all the premises of mathematics are concerned with these, gives, I believe, the precise statement of what philosophers have meant in asserting that mathematics is *à priori* [*sic*]. The fact is that, when once the apparatus of logic has been accepted, all mathematics necessarily follows...From what has now been said, the reader will perceive that the present work has to fulfil two objectives, first, to show that all mathematics follows from symbolic logic, and secondly to discover, as far as possible, what are the principles of symbolic logic itself. (Russell 1938[1903]: 8–9)

In accordance with these objectives, during the years 1903–1910 Russell and Whitehead collaborated and published a series of papers in which they considered various difficulties attendant upon the task of seeking (i) to discover the most parsimonious axiomatic logical system, and (ii) to derive the whole of mathematics from this basis in such a way as to avoid all 'fallacies'. Although, as mentioned above, much of their work involved synthesising the research of their predecessors and contemporaries, they also made numerous significant theoretical contributions themselves. Of these, perhaps the most controversial was the 'theory of logical types'. Whitehead and Russell had observed that the paradoxes of set theory invariably involved self-reference of one kind or another, hence their tendency to refer to them as 'vicious-circle fallacies'. Accordingly, the theory of logical types was designed to delimit the extent of permissible self-reference in an attempt to avoid the paradoxes. As they later explained,

> An analysis of the paradoxes to be avoided shows that they all result from a certain kind of vicious circle. The vicious circles in question arise from supposing that a collection of objects may contain members which can only be defined by means of the collection as a whole...The principle which enables us to avoid illegitimate totalities may be stated as follows: 'whatever includes *all* of a collection must not be one of the collection'. (Whitehead and Russell 1925[1910]: 37)

Although an arbitrary and rather elaborate 'principle', the theory at least provided a practical way of avoiding paradoxes while developing set-theoretical concepts from the axioms of a given logical system.[19]

Whitehead and Russell's decade of research into the feasibility of their Logicist project resulted in the publication of *Principia Mathematica* (hereafter *PM*) during the years 1910–1913. The influence of *PM* upon the development of logic during the twentieth century cannot really be overestimated. Although it contains inevitable inconsistencies and obscurities, this work still constitutes the most profound attempt to reduce mathematics to logic. Consequently, it is necessary to consider the form and content of *PM* in some detail.[20]

The various chapters of *PM* were subdivided in sections which were further subdivided into 'numbers', indicated by an asterix and a numeral (i.e., *1), which served to facilitate cross-references. In numbers *1–*5, the so-called 'theory of deduction' was developed, and this effectively constituted the propositional calculus. Accordingly variables were introduced to denote elementary propositions (e.g., p, q) and the fundamental logical operators negation ('$\neg$'), disjunction ('$\vee$'), conjunction ('$\wedge$'), and implication ('$\rightarrow$') were presented and defined along with primitive propositions. This latter group includes informal statements of the type 'Anything implied by a true proposition is true', and these were used to enable more complex propositions to be derived. The logical operators, listed above, were not all assumed to be primitive. Rather, only disjunction and negation were defined directly, and the definitions of the other operators were constructed from these. For instance, using the symbol '$=_{df}$' to denote definition, implication can be defined as

$$p \rightarrow q =_{df} \neg p \vee q \qquad (2.4)$$

indicating that the statement 'p implies q' and the statement 'either not-p or q' are functionally equivalent. From this minimal basis, essential non-primitive propositions were then derived. For example, the 'principle of tautology' is asserted (i.e., '$\vdash$') as

$$\vdash (p \vee p) \rightarrow p \qquad (2.5)$$

and this proposition is associated with the symbol 'Taut' in order to facilitate future reference.

Having established the basic propositional calculus in this manner, Whitehead and Russell then introduced the predicate calculus, and this was accomplished in numbers *9–*14, where the propositions established for the propositional calculus were simply extended so that they could be applied to functions taking variables as arguments (i.e., $\phi(x)$). In addition, the universal operator,

'∀', was introduced, and statements of the form '$\forall x[\phi(x)]$' were taken to mean 'For all x it is the case that $\phi(x)$ is true'. Using the existing formalisms, the existential operator was then defined in terms of the universal operator and negation as follows

$$\exists x[\phi(x)] =_{df} \neg[\forall x [\neg\phi(x)]] \tag{2.6}$$

where, as previously, '$=df$' indicates that the definiendum is being defined. With the basics of the predicate calculus established for 1-place propositional functions, Whitehead and Russell extended the framework so that n-place functions could be handled, and, having introduced the predicate calculus in this manner, number *20 prepared the ground for many of the later technical developments by introducing the calculi of classes and relations. 'Class' is the word that is used in *PM* for Cantorian sets. This term derives from pre-Cantorian theories of aggregates, and, in the first years of the 1900s, Whitehead and Russell began to use it as the English equivalent of Cantor's term '*Menge*'.[21] As defined in *PM*, classes are understood to be groups of variables that satisfy propositional functions of the form '$\phi(x)$'. Class membership can therefore be defined as

$$\vdash x \in \hat{z}[\phi(z)] \equiv \phi(x) \tag{2.7}$$

where '$\equiv$' indicates bidirectional implication. Here '$\hat{z}$' constitutes the class determined by the function ϕ, so (2.7) indicates that the statement 'x is a member of the class determined by the function ϕ' implies the statement '$\phi(x)$ is true' (and vice versa). The definition of relation follows on from the function-based definition of classes since, in *PM*, relations are understood to specify a 'class of couples'. In other words, the variable pair (x, y) is a member of the class of couples associated with the relation R, so long as the statement '$x R y$' holds for x and y. Since any 2-place propositional function determines a relation, there is a clearly defined connection between functions and relations, and this connection is captured by the equivalence

$$\vdash R = \hat{x}\hat{y}\phi(x, y) \equiv x R y \equiv_{x,y} \phi(x, y) \tag{2.8}$$

Upon this theoretical basis, the calculus of relations was developed in numbers *23–*38, during which time various essential propositions were offered in convenient shorthand notations. For instance, if the relation R implies the relation S, then the notation

$$R \subset S = x R y \rightarrow_{x,y} x S y \tag{2.9}$$

was used to prevent laborious use of unwieldy symbolism.

As *PM* continued, the central task of deriving the rudiments of mathematics (i.e., the essentials of number theory) was accomplished. Finite arithmetic was obtained first (*100–*106) before the leap to the transfinite realm was made (*118–*126). Eventually the general theory of series was presented (*200–*276), which led to the introduction of vector families (*330–*375). The whole project had begun as a simple attempt to provide a revised version of Russell's *Principles of Mathematics* and, after ten years of continuous labour, it had resulted in the publication of three monumental volumes.

The general reception of *PM* was complex, and some specific aspects of its influence and subsequent development will be discussed in chapter 3. It is only necessary here to indicate that during the 1920s and 1930s many researchers attempted to simplify and/or extend the system Whitehead and Russell had constructed. After *PM* and the foundational debates of the 1920s (discussed in the following sections), the desire to derive the whole of mathematics from logic waned rather, though research into logic as an independent discipline continued unabated. From the 1950s onwards various non-classical logics such as conditional logic, fuzzy logic, and quantum logic began to receive more attention, and there were numerous attempts to use techniques derived from modern symbolic logic to analyse natural language (as discussed in chapter 3).[22] Nevertheless, despite the countless developments and changes that have occurred since its first appearance, *PM* remains an astonishing testament to the ambition of the Logicist movement in the early twentieth century.

2.6   Formalism

The foundational movement that came to be known as Formalism, and which came to be viewed as an alternative to Logicism, was associated primarily with David Hilbert, one of the most influential mathematicians of the late nineteenth and early twentieth centuries.[23] Hilbert's early work was devoted to a range of topics in number theory, analysis, and algebra, and his interest in foundational issues was not signalled until the publication of his *Foundations of Geometry* in 1899. In this booklet, Hilbert attempted to provide a viable axiomatic foundation for geometry, just as Russell had attempted to do two years previously. General dissatisfaction with the existing axiomatic-deductive geometrical systems (especially Euclid's *Elements*) had been provoked during the nineteenth century by the proliferation of non-Euclidean geometries which substantially undermined the role of spatial intuition as a means of validating geometrical arguments. By contrast with the classical Euclidean methodology, Hilbert endeavoured to remove all latent remnants of geometric intuition by exploiting the correspondence between geometry and arithmetic. He argued that geometric relations could be interpreted as arithmetic relations, in which case the validity of axiomatic-deductive geometrical systems could be guaranteed without the need for intuition-based arguments, assuming (of course) that arithmetic itself was constructed upon a secure basis. This kind of relativistic foundational approach is reminiscent of the attempts to secure analysis by means of number theory that were discussed in section 2.3.

Given the ultimate dependence of geometry upon arithmetic (or, more specifically, the theory of real numbers), as advocated by Hilbert in *Foundations of Geometry*, it was perhaps inevitable that he should have begun to explore the axiomatic basis of number theory itself in the early 1900s, and, accordingly, he considered the implications of such a task explicitly in his 1900 paper 'Concerning the Concept of Number'. However, it was not until 1904 that he began to address the issue of mathematical foundations in general, and he seems to have been galvanised into action primarily by the paradoxes of set theory that had been collected and discussed by Russell in his *Principles of Mathematics*, though Hilbert had been familiar with some of the difficulties since the late 1890s.[24] While agreeing with Russell that the paradoxes undermined set theory as currently formulated, Hilbert dismissed the assertion that they could be eliminated only by deriving mathematics from a small set of logical axioms. The Logicist research programme was misguided, Hilbert maintained, primarily because logic utilises various mathematical concepts that are later derived from it, thus inducing a fatal circularity:

> Arithmetic is often considered to be part of logic, and the traditional fundamental logical notions are usually presupposed when it is a question of establishing a foundation for arithmetic. If we observe attentively, however, we realise that in the traditional exposition of the laws of logic certain fundamental arithmetic notions are already used, for example, the notion of set and, to some extent, also that of number. Thus we already find ourselves turning in a circle, and that is why a partly simultaneous development of the laws of logic and of arithmetic is required if paradoxes are to be avoided. (Hilbert 1967b[1904]: 131)

This quotation is taken from Hilbert's 1904 paper 'Concerning the Foundations of Logic and Arithmetic', which is often regarded as the earliest statement of his Formalist manifesto, and there is no doubt that in this paper Hilbert introduced several of the key ideas that were to dominate his mature foundational work.

During the 1910s Hilbert was enchanted by *PM* and started to write more enthusiastically about logic as a result. In particular, he came to admire the powerful symbolic language that Whitehead and Russell had developed in order to facilitate their logical deductions.[25] Despite his augmented appreciation, though, Hilbert continued to maintain that the Logicist movement was flawed due to the aforementioned circularity inherent in the strategy it adopted. However, during this period he felt compelled not only to demonstrate the weaknesses of the renewed Logicist agenda, but also to invalidate the Intuitionist arguments (discussed in section 2.7) that were beginning to permeate the consciousness of the international mathematical community. Goaded into activity, therefore, by these alternative foundational movements, Hilbert began to present, with greater clarity, his own proposal for salvaging classical mathematics from the paradoxes of set theory. As a result, in a series of publications that appeared during the years 1918–1934, frequently aided by his assistant Paul Bernays (1888–1977), Hilbert developed his *'Beweistheorie'* (i.e., 'proof theory'), which was intended explicitly to define his Formalist position concerning the question of foundations. As Hilbert's theory evolved over the years, many of the technical details altered, but the underlying principles remained fairly constant. Therefore, rather than attempting to provide a superficial overview of the complete life-cycle of the theory, one particular mature expression of it will be considered in some detail here in order to convey Hilbert's main aims and strategies. The version of the theory discussed will be that presented in the 1927 paper 'The Foundations of Mathematics'. The exposition Hilbert offered in this paper is comparatively lucid and reveals many of the abiding concerns that were later to be distorted and exaggerated in countless more extreme accounts, some of which will be considered in section 2.8.

'The Foundations of Mathematics' begins with a clear statement of intent that effectively constitutes a non-technical overview of the method developed in the whole paper:

> I should like to eliminate once and for all the questions regarding the foundations of mathematics, in the form in which they are now posed, by turning every mathematical proposition into a formula that can be concretely exhibited and strictly derived, thus recasting mathematical definitions and inferences in such a way that they are unshakable and yet provide an adequate picture of the whole science. (Hilbert 1967a[1927]: 464)

This passage clearly indicates that Hilbert's proof theory involved two related tasks. First, a procedure was required that enabled 'every mathematical proposition' to be converted into a 'formula', then it must be demonstrated that the formulae obtained could be 'strictly derived'. The first task stipulates that mathematical statements must be formalised (i.e., converted into strings of precisely defined symbols) so that mathematics as a whole can be viewed simply as 'an inventory of formulae' (Hilbert 1967a[1927]: 465), and more will be said about the process of formalisation later. The second task involves the derivation of the formulae within a given system. The overriding concern here is with the nature of the proof techniques that are utilised, hence Hilbert's use of the compound noun '*Beweistheorie*'. Obviously, since this task involves the manipulation of strings of symbols that represent mathematical propositions, it can be said to be characterised by a certain (not necessarily vicious) circularity: proof-theoretical mathematical techniques are used to determine the validity of (suitably encoded) mathematical propositions. It is this apparent self-reference that caused the second of Hilbert's tasks to be referred to as 'metamathematics'; that is, mathematics about mathematics.

Having delineated his basic intentions at the start of the paper, Hilbert immediately proceeds to introduce the fundamental machinery he requires, and the three main components he presents are a set of logical operators, a general proof schema, and a set of axioms. The logical operators are unremarkable, and they include symbols for implication, conjunction, disjunction, and negation, as well as universal and existential operators. These are all common to *PM*-style systems, though (as shown later) Hilbert adopts definitions for the last two that differ from those offered in *PM*. The general proof schema Hilbert presents, however, is of greater interest. In the paper a mathematical proof is informally defined (rather unsatisfactorily) as 'an array that must be given as such to our perceptual intuition' (Hilbert 1967a[1927]: 465), and (more helpfully) it is stated that a proof consists of a sequence of inferences. The specific proof schema Hilbert presents takes the form

$$\frac{\mathfrak{G} \quad \mathfrak{G} \to \mathfrak{F}}{\mathfrak{F}} \qquad (2.10)$$

and it defines the type of inference that is permitted in proof construction. The symbols $\mathfrak{G}$ and $\mathfrak{F}$ in schema (2.10) indicate formulae (i.e., mathematical proposition converted into the specified formal symbolism) which are either (i) axioms in the system, (ii) propositions derived from (i) by substitution, (iii) the end formulae of a previous valid proof, or (iv) propositions derived from (iii) by means of substitution. In schema (2.10), $\mathfrak{G}$ and the implication $\mathfrak{G} \to \mathfrak{F}$ are given, with the result that $\mathfrak{F}$ can be inferred. A formula, $\mathfrak{F}$, therefore, is said to be provable if it is an axiom in the system, or if it is the final formula in a proof. This methodology enables proofs to be viewed as sequences of logical inferences that enable formulae to be derived within a given axiomatic system. It is crucial for Hilbert's project that the procedural definition of a proof, as outlined above, is clear and unambiguous, since, as he states later in the paper, it is imperative that 'a formalised proof, like a numeral, is a concrete and surveyable object' (Hilbert 1967a[1927]: 471). It is the property of being 'surveyable' that is so important: if a proof cannot be checked in an infallible manner, then mathematics cannot be raised upon a secure proof-theoretical foundation.

The axioms, mentioned above, that Hilbert introduces in his paper are subdivided into six main categories:

- Group I: Axioms of Implication (e.g., $A \rightarrow (B \rightarrow A)$)
- Group II: Axioms of Conjunction and Disjunction (e.g., $(A \wedge B) \rightarrow A$)
- Group III: Axioms of Negation (e.g., $\neg\neg A = A$)
- Group IV: The ϵ-axiom: $A(a) \rightarrow A(\epsilon(A))$
- Group V: Axioms of Equality (e.g., $a = a$)
- Group VI: Axioms of Number (e.g., $a' \neq 0$, where 'a'' means 'the number following a')

The axioms in groups I–IV are referred to as 'the logical axioms', while those in groups V–VI are called 'mathematical axioms' since they involve number-theoretic concepts. Once again, this highlights the difference between Formalism and Logicism: Hilbert assumes that certain mathematical objects, such as the numeral '1', are pre-theoretical, existing in the intuition as a thought-object ('*Gedankeding*'), while Whitehead and Russell seek to derive even such basic objects from the principles of logic. The axiom group that demands most attention is group IV, which contains the ϵ-axiom. This axiom is required in order to enable transfinite arithmetic to be incorporated within the basic proof-theoretical framework. More practically, it also permits the vague notions of 'all' and 'there exists' to be defined. As shown above, the axiom takes the form '$A(a) \rightarrow A(\epsilon(A))$', where $\epsilon(A)$ denotes an object for which the proposition $A(a)$ holds, if it holds for any proposition at all. Consequently, the universal and existential operators can be defined as follows:

$$\forall x[A(x)] \equiv A(\epsilon(\neg A)) \tag{2.11}$$

$$\exists x[A(x)] \equiv A(\epsilon(A)) \tag{2.12}$$

These definitions should be compared with those used by Whitehead and Russell in *PM*, and included in (2.6) above. As mentioned previously, Hilbert's use of the ϵ-axiom (which uses the function $\epsilon(x)$) enabled him to construct proofs for transfinite arithmetic in accordance with the strictures of proof theory. However, while the ϵ-function facilitated the construction of such proofs, Hilbert often sought to eliminate the function at a later stage in a given derivation. In order to accomplish this he made extensive use of recursion and recursive functions. Since this aspect of Hilbert's work was partly responsible for the advancement of recursive function theory in the early twentieth century, it will be considered in more detail in that context in section 3.3.

Armed with his set of operators, his proof schema, and his axioms, Hilbert was now able to address the issue of proof construction. The central task was to construct a metamathematical proof that would demonstrate the validity of a given axiom set. For Hilbert, the validity of such a set was always closely related to the technical notions of completeness and consistency. The requirement of completeness simply demands that all well-formed formulae, derived within a given system, can be shown to be either true or false. As for the requirement of consistency, from a proof-theoretical perspective, a given axiom set is considered to be consistent if no formulae taking the form '$a \neq a$' can ever be derived. In other words, a consistent axiom set will never allow contradictions to be proved. The task of proof theory in part, therefore, is to secure the axiomatic system underlying the whole of mathematics by establishing its consistency. The nature of this task, for Hilbert at least, was very different from the task of converting mathematical propositions into formal strings of symbols. As he states in the 1927 paper,

> To prove consistency we therefore need only show that $0 \neq 0$ cannot be obtained from our axioms by the rules in force as the end formula of a proof, hence that $0 \neq 0$ is not a provable formula. And this is a task that fundamentally lies within the province of intuition, just as much as does in contentual number theory the task, say, of proving the irrationality of $\sqrt{2}$ (Hilbert 1967a[1927]: 471)

Statements such as this are not atypical. Hilbert repeatedly emphasised the contentual nature of the metamathematical aspects of proof theory. For instance, in a 1922 paper, while providing an overview of proof theory, he observes:

> In addition to this proper mathematics, there appears a mathematics that is to some extent new, a *metamathematics* which serves to safeguard it by protecting it from the terror of unnecessary prohibitions as well as from the difficulty of paradoxes. In this metamathematics – in contrast to the purely formal modes of inference in mathematics proper – we apply contentual inference; in particular, to the proof of the consistency of the axioms. (Hilbert 1998[1922]: 212)

The emphasis here is absolutely clear: although formal (i.e., meaning-less) methods may be used in mathematics proper, such methods *cannot* be used during the metamathematical stage of analysis, indicating that, for Hilbert at least, proof theory was considerably more than a game involving the manipulation of meaningless symbols. Statements such as the above, with their focus upon the differences between formalisation and metamathematical analysis, should be recalled when the nature of Hilbertian Formalism is considered. A common misconception presents Hilbert as wanting to reduce the whole of mathematics to a contentless exercise in symbol manipulation that is performed in accordance with clearly defined rules. From this perspective, in the Formalist game it is the relationship between the strings of symbols that is crucial, and the meaning either of the symbols themselves or of the strings they form is deemed to be irrelevant. This misconstrual of Hilbert's programme is partly due to the practice of extracting certain of his comments from out of their immediate context. For instance, as mentioned above, part of Hilbert's contribution in his *Foundations of Geometry* was to demonstrate that the meaning of the geometrical objects he considered need not be accommodated in order to analyse them coherently. In other words, statements about lines, points, and planes could just as readily be interpreted as statements about arithmetic objects, or, as Hilbert allegedly put it 'tables, chairs and beer-mugs!' (quoted in Grattan-Guinness 2000: 208). However, this conventional misinterpretation of Hilbert's programme is also the result of his distinction between the formalisation process and the metamathematical process being ignored. On numerous occasions, for instance, Hilbert emphasised that the task of converting mathematical propositions into a formal symbolic language was a mechanical procedure that did not rely upon considerations of meaning. In his 1927 paper, for example, he states that 'in my theory, contentual inference is replaced by the manipulation of signs according to rules' (Hilbert 1967a[1927]: 467). Although this observation refers only to the pre-metamathematical stage of analysis, comments such as these (when extracted out of context) appear to suggest that it is the formal relationships between strings of symbols that matter, not the meaning of the strings themselves, even during the metamathematical manipulations of these strings. It was the (mis)perceived extremity of this emphasis on the formal properties of mathematical statements that caused Brouwer to refer to Hilbert's programme as 'formalisme'. However, as demonstrated above, Hilbert was never so extreme in his own brand of Formalism, and this observation has caused some commentators to recommend the avoidance of the term when discussing Hilbert, or at least to insist upon an accurate definition.[26] However, as discussed in section 2.8, it was a caricatured version of Hilbert's original theory that was popularised throughout North America and Europe during the 1930s and 1940s, and which ultimately influenced the development of syntactic theory in the twentieth century.

The fate of Formalism, or, more specifically, of proof theory, is well known. In 1931 the young Kurt Gödel published an incompleteness theorem which demonstrated that, if a formal system is strong enough to prove theorems from basic arithmetic, then there will always be theorems that are true but which cannot be proved within the system. In other words, Gödel demonstrated that the criterion of completeness was a chimera, and this proof appeared to invalidate the Formalist approach to the foundations problem. Nevertheless, despite Gödel's results, a number of mathematicians have continued to work within the general framework of proof theory and, as shown in chapter 3, the philosophy behind the theory has exerted a profound influence over many different disciplines.

2.7   Intuitionism

The third major foundational movement, which became known as Intuitionism, was originally associated with the Dutch mathematician Luitzen Brouwer (1881–1966), and it was intended to provide a valid alternative both to Logicism and (incipient) Formalism.[27] Brouwer signalled his preoccupation with foundational issues as early as 1907, when he submitted a doctoral thesis on the subject, *Concerning the Foundations of Mathematics*. Although he later refined considerably the ideas presented in this early work, the thesis nevertheless outlines the basic preoccupations that remained remarkably constant throughout his long career. For instance, in chapter 2 of his thesis, Brouwer explicitly rejects the assumption that mathematical objects and the symbols used to express them are equivalent, arguing instead that thought and language are largely separate. So crucial was this assumption to the whole Intuitionist enterprise that Brouwer was later to refer to it as 'the first act of Intuitionism' (Mancosu 1998: 8–9). The inevitable result of this act was that he came to view mathematics primarily as a process of isolated mental construction, accomplished by the individual mathematician, which must then be (imperfectly) communicated to others by means of language, either a natural language or, most frequently in the mathematical literature, some kind of formal symbolic language. Consequently, intuition is understood to provide the foundation for all of mathematics, and the Logicist and Formalist programmes, with their various ways of prioritising linguistic forms, are deemed to be utterly misguided since they consistently fail to recognise this crucial fact.

While Brouwer's characteristic approach to the foundations problem was outlined in his doctoral thesis, he seems to have felt that he had to establish himself as a leading mathematician if his nascent Intuitionist philosophy were ever to be taken seriously by the international mathematical community. Consequently, during the years 1908–1912 he swiftly turned himself into the leading expert in algebraic topology, publishing around forty papers in the space of four years. As a result, his reputation as a leading mathematician was quickly secured.[28] Now, with his professional career established, he promptly returned to his abiding preoccupation with the task of elaborating an intuition-based theory of mathematics, and this return to foundational considerations marked the start of his sustained attempt to develop Intuitionism as a valid philosophical position. The public renewal of the Intuitionist programme effectively began on 14 October 1912, when Brouwer delivered a paper entitled 'Intuitionism and Formalism'. This inaugural address largely restated the case as outlined in his doctoral thesis, though, to some extent it anticipated future developments by focusing more of the discussion upon set-theoretical concerns. The research programme (re)initiated by the presentation of this paper continued unabated until 1928, and, as it gathered momentum, it began to arouse significant disquiet and, occasionally, acrimonious controversy. The main cause of complaint was that Brouwer's reformulation of the foundations problem jeopardised the validity of significant portions of classical mathematics. Certain individuals began to sense that the old mathematical establishment was beginning to crumble, and, if Hermann Weyl (one of Brouwer's early converts) was to be believed, 'Brouwer, das ist die Revolution!'[29] (quoted in van Stigt 1990: 71).

During the 1920s Brouwer began to articulate how, in his markedly solipsistic philosophy, mathematics could be viewed as the task of creating objects in the individual consciousness by means of constructive procedures, and he accomplished this mainly by devising specific techniques that could be used within a strict Intuitionistic framework. For instance, although his attitude towards logic had been wholly negative during the 1910s, he became more accepting during the 1920s, though he still refused to countenance full-blown *PM*-style classical logic. Perhaps his most provocative stance in this respect was characterised by his rejection of the so-called 'principle of the excluded middle'. This principle had played a fundamental role in logic since Aristotle, and, essentially, it claims that all propositions are either true or false, a claim which in turn implies that all mathematical statements can be shown to be either true or false. Brouwer rejected this assumption and, as a result, developed what has since become known as 'intuitionist logic'.[30]

In addition to his reformulation of classical logic upon intuitionistic principles, Brouwer also concerned himself with the nature of the real number continuum, and came to despise the standard set-theoretic definition that had emerged from the work of Weierstrass, Dedekind, and Cantor. For Brouwer, the continuum was a primitive concept that could not be constructed from more elementary entities. In particular, it could certainly not be built up from sets of discrete points, and therefore was not an arithmetic manifold of real numbers as Cantor (and others) had supposed. Consequently, in a series of papers published in the 1920s, he began to devise an intuitionistic version of set theory based upon a dynamic conception of continuity in which points on the real number line were characterised as convergent sequences of nested intervals that were generated by the free choice of the individual consciousness. In order to achieve this ambitious project, Brouwer sometimes extended existing set-theoretical techniques and sometimes devised his own radical new methods, many of which outraged various sections of the conservative mathematical establishment.[31]

While Brouwer's labours impressed many, the unwieldy nature of the constructive procedures demanded by an unremitting adherence to Intuitionistic principles dissuaded all but a small coterie of devoted followers (the foremost of whom was Arend Heyting (1898–1980)) from adopting Brouwer's methods as practical tools, and there is no doubt that Brouwer was discouraged by this lack of general acceptance. His disquiet increased in the 1920s when the Formalism–Intuitionism debate became a personal feud between himself and Hilbert, resulting in his dismissal by the latter, in 1928, from the editorial board of the journal *Mathematische Annalen* (*Mathematical Annals*). After these final disputes Brouwer retreated into relative obscurity, from which he did not emerge until the 1950s, when he toured the world as an itinerant lecturer, still preaching the Intuitionist gospel. These lectures seem to have been received by his audiences with considerable warmth, although he was mainly viewed as a curious relic, a remarkable remnant of an earlier age when anxieties about the foundations of mathematics were obsessively debated by professional mathematicians, logicians, and philosophers alike.

2.8 Evangelism and pedagogy

Having considered the work of the main participants in the foundational debates of the early twentieth century, it is now necessary briefly to discuss some of the later publications that communicated many of the central arguments summarised in the preceding sections to a wider audience. The survey offered here makes no claim to be exhaustively comprehensive. Indeed, such was the proliferation of books and articles concerning the perceived foundations crisis that appeared during the years 1910–1960, that several sizable tomes could be devoted solely to the task of exploring the way in which the work of Russell, Hilbert, Brouwer, and others was interpreted, reformulated, modified, and utilised for evangelical and pedagogic purposes by later generations. Consequently, some kind of selection process is required, and the texts referred to in this section simply happen to be those that are cited most frequently in linguistics papers published during the first half of the twentieth century. As a result, the following discussion intentionally anticipates some of the main themes of chapter 3, functioning simultaneously as a postlude to the current chapter and a prelude to the next.

One of the first textbooks that attempted to provide a detailed summary of pre-1910 developments in various branches of mathematics was John Young's (1879–1932) *Fundamental Concepts of Algebra and Geometry*. The text was published in 1911, but it was based upon a series of lectures that had been delivered at the University of Illinois in 1909. Consequently, Young was not able to consider the implications of *PM*, the first volume of which appeared in 1910, but he did provide a thorough introduction to a wide range of topics, including Euclidean and non-Euclidean geometry, logic, set theory, number theory, and numerous other subjects. He openly declared that his primary aim was to provide 'an elementary account of the logical foundations of algebra and geometry' (Young 1911: v), a remark that possibly indicates some kind of sympathy with the Logicist movement, and he repeatedly stresses the fact that mathematical propositions are 'logically connected' (Young 1911: 1). However, he also admits that throughout the book he has adopted a 'formal point of view' (Young 1911: v), and certainly his knowledge of Hilbert's proto-Formalist work is revealed in chapters 13 and 14, when he discusses Hilbert's axiomatic approach to geometry in some detail. In this context it is striking that by 1911 the task of providing a logical foundation for specific branches of mathematics was already associated with the Formalist programme.

Although, as mentioned above, Young's text was not able to provide a discussion either of *PM* or of Hilbert's mature proof theory, other textbooks eventually appeared that covered these topics in considerable detail. Often these publications were aimed at advanced undergraduates, or postgraduates in their first years of research, and they attempted primarily to summarise existing results in symbolic logic and metamathematics in a coherent fashion. An early example of this type of textbook was Quine's *Mathematical Logic*, which first appeared in 1940 (reprinted in 1951) and which provided a clear overview of the rudiments of *PM*-style symbolic logic, including chapters on statements, quantification, the theory of classes, relations, numbers, and logical syntax. As will be shown in section 3.7, the theory of logical syntax developed considerably during the 1930s and 1940s, largely due to the influence of Carnap, who refined ideas that Hilbert had introduced. Quine's interest in the syntax of formal languages is apparent throughout his book; he devoted a whole chapter to the topic, and his presentation is conspicuously influenced by Formalism. For instance, while discussing the syntax of formal logical systems, he introduces an alphabet of primitive symbols and adds, with reference to strings formed from this basic symbol set, 'all these characterizations are *formal systems*, in that they speak only of the typographical constitution of the expressions in question and do not refer to the meanings of these expressions' (Quine 1940: 283), and it is this emphasis on the form, rather than the content, of symbolic expressions that reveals the influence of Hilbert's proof theory (as mediated by Carnap). As will become apparent below, such observations became the norm in introductory texts of this kind during the 1940s and 1950s.

Another presentation of the rudiments of symbolic logic appeared when Church published his *Introduction to Mathematical Logic: Part 1* in 1944 – a text that (re)appeared in a revised and expanded form in 1956. Like Quine, Church presented the same basic topics which, by the mid-1950s, were rapidly becoming an incantational mantra (i.e., primitive symbols, variables, quantifiers, propositional calculus, first-order predicate calculus, second-order predicate calculus, and so on), and his Formalist agenda is expressed unambiguously when he observes that 'traditionally, (formal) logic is concerned with the analysis of sentences or of propositions and of proofs with attention to the *form* in abstraction from the *matter*' (Church 1956: 1). It is revealing that the task of using logic to analyse a proof could already be described as traditional, since this indicates the speed with which Hilbert's metamathematical programme had been accepted. Church goes on to discuss the specific topic of the syntax of logical systems in a subsection of his introduction, and he draws a distinction between natural and formal languages. Like Russell, Church felt that natural languages were far more complicated than formal (i.e., artificial) languages since they had 'evolved over a long period of history to serve practical purposes of facility of communication' (Church 1956: 3). Consequently, when Church used the term syntax, he was referring specifically to the syntax of formal languages, rather than natural languages, and he made a further distinction between 'elementary' and 'theoretical' syntax. Elementary syntax is concerned with 'setting up the logistic system and with the verification of particular well-formed formulas, axioms, immediate inferences, and proofs', while theoretical syntax constitutes 'the general mathematical theory of a logistic system or systems and is concerned with all the consequences of their formal structure (in abstraction from the interpretation)' (Church 1956: 59). Clearly, this approach is rooted in Hilbert's proof theory, since the distinction is essentially that between mathematics proper (i.e., proving theorems *in* a logical system) and metamathematics (i.e., proving theorems *about* a logical system). Note, though, that, for Church, the 'interpretation' of the system is irrelevant *even during the metamathematical stage*, while, as indicated in section 2.6, for Hilbert at least, meaning *was* involved in metamathematical considerations. Church's recommended methodology is an example of the sort of extreme Formalism that came to dominate in the 1940s, at the expense of Hilbert's more cautious and subtle approach. It is also significant that, with reference to formal systems, Church remarks that 'like any branch of mathematics, theoretical syntax may, and ultimately must, be studied by the axiomatic method' (Church 1956: 59), since, as will be shown in section 3.2, linguists (particularly syntacticians) became increasingly interested in the axiomatic-deductive method during the first decades of the twentieth century, and the method was ultimately to influence the development of TGG considerably.

Although, as indicated above, Church's text draws upon Formalism, while introducing the rudiments of symbolic logic, it is not primarily intended as an introduction to proof theory. However, an authoritative exposition of the theory did appear in 1952, when Kleene published his *Introduction to Metamathematics*. Kleene's debt to Hilbert is clear from the title alone, and, since the book is intended to be an introduction to proof theory in its entirety, it covers more topics than the introductions to logic discussed above. For instance, in addition to the obligatory chapters on propositional and predicate calculus, it also contains sections on set theory, formal system theory, and the general theory of recursive functions. As expected, the need to avoid meanings, or 'interpretations', when manipulating strings of symbols in a formal system, is repeatedly stressed. For instance, while introducing the notion of a formal system, Kleene remarks that it must be 'described and investigated, by finitary methods and without making use of an interpretation of the system' (Kleene 1952: 69). Later, the above advice is restated in a more elaborate (and rather ungainly) form when the primitive symbols of the system are introduced:

> We reiterate that the interpretations are extraneous to the description of the formal system as such. It must be possible to proceed regarding the formal symbols as mere marks, and not as symbols in the sense of symbols for something which they symbolize or signify. (Kleene 1952: 70)

So, the symbols in a formal system must be manipulated without worrying about that which they denote, and, just in case there could be any lingering doubts, on the very next page Kleene stresses again that 'in metamathematics we must treat the formal symbols as meaningless' (Kleene 1952: 71). These passages indicate that, like Church's presentation, Kleene's text can be viewed as yet another example of the more extreme Formalist position that came to characterise pedagogic texts during the 1940s and 1950s.

One other book, also published in 1952, that deserves comment in this context is Raymond Wilder's *Introduction to the Foundations of Mathematics*. While Church and Kleene were concerned with presenting the technical apparatus of symbolic logic and proof theory respectively, reserving an historical overview of the development of these theories only for footnotes and asides, Wilder wanted to provide a detailed historical survey of the whole foundations crisis. Consequently, in addition to the expected topics, his text includes chapters on the axiomatic-deductive method, set theory, number theory along with separate sections on Logicism, Intuitionism, and Formalism. It is of particular interest that Wilder's book was directly inspired by Young's text, discussed above. As Wilder explains in his introduction,

> In a general way, the idea of the book is similar to that which motivated J. W. Young's *Fundamental Concepts of Algebra and Geometry*, first published in 1911. In 1932 I discussed with Professor Young the desirability of a book such as this one; he agreed thoroughly that it was desirable to write it, if only to have available a book on foundational concepts that will take into account the great strides that have been made in Foundations since the publication of his book. (Wilder 1952: vi)

Clearly, then, by the early 1950s there was an interest not only in the mathematical techniques that emerged from the foundations crisis, but also in the cultural and intellectual history of the period, and Wilder's influential text was consciously designed to cater for this need.

The texts mentioned so far are all either mathematical or logical textbooks that attempted to provide insights into fundamental results in logic and metamathematics. However, other publications began to appear during the 1940s and 1950s that emphasised the wider utility of some of the techniques developed in these areas. For instance, a number of texts attempted to argue that logic could be used to facilitate the analysis of natural language. Two influential texts of this type are Hans Reichenbach's *Elements of Symbolic Logic* (1947) and Paul Rosenbloom's *Elements of Mathematical Logic* (1950). Reichenbach's text is a curious mixture of conventional expository sections that introduce standard topics, and idiosyncratic sections that are mainly concerned with his own research interests. The most significant chapter from the viewpoint of linguistic theory is chapter 7, entitled 'Analysis of Conversational Language', in which Reichenbach outlines his plans for 'a logistic grammar', which stems

52 *The consequences of analysis*

from 'the desire to connect logic with the natural use of language' (Reichenbach 1947: vi). Although the details of Reichenbach's system need not be considered here, it is important to note that his basic intention was to create a grammar for the English language based upon propositional functions. For instance, he observed that the declarative sentence 'x loves y' could be represented by the propositional function '$f(x, y)$', where 'f' corresponds to the verb 'love', and his interest in this sort of function-theoretic grammar was motivated by a dissatisfaction with traditional subject-predicate analysis. Indeed, Reichenbach claimed that the standard subject-predicate analysis 'does violence to the structure of the sentence' (Reichenbach 1947: 252). As an example, he considers the sentence 'Peter is taller than Paul' and claims that this structure is inadequately analysed by classifying 'Peter' as subject and the rest as the predicate, since clearly, in this example, there is some kind of functional similarity between 'Peter' and 'Paul', and therefore this similarity (as well as the obvious functional differences) should be captured by a sufficiently detailed analysis. He goes on to claim that a grammar based on propositional functions like those mentioned above could capture these structural similarities more accurately than subject-predicate analysis. Although Reichenbach's work was never developed extensively by professional linguists, his claim that natural language and logic are more compatible than was commonly supposed at the time intrigued mathematically minded linguists during the 1950s, as will be shown in section 3.4.

While not as radical as Reichenbach's text, Rosenbloom's small volume also implied that the syntax of formal logical systems and the syntax of natural language are essentially identical. His main discussion of this issue is contained in chapter 4, entitled 'The General Syntax of Language', and the definition of a language that he offers is certainly sufficiently broad to include both formal and natural languages.

> A language consists of certain signs, and certain strings of these signs. Its syntax consists of rules for classifying and transforming these strings. The *alphabet* of a language consists of certain basic signs, usually in finite number [*sic*]. By a *string* we mean a finite sequence of signs. A string is exhibited by writing its signs in linear order from left to right. (Rosenbloom 1950: 152)

Once again the Formalist emphasis on inscription (i.e., the writing of finite sequences of signs) is apparent here, and, in this respect, the definition given above is not particularly unusual. What is of interest, though, is the way in which Rosenbloom goes on to discuss the differences between formal and natural languages. For instance, he implies that these two types of language differ in degree rather than in kind:

> As in all natural languages, including Esperanto, the rules of word and sentence formation in English are so complicated and full of irregularities and exceptions that it is almost impossible to get a general view of the structure of the language, and to make generally valid statements about the language. It is for this reason that mathematicians and logicians prefer to work with languages like $\mathbf{L}_3$ [a formal language defined earlier in the text] with very simple and regular structures. (Rosenbloom 1950: 153)

The implication, then, is that, although English and other natural languages are bafflingly complex, and although mathematicians and philosophers find it easier to work with artificially constructed languages, there is no reason *in principle* why natural languages cannot be subjected to the same kinds of formal analysis as their artificial cousins. As will be shown in chapter 3, this is exactly the sort of approach that certain linguists gradually adopted in the the 1940s and 1950s, and it is no coincidence that Chomsky used Rosenbloom's text as one of his main sources of information concerning formal syntax during the early 1950s.

3 *Mathematical linguistics*

3.1 Chapter overview

The purpose of this chapter is to summarise some of the developments, associated with the formal sciences, that grew out of the foundations debates of the early decades of the twentieth century, and to examine the way in which they exerted an influence upon the formulation of linguistic theory. The basic strategy is to focus upon particular techniques or theories that were ultimately to be involved in the creation of TGG. Consequently, it should be remembered throughout that this chapter is necessarily selective, and that it does not attempt to provide an exhaustive coverage of all the associations between mathematics and linguistics that were mooted during the first half of the twentieth century. The first subject, discussed in section 3.2, is the use of the axiomatic-deductive method, and detailed attention is given to the work of Bloomfield, Bloch, and Harwood. Recursive function theory is considered next, in section 3.3, with specific reference to the work of Gödel, Kleene, Post, and Bar-Hillel. In section 3.4 the work of the Lvov-Warsaw school of logicians is assessed, and particular emphasis is placed upon the way in which some of Ajdukiewicz's research into logical systems was revived by Bar-Hillel in the early 1950s. The evolution of constructional system theory is considered in section 3.5, and the associations between Carnap and Goodman are explored, while, in section 3.6, the extreme philosophical stance that came to be known as constructive nominalism is presented. The crucial topic of formal syntax is examined in section 3.7, and the main focus is on the work of Carnap, Bloomfield, Hjelmslev, and Harris. Finally, in section 3.8 the diverse strands of the chapter are brought together by considering the general response of linguists working in the early 1950s to the gradual mathematisation of large parts of their discipline.

3.2 Axiomatics

As indicated in chapter 2, the debates concerning the foundations of mathematics that raged during the early 1900s generated considerable interest at the time, and the details of the various foundational strategies proposed by the main participants were discussed in introductory texts such as those by Young, Quine, Church, Kleene, and Wilder (as summarised in section 2.8), all of which were accessible to mathematically inclined linguists. Without doubt the most significant linguist actually to follow the progress of the foundational debates closely at the time was Leonard Bloomfield (1887–1949), and the first of Bloomfield's publications to reveal the extent of his preoccupation with mathematics was his 1926 paper 'A Set of Postulates for the Science of Language'. In this short paper Bloomfield suggested that linguists should start to use the same basic axiomatic-deductive method which had transformed the study of arithmetic and geometry in the nineteenth century. Bloomfield uses the term 'postulates' instead of axioms, and, at the start of his paper, he explains why a postulational approach could benefit linguistics:

> The method of postulates (that is, assumptions or axioms) and definitions is fully adequate to mathematics; as for other sciences, the more complex their subject-matter, the less amenable they are to this method, since, under it, every description or historical fact becomes the subject of a new postulate ... Nevertheless, the postulational method can further the study of language, because it forces us to state explicitly whatever we assume, to define our terms, and to decide what things may exist independently and what things are interdependent. (Bloomfield 1926: 153)

As far as Bloomfield was concerned, then, the axiomatic-deductive method was of value since it could introduce new rigour (in the Cauchian sense) into linguistics, just as it had been used to render mathematics more exact during the nineteenth century. The comparison with Cauchy's rigorisation programme is not vacuous, since the emphasis in the above passage is upon stating assumptions 'explicitly', and determining which aspects of a given theory are 'interdependent' and which can be treated 'independently'. In this way, Bloomfield appears to be recommending a reformulation of linguistics that is similar both in spirit and methodology to the reformulation of the calculus that Cauchy proposed at the beginning of the nineteenth century (as discussed in section 2.3). In order to clarify how this new rigorisation programme for linguistics might be accomplished, Bloomfield explicitly states later in the paper that, by the judicious use of axioms, definitions, and deduction, 'certain errors can be avoided or corrected by examining and formulating our (at present tacit) assumptions and defining our (often undefined) terms' (Bloomfield 1926: 153). In other words, when compared to more fully developed formal sciences (such as mathematics), linguistics appeared to be infested with errors that could be avoided if an axiomatic-deductive approach were adopted, and, in accordance with this proposal, Bloomfield introduced a set of postulates that could provide a secure foundation for the whole of linguistics. The particular postulates he introduced included definitions and assumptions such as[1]

> **Definition**: An act of speech is an utterance.
> **Assumption**: Within certain communities successive utterances are alike or partly alike.

It is significant that, although Bloomfield recommended the use of a basic postulational methodology because it could make linguistics more precise, as these examples indicate, he did not attempt to introduce a formal language (*à la PM*) that would enable the axioms of linguistics to be converted into unambiguous sequences of precisely defined symbols. However, as will be shown below, this extension was accomplished by a later generation of linguistics.

The text that Bloomfield cites as the main source of his information concerning the axiomatic-deductive method is Young's 1911 text *Lectures on the Fundamental Concepts of Algebra and Geometry* (discussed in section 2.8), and, given Bloomfield's knowledge of this work, it is reasonable to suppose that, by 1926 at least, he was broadly familiar with all the pre-1911 topics summarised in chapter 2 above, since they are all discussed in Young's book. In addition to this direct inspiration from the pedagogical mathematical literature, Bloomfield was persuaded by the work of the psychologist Albert Weiss (1879–1931) that mathematical procedures could be usefully employed in the mind-based sciences. For instance, in a 1925 paper, Weiss had proposed a set of postulates for psychology, and this attempt at axiomatisation partly inspired Bloomfield's proposal for the reform of the methodology of linguistics.[2] Clearly, therefore, by 1926 Bloomfield was intrigued by the precise nature of the relationship between mathematics and cognitive phenomena such as natural language, and, far from being an ephemeral fad, his interest in this topic seems to have increased during the years following 1926. For instance, there are various comments concerning the relationship between language and mathematics in his most famous and influential book, *Language*, which appeared in 1933. To take one example, at one point he refers to mathematics as 'the ideal use of language' (Bloomfield 1933: 29), and later declares (rather provocatively) that one of the tasks confronting the practising linguist is to 'reveal the verbal character of mathematics'

(Bloomfield 1933: 507). Although Bloomfield does not state explicitly in *Language* how such a task could best be accomplished, this remark certainly suggests that by the early 1930s he had begun to consider the possibility of using techniques from linguistics in order to analyse mathematics, rather than merely using mathematical procedures to explore fundamental properties of language.[3]

Despite Bloomfield's great influence upon research into natural language, his acknowledged enthusiasm for the axiomatic-deductive method and, in particular, his proposed set of postulates for linguistics did not immediately inspire other linguists to employ similar techniques. Indeed, it was not until the late 1940s that other researchers began to develop the basic methodology he had outlined in his 1926 paper. For instance, in 1948 Bernard Bloch (1907–1965) published 'A Set of Postulates for Phonemic Analysis', in which he referred directly to Bloomfield's earlier work:

> Leonard Bloomfield was the first to state explicitly some of the assumptions that underlie the methods of linguistic science; his formulation of these axioms ... has remained for more than twenty years the only attempt of its kind. We may find it necessary now, in the light of recent theoretical discussion, to make certain changes of detail in his list of assumptions; but the importance of his article as a contribution to linguistic theory is undiminished. Whoever undertakes, in future, to apply the postulational approach to linguistics will find his task made easier by the model that Bloomfield has provided. (Bloch 1948: 3)

This passage indicates that Bloch's own attempt to provide a set of axioms for phonemic analysis was partly inspired by Bloomfield's work, although his observation that due to 'recent theoretical discussion' the exact system Bloomfield proposed would have to be altered, indicates that he was aware of the limitations of the 1926 postulate set. As a result, Bloch himself made several 'changes of detail' to Bloomfield's system. For instance, he rejected Bloomfield's assumption that phonemes are actually present in sound waves, adopting instead the (then) contemporary view that phonemes are abstract linguistic units. Nevertheless, despite these alterations, the basic postulational methodology Bloch used was identical to that proposed by Bloomfield. In particular, Bloch's postulates are expressed as statements in English, and these are intended unambiguously to define all phenomena associated with phonemic analysis. For instance, Bloch's first postulate and first definition take the form[4]

1.1 Postulate 1: There are communities of human beings who interact partly by the use of conventional auditory signs.
1.2 Definition: Such a community is a *speech-community*.

As these examples indicate, like Bloomfield, Bloch made no attempt to convert his postulates into a precisely defined formal language, and was content with a natural language exposition of his system.

Bloch's 1948 postulate set for phonemic analysis heralded a renewed interest in the axiomatic-deductive method amongst the North American linguistics community, and the intensity of this renewal is indicated by the rapid increase in the number of axiomatic-deductive linguistic theories that began to appear during the late 1940s and early 1950s. To consider just one example,[5] in 1955 F. W. Harwood (dates unknown) published a paper entitled 'Axiomatic Syntax: The Construction and Evaluation of a Syntactic Calculus', and it is revealing that, in this paper, Harwood cites neither Bloomfield's nor Bloch's work directly, declaring instead that the methodology outlined constitutes an attempt to apply 'ideas from the field of mathematical logic' in a linguistic context (Harwood 1955: 409). This remark suggests that, while Bloomfield had been inspired primarily by work in geometry (and psychology), and while Bloch had consciously sought to revive Bloomfield's method, Harwood had been influenced directly by advances in symbolic logic, though he does also mention Bar-Hillel explicitly, demonstrating that he was aware of the contemporaneous interest in adapting techniques derived from mathematics in order to facilitate syntactic analysis. The extent of Harwood's indebtedness to research into logic is apparent from the kind of terminology and formal machinery utilised in the paper. For instance, his basic intention is to discuss 'methods for presenting syntactic information in the form of a calculus, and for measuring its goodness of fit to a language' (Harwood 1955: 409). More precisely, he proposes a system that has access to a finite word list, and which combines the words in this list in various principled ways in order to generate sentences in a given language. Harwood views sentences as 'a serially ordered set of positions, 1, 2, ..., p, each filled by one of the words on our list' (Harwood 1955: 410). Consequently, the sentence 'John discovered the path' is a 4-positional sentence. Having defined these terms, Harwood continues:

> Now a set of p positions may be filled from a finite list of r words, $w_1, w_2, \ldots, w_r$, in r^p ways; we shall call the N possible p-positions sequences of $w_{1...r}$. Let Lp be a subset of the N possible p-positional sequences of $w_{1...r}$ which occur as sentences in the language L and $-Lp$ (read not Lp) the remainder. (Harwood 1955: 410)

This formulation indicates that, in Harwood's scheme, the set of sentences in language L can be subdivided into two disjoint subsets; namely, the set of grammatical sentences Lp and the set of ungrammatical sentences $-Lp$. He continues:

> An axiomatic system S operating on $w_{1...r}$ divides the N possible p-positional sequences of $w_{1...r}$ into a subset Kp which are derivable in S, and $-Kp$ the remainder which are not derivable. (Harwood 1955: 410)

In other words, given the binary grammaticality assumption introduced above, it is the task of an axiomatic syntactic system such as S to divide the set of possible sentences into two distinct subsets; namely, Kp, the set of derivable sequences, and $-Kp$, the set of non-derivable sequences. Obviously, the more closely Kp approximates to Lp, defined above, the better the system S performs. In practice, Harwood's theory requires the following elements in order to achieve its purpose (see Harwood 1955: 410):

- A finite set of words, $w_{1...r}$, which are divided into classes, $C_{1...m}$, so that $C_{1...m}$ can be used as variables of which the words in these classes are the values.
- An initial set of sequences of $C_{1...m}$.
- A set of procedure rules for deriving further sequences from the initial set.

As an example of a procedure rule, Harwood offers the following: 'Given $C_a C_i$ as an initial sequence and $C_i \rightarrow C_j$ as a procedure rule we may derive $C_a C_j$' (Harwood 1955: 410). This example illustrates the way in which one sequence can be derived from an existing sequence, and it obviously resembles Hilbert's proof schema given as (2.10) above since it uses logical implication in order to derive a particular sequence. In passing, it should be noted that, while Harwood discusses the fact that Kp should approximate as closely as possible to Lp, he is compelled to address the issue of compactness; that is, he suggests that the system S should be constructed as economically as possible. Specifically, he states that 'compactness is an important and measurable feature' (Harwood 1955: 411), and this concern for compact grammars will become the focus of attention in section 4.3 when simplicity criteria are discussed in relation to TGG.

As this brief overview clearly demonstrates, by 1955 expositions written in natural language outlining axiomatic-deductive systems that could be used to analyse natural languages were no longer considered adequate by certain researchers. Taking Harwood as an example, as the above quotations indicate, he specifically introduced a formal symbolic language that enabled him to state his initial assumptions more precisely than either Bloomfield or Bloch, with the result that the degree of ambiguity in the system he develops is significantly reduced. In addition, it is important to recognise that one of the most revealing characteristics of Harwood's system is the assumption that all sentences (i.e., word sequences) in a given language can be classified as belonging either to the subset Kp (i.e., the set of derivable sentences) or the subset $-Kp$ (i.e., the set of all non-derivable sentences). This classificatory system demonstrates that one of the natural consequences of adopting a strict axiomatic-deductive approach to syntactic theory is the assumption that grammaticality is a binary, set-theoretical concept: given the set of all sentences in a given language, each sentence can be shown to be either grammatical (i.e., derivable) or ungrammatical (i.e., non-derivable), and consequently a given sentence must belong to one of these two disjoint subsets. Some of the issues involved here will be considered further in chapters 4 and 5. The main point is that, as Harwood's work demonstrates, by the mid-1950s the use of the axiomatic-deductive method in linguistics, particularly syntax, had been revived by certain linguists, following Bloomfield's initial 1926 proposal, and made more precise by the use of formal symbolic languages, ultimately derived from systems of logic. This advance had profound consequences for the development of TGG, and, as will be shown in section 5.7, it was the axiomatic-deductive nature of TGG that bedazzled some of its earliest commentators.[6]

3.3 Recursive definitions

As indicated in section 3.2, one consequence of the influence of the axiomatic-deductive method upon linguistics was the emergence in the 1950s of systems of 'axiomatic syntax' (to use Harwood's phrase), and, given the language-based emphasis of Hilbert's axiomatic-deductive proof theory (which in turn drew upon Whitehead and Russell's language-based axiomatic-deductive Logicism), it was perhaps inevitable that other proof-theoretical techniques would eventually be employed in a linguistic context. As mentioned briefly in section 2.6, one of the most distinctive features of Hilbertian Formalism was the emphasis it placed upon the use of finite methods during the process of mathematical proof construction, and recursive functions came to be viewed as important tools for this purpose. Consequently, numerous researchers advanced recursive function theory during the 1930s and 1940s, and in the early 1950s recursive components began to be explicitly introduced into syntactic theory. Since the initial TGG formalism utilised such components, it is necessary to consider the manner in which these ideas migrated from proof theory to linguistics.[7] Before providing explicit definitions of various kinds of recursive functions, though, it is necessary first to outline the lineage of the main ideas considered in the following paragraphs, since the development of recursive function theory is convoluted and problematic.

In summary, then, the basic concept of a recursive function had been introduced in the nineteenth century, and such functions were deployed by Dedekind during his investigations into the nature of the real numbers. In turn, Dedekind's use of recursive functions influenced Peano, who used such techniques while defining mathematical induction (as in Peano 1959a[1889]), and a number of leading mathematicians and logicians developed the theory further before Hilbert began to advocate its use within the context of Formalism. However, the basic theory was endowed with especial significance when Gödel used primitive recursive functions in his celebrated incompleteness theorem of 1931, and again when he introduced general recursive functions in 1934. Gödel's work was advanced by Church, Kleene, Alan Turing (1912–1954), and Emil Post (1897–1954) during the 1930s and 1940s, and, specifically, it was demonstrated that recursive function theory, λ-calculus, and computability theory provided alternative, but equivalent, formal expositions of the informal notion of effective calculability. Crucially, the notion of recursively enumerable sets was introduced by Church in 1936, before being reformulated with renewed impetus by Post in 1944.

While the above overview provides a (very) brief summary of the basic development of recursive function theory from the late nineteenth century to the 1940s, it perhaps insufficiently stresses that the history of the theory from the late 1930s to the present is peculiarly convoluted, since it came to be intricately intertwined both with the notion of λ-definability and with the theory of computability. While some of the consequences of this conflux are discussed in the conclusion, the following paragraphs will not consider the relationship between recursion, λ-calculus, and computability in detail, since the main focus must be upon Gödelian recursive function theory. The explanation for this is simple: the notions of induction by definition and recursively enumerable sets, which were both primarily associated with Gödelian recursive function theory, influenced the development of syntactic theory most profoundly in the 1950s, and therefore these aspects of the theory require focused consideration. Having specified the limits of the ensuing discussion in this manner, it is necessary now to define recursive functions more precisely.

If a given recursive function is viewed as a number-theoretic function that is defined upon the domain of non-negative integers, then, informally, the characteristic feature of such a function is that each value it calculates is specified in terms of previous values that the same function has already calculated. In other words, recursive functions are associated with a particular kind of self-reference, and this can be cited as a defining property. In the context of number-theoretic functions and predicates, then, recursive definitions consist of a pair of equations, the first of which determines the condition that terminates the recursion, and the second of which constitutes the recursive step. For instance, consider the following pair of equations:

$$\phi(0) = q \tag{3.1}$$
$$\phi(y') = \chi(y, \phi(y)) \tag{3.2}$$

Here $q, y, y' \in \mathbb{N}$, where y' indicates the successor of y (i.e., $y' = y + 1$). In this pair of equations (3.1) defines the termination condition since, when the function ϕ is called with 0 as its argument, it will simply return the natural number q. By contrast, equation (3.2) defines the recursive step since, if the function ϕ is called with the natural number y' as its argument, then the value for $\phi(y')$ is calculated by calling the function χ which takes two arguments – namely, the natural number y (i.e., $y' - 1$) and the function $\phi(y)$. To consider a concrete example, if add$(x, y) = x + y$ and add$(0, x) = x$, and 'add' is called in order to sum the numbers 4 and 1, then the value returned by the function is calculated as follows:

1. add(4, 1) = add(3, 1) + 1
2. add(3, 1) = add(2, 1) + 1
3. add(2, 1) = add(1, 1) + 1
4. add(1, 1) = add(0, 1) + 1
5. add(0, 1) = 1
6. add(1, 1) = 1 + 1 = 2
7. add(2, 1) = (1 + 1) + 1 = 3
8. add(3, 1) = ((1 + 1) + 1) + 1 = 4
9. add(4, 1) = (((1 + 1) + 1) + 1) + 1 = 5

In this example, the initial function call, add(4, 1) triggers a sequence of four recursive function calls which only terminates in line 5 when add(0, 1) is reached. Once the recursion has been halted in this manner, the values that are returned by each recursive call are calculated. Equation pairs of the kind defined in (3.1) and (3.2) were used by Peano in order to define mathematical induction, and they have always been at the core of recursive function theory.

As indicated in section 2.6, Hilbert's interest in primitive recursive functions was primarily due to the fact that they could replace ϵ-functions in mathematical proofs, and in order to appreciate why this might be desirable, it is worth emphasising the relationship between recursive functions and proof by induction.

In mathematics an inductive proof attempts to prove a given theorem by establishing that the theorem holds for the first case and for the $n + 1^{\text{th}}$ case. Since the proof is obtained for both an initial instance and a general successor, then the proof is understood to hold for all cases, since any case can be derived from the initial instance by repeated applications of the inductive step. Consequently, although an inductive proof is finite, it covers an infinite number of cases. Primitive recursive functions permit the same type of iterated inference and, consequently, Hilbert believed that such functions could guarantee the validity of proofs which previously had to utilise ϵ-functions. Accordingly, the notion of recursion was established at the core of Formalism and, as a result, it received considerable attention from other mathematicians. Indeed, the relationship between recursive functions and induction is extremely close, to the extent that recursion can be viewed as definition by induction (e.g., Kleene 1952: 217). Further, the fact that recursive functions enable finite proof techniques to be employed was noted by many researchers, and this was often cited as a desirable and characteristic property. For example, Gödel stated explicitly that '[r]ecursive functions have the important property that, for each given set of values of the arguments, the value of the function can be computed by a finite procedure' (Gödel 1986b[1934]: 348). One obvious question that arises from considerations of this kind can be expressed as follows: which classes of number-theoretic functions can be defined recursively? The answer to this question was developed during the 1930s, primarily by Gödel, and later elaborated by his successors, especially Kleene. One crucial notion that was advanced as a result of this research was that of primitive recursion. Formally, a function is classified as being a primitive recursive function if it is definable by a series of applications of the following equations:[8]

$$\phi(x) = x' \tag{3.3}$$

$$\phi(x_1, x_2, \ldots, x_n) = q \tag{3.4}$$

$$\phi(x_1, x_2, \ldots, x_n) = x_i \tag{3.5}$$

$$\phi(x_1, x_2, \ldots, x_n) = \psi(\chi_1(x_1, x_2, \ldots, x_n), \ldots, \chi_m(x_1, x_2, \ldots, x_n)) \tag{3.6}$$

$$\phi(0) = q \tag{3.7}$$

$$\phi(y') = \chi(y, \phi(y)) \tag{3.8}$$

$$\phi(0, x_2, \ldots, x_n) = \psi(x_2, \ldots, x_n) \tag{3.9}$$

$$\phi(y', x_2, \ldots, x_n) = \chi(y, \phi(y, x_2, \ldots, x_n), x_2, \ldots, x_n) \tag{3.10}$$

The equations above define number-theoretic functions when n and m are positive integers, i is an integer such that $1 \leq i \leq n$, q is a natural number, and $\phi, \psi, \chi, \chi_1 \ldots \chi_m$ are number-theoretic functions that take the indicated numbers of arguments. In Kleene's terminology, a function that satisfies the equation in (3.3) is called the successor function; a function that satisfies (3.4) is called a constant function; a function that satisfies (3.3–3.4), or (3.5) is called an initial function; a function that satisfies (3.6), (3.7–3.8), or (3.9–3.10) is called an immediate dependent of other functions (e.g., the χ functions). Consequently, a function ϕ is called a primitive recursive function if there is a finite sequence of occurrences of functions, $\phi_1, \phi_2, \ldots, \phi_k$, where $k \geq 1$, such that each function of the sequence is either an initial function, or an immediate dependent of preceding functions of the sequence, and the last function ϕ_k is the function ϕ.

While the equations given above can be used to define primitive recursive functions, Gödel soon realised that there were certain effectively calculable functions that were not primitive recursive (for instance, functions that were defined by induction in respect to two variables simultaneously), and, consequently, he defined a wider class of functions called general recursive functions. In essence, a function ϕ is a general recursive function with respect to the functions $\psi_1, \ldots, \psi_n$ if there is a system of equations which defines ϕ recursively from $\psi_1, \ldots, \psi_n$.[9]

Given the definitions of primitive and general recursive functions, a number of researchers began to consider the consequences of recursive function theory. For instance, in 1936 Church introduced the idea of a recursively enumerable set, and this basic idea was influentially expanded by Post in the early 1940s (especially Post 1944). In essence, a set of non-negative natural numbers, $\mathcal{A}$, is recursively enumerable if there is a general recursive function ϕ which enumerates the members of the set. In other words, the set $\mathcal{A}$ is recursively enumerable if $\phi(0) \in \mathcal{A}$, $\phi(1) \in \mathcal{A}$, $\phi(2) \in \mathcal{A}$, ... where ϕ is a general recursive function, and where the sequence constitutes an enumeration of the members of $\mathcal{A}$. From the perspective of syntactic theory, it is of considerable interest that Post used the verb 'to generate' in order to describe the process of obtaining members of sets using recursive devices (such as general recursive functions), and was therefore able to speak of 'generated sets' (Post 1944: 286). Critically, Post viewed the task of enumerating the members of a recursively enumerable set as a generational problem. The implications of this will be considered when TGG is discussed in section 5.6.

As with the axiomatic-deductive approaches discussed in section 3.2, during the 1950s recursive function theory began to be investigated by mathematically minded linguists who were keen to explore the methodology of the formal sciences in the hope of finding techniques that could make linguistic research more rigorous. One of the first explicit discussions of the benefits of recursive definitions in linguistic theory was contained in Bar-Hillel's short paper 'On Recursive Definitions in Empirical Science' which appeared in 1953.[10] As the title suggests, Bar-Hillel's main intention in this work was to argue that recursive definitions need not only be used in formal mathematical situations, but could also be used beneficially in the context of the empirical sciences. As an example of elementary recursion, Bar-Hillel considers Peano's Immediate-Successor (IS) function, which he had encountered in Kleene's *Introduction to Metamathematics*,[11] and, following Kleene, Bar-Hillel provides a two-part definition of this function:

Definition 3.1: The IS Function (Recursive)
1. $a + 1 = a'$
2. $a + n' = (a + n)'$

Definition 3.1 can be directly compared with the equation pair (3.1)–(3.2) above, since, in both cases, the recursion is induced by the second step. Having considered the basic implications of adopting such definitions in a mathematical context, Bar-Hillel goes on to suggest that, in the empirical sciences, definitions have often included statements that are actually recursive, even though this property has not been explicitly acknowledged. In order to illustrate his point he states that, 'for a change' (Bar-Hillel 1953a: 163), he will consider several examples from linguistics. As implied, this manoeuvre is rather unexpected, since recursive definitions had usually been considered in relation to the formal sciences (especially proof theory), and had not been explicitly utilised previously in the context of linguistic theory. In his discussion of this subject, though, Bar-Hillel adopts a purely language-based approach by using English as a metalanguage and by employing it to analyse his chosen object language, French. At the beginning of his analysis, he introduces the following definition (see Bar-Hillel 1953a: 163):[12]

Definition 3.2: Sentence (Recursive in Disguise)
x will be called a *sentence* (in French) if (and only if) x is a sequence of a nominal and a (intransitive) verbal, or a sequence of a nominal, a (transitive) verbal and a nominal or, . . ., or a sequence of a sentence, the word 'et', and a sentence, or, . . .

In this definition, the terms 'nominal' and 'verbal' can be understood to mean 'noun phrase' and 'verb' respectively, and it is important to note that this definition seeks to define sentences which can be infinitely long, in terms of subcomponents combined by means of the conjunction 'et'. Having introduced definition 3.2, Bar-Hillel proceeds to demonstrate that although it does not explicitly manifest the two-part structure of a recursive definition, it is nevertheless 'recursive in disguise', and he accomplishes this by restating the definition of a sentence as follows (see Bar-Hillel 1953a: 163):

> **Definition 3.3: Sentence (Recursive)**
> 1. x is a *sentence*$_1$ (a *simple sentence*) $=_{df}$ x is a sequence of a nominal and a (intransitive) verbal or a sequence of a nominal, a (transitive) verbal, and a nominal, or ...
>
> 2. x is a *sentence*$_{n+1}$ (a *compound sentence* of the $n + 1^{th}$ order) $=_{df}$ x is a sequence of a sentence$_p$, the word 'et', and a sentence$_m$, where either p or m (or both) are equal to n and none is greater than n, or ...

Expressed in this fashion, the definition of a sentence now takes the familiar form of 'a pair of simultaneous recursive definitions', and, Bar-Hillel goes on to claim that it is 'simple' to check that a given compound sentence is 'a proper French sentence', since the structure can be iteratively broken down into smaller units until the basic constituent units (i.e., clauses) are obtained (Bar-Hillel 1953a: 164). If this can be achieved, then the sentence is 'proper', if not then (presumably) it is improper (i.e., ungrammatical). Once again it is clear that one of the consequences of a mathematical (in this case, recursive) approach to syntax is that grammaticality is most naturally expressed in binary terms: if a sentence can be analysed in accordance with the posited recursive definition, then it is grammatical, if not, then it is ungrammatical. Bar-Hillel ends his short paper with a rallying cry which, though expressed in very general terms, was bound to intrigue any linguists who were even remotely interested in the relationship between the formal sciences and linguistic theory:

> In conclusion, let me say that, in view of the role played by recursive definitions in concept formation in empirical science, it is the task of the methodologists to dedicate time and effort to the evaluation of their precise import in different fields of inquiry and the task of the scientists to become acquainted with the recent investigations on recursive definitions to a degree, at least, that would free them from the misconceptions that have so frequently been connected with their occurrence in disguise. (Bar-Hillel 1953a: 165)

The basic thrust of the above passage is that certain fields of empirical enquiry were infested with 'misconceptions' primarily because they failed to realise that they were concerned with phenomena that could most easily be defined recursively. Given the topic of Bar-Hillel's own discussion – namely, natural language – it would be difficult to avoid the conclusion that linguistics is one of the empirical sciences that was bedevilled by such misconceptions. With its emphasis on greater explicitness and the avoidance of misrepresentation, it is striking how similar the tone of this passage is to Bloomfield's 1926 plea for the avoidance of 'error' in linguistic research, and certainly Bar-Hillel's desire for precision was swiftly becoming a characteristic feature of the work of those linguists interested in making their discipline more mathematical. This attitude has already been identified in the work of Bloomfield, Bloch, and Harwood, and these are only a few of the researchers who were actively involved in the process of rigorisation. Others will be mentioned later. Certainly, though, Bar-Hillel's use of recursive definitions to analyse the structure of sentences in natural language can be viewed as one manifestation of this pervasive desire for the mathematisation of syntactic analysis, which became such a characteristic feature of certain kinds of linguistic research in the mid-twentieth century. Significantly, Bar-Hillel's ideas intrigued Chomsky in the early 1950s, and in section 5.6, the influence of recursive function theory upon TGG will be considered directly.

3.4 Logical systems

As mentioned briefly in section 2.5, after the publication of *PM* the development of symbolic logic became complex and fragmented as new groups of researchers emerged, often gathered around particular academic institutes, and often inspired by the desire of improving or extending or replacing the logical system offered by Whitehead and Russell. While the work of one of these groups, the Vienna Circle, will be discussed in section 3.5, in this section some of the research associated with another post-*PM* group of logicians – namely, the Lvov-Warsaw school – will be considered.

The Lvov-Warsaw school developed in the early twentieth century under the leadership of Kazimierz Tawardowski (1866–1938) who moved from Vienna to Lvov in 1895. Although trained mainly in philosophy and psychology, Tawardowski started lecturing on logic soon after being appointed, and gradually a whole generation of Polish logicians matured under his guidance. Dominant amongst these were Jan Lukasiewicz (1878–1956), Stanislow Leśniewski (1886–1939), Kazimierz Ajdukiewicz (1890–1963), and Alfred Tarski (1902–1983). Although the individual members of the school pursued many different research interests, much of their work was inspired by perceived limitations and weaknesses in the logical system presented in *PM*. For reasons that will become apparent later, only the work of Leśniewski and Ajdukiewicz will be considered here.[13]

Leśniewski studied under Tawardowski, and was appointed to the position of Chair of Philosophy at Warsaw in 1915. His most significant contribution to the development of logic was the tripartite logical system he devised, and which was intended to provide a more secure basis for mathematics than the system contained in *PM*. The ambitious nature of this work alone is revealing, since the very fact that Leśniewski attempted such a project indicates that, during the 1920s, the Logicist movement was still very much alive. His main doubts about the *PM* system concerned the imperfections inherent in the kind of formal symbolic language it employed, and he was particularly concerned by the dubious validity of Whitehead and Russell's assertion operator. For instance, Leśniewski juxtaposed the proposition 'p' and the assertion '$\vdash p$' and asked whether the two propositions have the same meaning or not. Indeed, he even asked whether the latter was actually a proposition at all (Leśniewski 1992c[1927]: 181–196). As for the controversial theory of logical types, Leśniewski argued that it was unclear whether the theory defined an ontological or a semantic hierarchy, and, besides, he was convinced that the theory was too intricate to serve as a basic, intuitive part of a logical system (Leśniewski 1992b[1914]: 115–128). Accordingly, motivated by these concerns, Leśniewski gradually developed his own alternative to *PM* during the years 1914–1939, and his system was characterised by a tripartite structure, the main components of which he referred to as 'protothesis', 'ontology', and 'mereology'.[14] Protothesis and ontology, taken together, provided the logical foundation of the whole system, the former being a generalised sentential calculus based upon the notion of equivalence, the latter being a nominal calculus with the function 'ϵ' (i.e., a stylised form of the ϵ that appears at the start of the word 'ἐστί' [Greek: 'it is']) as its primitive term. The logical core provided by these components was equal in power to that contained in *PM*. The third component of Leśniewski's system, mereology, was an extralogical theory based upon the single primitive non-logical constant 'Part'. In essence, mereology was a reformulation of Cantorian set theory in which set membership was transitive rather than intransitive. For instance, in classical set theory, given the fact that (i) $x \in A$ and (ii) $A \in B$, it does not necessarily follow that $x \in B$, while in mereology, if (i) and (ii) hold, then $x \in B$ follows.

One of the reasons for preferring this kind of set theory was that it enabled Russell's paradox to be avoided when deriving set theory from logical axioms without having to resort to elaborate and artificial methods. However, Leśniewski was also motivated to construct his transitive alternative to classical set theory by his nominalistic beliefs. These beliefs were manifest in his assertion that only individuals exist and that, therefore, aggregates or collections of any kind should not be manipulated as independent entities, but should rather be defined in terms of their individual elements (see Leśniewski 1992c[1927]: 229–230, especially Axiom II). Consequently, classical sets must be consistently rejected. This extreme stance can be seen as a direct reaction to the paradoxes of set theory: if the theory as standardly formulated permitted contradictions, then it must be reformulated, and nominalism, with its focus on individual entities and its refusal to accept the abstract notion of a set, constitutes an intellectually plausible alternative framework. With specific reference to formal symbolic languages, Leśniewski's nominalism caused him to view them as finite sequences of inscriptions that could be combined in various ways to produce longer sequences, and these methods largely anticipated the kind of approach espoused by the architects of constructive nominalism in the 1940s, as will be shown in sections 3.5 and 3.6.

As indicated above, perceived flaws in *PM* inspired Leśniewski to devise a viable alternative, and Whitehead and Russell's work also provoked Ajdukiewicz, who was one of Leśniewski's young contemporaries at Warsaw. Rather than focusing on the Logicist foundational programme, though, Ajdukiewicz was more concerned with the task of exploring the syntax and semantics of formal logical languages of the type synthesised by Whitehead and Russell. In particular, he was interested in the differences that existed between such languages and natural languages. Therefore, in a series of papers, starting with 'On the Meaning of Expressions' in 1931, he considered various technical aspects of semantics and syntax. Often in his published work he chose to focus on well-defined formal languages simply because, by contrast, natural languages suffered from 'vagueness and lack of clarity' (Ajdukiewicz 1978b[1931]: 26). Nevertheless, he was always keen to consider his conclusions in relation to natural languages. In particular, in much of this work, Ajdukiewicz repeatedly emphasised the close connection between syntax and semantics, and he sought to specify various sets of 'meaning-rules' (Ajdukiewicz 1978a[1934]: 57) for natural language. Since he often advocated a relativistic view of language, with a pronounced concentration on situational interpretation, his work in this area can be viewed (to some extent) as a kind of proto-pragmatics.[15]

Ajdukiewicz's main contribution to syntactic theory, though, was 'Syntactic Connexion' (1936), and, at the very start of this paper, he indicated that his interest in the syntax of formal languages was inspired by the paradoxes of set theory and the Logicist movement that sought to eliminate them: 'the discovery of the antinomies, and the method of their resolution, have made problems of linguistic syntax the most important problems of logic' (Ajdukiewicz 1978a[1936]: 118). Consequently, he was motivated by the paradoxes of set theory ultimately to devise a system of syntactic analysis that would facilitate the analysis of 'syntactic connexion'. Towards the end of the paper, Ajdukiewicz provides a reasonable definition of 'connexion', but, initially he illustrates the concept by means of an example: the sequence of words 'John loves Ann' possesses the property of syntactic connection, whereas the sequence 'Perhaps horse of will however shine' does not (Ajdukiewicz 1978a[1936]: 118). As this example indicates, Ajdukiewicz's notion of 'connexion' is associated with the traditional idea of grammaticality, and the basic task for the type of analytic syntactic system he develops in the paper is to demonstrate that the first sentence is connected (i.e., grammatical), while the second is not. It is important to note, though, that syntactic connection of this kind does not correspond directly to the Formalist notion of syntactic well-formedness, since, for Ajdukiewicz, syntactic connection is developed as a theory of semantic categories, while well-formedness is determined without reference to meaning. In elaborating his ideas, Ajdukiewicz states that he was primarily influenced by the work of his compatriot Leśniewski, but that he was also motivated by Russell and Whitehead's theory of types. As will be discussed below, the theory of syntactic connection that Ajdukiewicz propounded in turn came to inspire the development of the theory of Categorial Grammar in the 1950s.

The basic methodology that Ajdukiewicz outlined in his main presentations of his theory involved a hierarchy of semantic categories which were represented by indices of the form

$$s, n, \frac{s}{n}, \frac{s}{nn}, \ldots, \frac{s}{s}, \frac{s}{ss}, \ldots, \frac{n}{n}, \frac{n}{nn}, \ldots, \frac{n}{s}, \frac{n}{ss}, \ldots \quad (3.11)$$

When this analytic strategy was applied specifically to natural language, each basic part of speech was associated with one of these indices. For instance, the definite article 'the' was associated with the index 'n/n', while a noun such as 'lilac' was associated with the index 'n'. Consequently, in this manner, syntactic analysis can be accomplished by means of manipulating indices. It is crucial to note that, although Ajdukiewicz developed his system of syntactic analysis for formal languages, he clearly indicated that, as far as he was concerned, such techniques could usefully be applied to natural languages. This is yet another indication of the fact that, during the 1930s and 1940s, the supposed distance that was perceived to separate formal and natural languages appeared gradually to be diminishing.

Although the work of Ajdukiewicz was discussed by logicians, it was ignored by linguists until, in a 1953 paper entitled 'A Quasi-Arithmetical Notation for Syntactic Description', Bar-Hillel revived and adapted Ajdukiewicz's basic scheme. Bar-Hillel's initial statement of intent is of considerable interest:

> The purpose of this paper is to present the outline of a method of syntactic description that is new insofar as it combines methods developed by the Polish logician Kasimir [*sic*] Ajdukiewicz on the one hand and by American structural linguists on the other. (Bar-Hillel 1953b: 47)

The particular 'structural linguists' that Bar-Hillel cites in a footnote are Charles Fries (1887–1967) and Zellig Harris (1909–1992), both of whom can be broadly classified as post-Bloomfieldians. It is perhaps unnecessary to stress that Harris' work in particular was extremely influential during the 1940s and early 1950s. Indeed, his *Methods in Structural Linguistics* (hereafter *MSL*) (1951), with its emphasis on distributional discovery procedures, had helped to define the basic methodology of structural linguistics.[16] As will be shown in later chapters, Bar-Hillel's conviction that techniques derived from the formal sciences could be combined with methods developed by structural linguists is one that was voiced frequently, by various researchers, during the 1950s, and some of the reasons for the perceived association, or compatibility, between mathematical techniques and the methodology of structural linguists are considered in section 3.7. Suffice it to say here that, for Bar-Hillel, the connection was due to the fact that certain techniques derived from logic met the structuralist demand for analytic procedures that functioned in a mechanical fashion. However, in order fully to appreciate Bar-Hillel's work, it is crucial also to note that throughout his paper the emphasis is upon the *description* of sentential structure and not primarily upon the type of mechanical discovery procedures sought by Harris (and others). As Bar-Hillel puts it himself,

> We are not interested here in developing a method which a linguist might use to ARRIVE at an analysis of a linguistic corpus, but only in a new way in which he could PRESENT the results of his investigations. (Bar-Hillel 1953b: 47)

One possible implication of this statement is that, for Bar-Hillel, Harris-style discovery procedures are not of primary importance, and such an interpretation is reasonable since, as will be shown when TGG is considered in section 5.3, this lack of concern for discovery procedures was starting to become more prevalent amongst the generation of young linguists reaching intellectual maturity in the early 1950s. In particular, the rejection of such procedures was perceived to be one of the most radical aspects of mature TGG.

Whatever his underlying motivations may have been, though, once Bar-Hillel had indicated how Ajdukiewicz's approach to syntactic analysis could be combined with the methodology of structural linguistics, he started to outline the basic theory which (in linguistic circles) would later be referred to as Categorial Grammar. The basic approach involves the definition and manipulation of fundamental syntactic categories. For instance, given the sentence 'Poor John sleeps', following Ajdukiewicz, Bar-Hillel claims that this structure can be exhaustively analysed using the two categories 'n' and 's', which he defines as

- n: the category of 'name-like strings'.
- s: the category of sentences.

With these definitions in place, he then introduces the following derived categories:

- $n/[n]$: the category of those strings with an n to their right form a string that belongs to category n.
- s/n: the category of the string that with an n to the left forms a string belonging to the category s.

Given the above definitions, a categorial analysis of the sentence 'Poor John sleeps' simply requires the sentence to be associated with the index sequence

$$\frac{n}{[n]} n \frac{s}{n} \qquad (3.12)$$

In which '$n/[n]$' denotes the adjective 'poor', 'n' denotes the noun 'John', and 's/n' denotes the verb 'sleeps'. Consequently, the subsequence '$n/[n]n$' can be reduced to n, giving the 'first derivative' of (3.12)

$$n\frac{s}{n} \qquad (3.13)$$

which is turn can be reduced to 's', forming the 'second and last derivative' of the initial index sequence in (3.12). Since the last derivative of the string belongs to the category s, the sentence can be considered grammatical since it constitutes a legitimate sentence. As Bar-Hillel observes, and as the title of his paper indicates, the process sketched above is 'something like ordinary mathematical multiplication of fractions' (Bar-Hillel 1953b: 48), and, as suggested previously, it is the mechanical nature of this process that allows it to be fused with structuralist linguistic methods: using Bar-Hillel's analytical procedure, sentences of natural language can be converted into strings of well-defined symbols in a formal language, and then manipulated (without reference to meaning) as if they were part of an algebraic system.

As with the formal axiomatic approaches to syntactic theory that began to emerge in the 1950s (discussed in section 3.2), Bar-Hillel's work implies that the type of formal languages used in symbolic logic (particularly the techniques developed by Ajdukiewicz) are closely related to natural languages and that, therefore, methods developed to analyse the former can be readily adapted in order to provide analyses of the latter. Although the type of approach to syntactic analysis proposed by Bar-Hillel was never explicitly incorporated into the TGG framework, it clearly demonstrated that techniques from logical syntax could be utilised for the purpose of linguistic analysis, and this is of considerable interest since, as will be shown in chapter 5, TGG itself drew heavily upon the methodology of symbolic logic.

3.5   Constructional system theory

In the previous sections of this chapter the influences of three particular aspects of the formal sciences upon linguistics were considered – namely, the influence of the axiomatic-deductive method, the influence of recursive function theory, and the influence of logical syntax. In this section constructional system theory is described, since it too exerted a lasting influence over syntactic theory in the 1950s. The theory, which was initially proposed by Carnap, grew out of attempts to use the logical techniques of *PM* in order to solve traditional philosophical problems. In particular, the theory was to influence Chomsky directly while he was developing TGG, consequently it is necessary to consider its genesis in some detail.

Carnap published his first book, *The Logical Construction of the World* (from henceforth *LCW*), in 1928.[17] The intellectual odyssey that had led him towards the philosophical position adopted in this work had been protracted and tortuous. As a student at Jena and Buchenbach from 1910 to 1926 he had studied experimental physics, mathematical logic (with Frege), and philosophy. Although, as a result of these eclectic interests, he initially struggled to devise a research proposal that was acceptable to one single department, he was awarded his Ph.D. in 1921 and immediately began work on the *LCW*. The bulk of the text was written during the years 1922–1925 and publication occurred just before he travelled to Vienna, where he subsequently became one of the most prominent members of the heterogeneous collection of intellectuals and academics now known as the Vienna Circle. The Vienna Circle had its origins in the early 1900s when the Viennese students Hans Hahn (1879–1934), Otto Neurath (1882–1945), and

Phillip Frank (1884–1966) started discussing various ideas concerning the relationship between logic, mathematics, philosophy, and science. In 1921 Hahn returned to Vienna as a lecturer and managed to arrange for Moritz Schlick (1882–1936) to be appointed to the chair of inductive philosophy. Schlick was a physicist by training, but was preoccupied with various topics in epistemology and ethics. He began to lead coffee-house discussion groups in the early 1920s, and the Vienna Circle emerged out of these gatherings. Other key members of the group were Karl Menger (1902–1985) and Gödel, and (to put it simply) this disparate group was unified by a common desire to rescue philosophy from the clutches of the metaphysicians by making it as precise and as exacting as mathematics or physics. In particular, the members of the Circle sought to provide a secure foundation for the sciences, to reject metaphysics, and to utilise logical analysis for the purposes of philosophical enquiry. Consequently, given Carnap's interests, it is no surprise that, when he joined the Circle in 1925, he quickly established himself as one of its defining figures. Indeed, although *LCW* was completed before he travelled to Vienna, in later years the book came to be viewed as one of the seminal texts of the so-called logical positivist movement that was associated with the Vienna Circle, and, since the text exerted a profound influence over the work of Goodman and Quine (both of whom in turn influenced Chomsky), it is necessary briefly to summarise the philosophical project that the book describes.[18]

Writing in his 'Intellectual Autobiography' of 1963, Carnap recalled that during the 1920s he had made 'numerous attempts at analysing concepts of ordinary language relating to things in our environment and their observable properties and relations, and at constructing definitions of these concepts with the help of symbolic logic' (Carnap 1963: 16). It is intriguing that, from the outset, Carnap was interested in 'concepts of ordinary language', since this research was the start of his exploration of logical epistemology, which was ultimately to influence the development of syntactic theory. His general approach was to employ the logical system developed in *PM* as a tool for considering questions of knowledge acquisition. This basic project was certainly influenced by Russell's provocative 1914 publication *Our Knowledge of the External World*, which had considered the possibility of such an approach to epistemological questions.[19] Specifically, in *LCW*, Carnap was explicitly concerned with the task of creating a *Konstitutionssystem*, or 'constructional system', which he described as follows:

> The present investigations aim to establish a 'constructional system', that is, an epistemic-logical system of objects or concepts... Unlike other conceptual

systems, a constructional system undertakes more than the division of concepts into various kinds and the investigation of the differences and mutual relations between these kinds. In addition, it attempts a step-by-step derivation or 'construction' of all concepts from certain fundamental concepts, so that a genealogy of concepts results in which each one has its definite place. It is the main thesis of construction theory that all concepts can in this way be derived from a few fundamental concepts, and it is in this respect that it differs from most other ontologies. (Carnap 1967[1928]: 5)

More precisely, as Carnap goes on to explain, a constructional system is one which contains a set of basic elements and a set of basic relations which, taken together, constitute the basis of the whole system, with the consequence that all other objects ('*Gegenstanden*') in the system are ultimately defined in terms of this basis. In other words, the task confronting the philosopher working within the broad framework of logical epistemology involves the generation of a definitional genealogy for all the objects in the universe of discourse, starting from a basis of irreducible primitives and the fundamental relations that exist between them.

Before embarking upon the task of actually creating a epistemic-logical constructional system in *LCW*, Carnap considers at length various formal difficulties that must be confronted before any such system can be attempted. In particular, he identifies four main problems which he refers to as the problems of (i) basis, (ii) ascension form, (iii) object form, and (iv) system form. He succinctly summarises these problems as follows:

> To begin with, a basis must be chosen, a lowest level upon which all others are founded. Secondly, we must determine the recurrent forms through which we ascend from one level to the next. Thirdly, we must investigate how the objects of various types can be constructed through repeated applications of the ascension forms. The fourth question concerns the over-all form of the system as it results from the stratified arrangement of the object types. (Carnap 1967[1928]: 47)

Carnap acknowledges that problems (ii), (iii), and (iv) are closely related to problem (i), since the choice of basis largely determines the form of the objects created and the manner of their creation, and these two characteristics largely determine the nature of the system as a whole. Since the technical issues associated with this cluster of interconnected problems are of such fundamental importance to Carnap's logical-epistemic approach, and since they were also explored by his most influential successors, it is necessary to discuss some of them briefly here.

As mentioned above, in *LCW*, Carnap adopts the logical framework presented in *PM*. In other words, his system utilises logical constants (e.g., negation, disjunction, and so on), variables, logical operators (e.g., the universal and existential operators), n-place functions, and all the other machinery of symbolic logic as developed by Whitehead and Russell, and summarised in section 2.5. Consequently, the problem of the basis can be classified as an *extralogical* problem since it concerns the choice of the basic elements and relations that must be assumed in addition to the logical basis. The basic elements that Carnap uses in his system are unanalysable elementary experiences (*'Elementarerlebnisse'*). This choice illustrates the particular fusion of phenomenology and symbolic logic that characterises the project outlined in *LCW*, and, in his autobiography, Carnap indicated that it was this phenomenological concern that distinguished this work from his previous efforts.

> A change in approach occurred when I recognised, under the influence of the Gestalt psychology of Wertheimer and Köhler, that the customary method of analyzing material things into separate sense-data was inadequate – that an instantaneous visual field and perhaps even an instantaneous total experience is given as a unit, while the allegedly simple sense-data are the result of a process of abstraction. Therefore, I took as elements total instantaneous experience rather than single sense-data. I developed a method called 'quasi-analysis', which leads, on the basis of the similarity-relation among experiences, to the logical construction of those entities which are usually conceived as components. On the basis of a certain primitive relation among experiences, the method of quasi-analysis leads step by step to the various sensory domains – first to the visual domain, then to the positions in the visual field, the colors, and their similarity system, the temporal order, and the like. (Carnap 1963: 16–17)

The 'similarity-relation' referred to above constituted the only extralogical relation that was incorporated in the basis of the system. This relation, 'Rs', is paraphrased as 'the recollection of similarity'. In other words, the relational statement 'x Rs y' indicates 'x and y are elementary experiences which are recognised as part similar through the comparison of a memory image of x with y' (Carnap 1967[1928]: 127). From this single extralogical primitive, Carnap was able to derive more complex relations such as 'part-identity'. Although, as indicated above, these relations are all extralogical constructs, it is clear both from the notation used and the manner in which they are defined that Carnap had been profoundly influenced by the theory of relations that Whitehead and Russell had presented in *PM* (especially numbers *23–*38, briefly considered in section 2.5 above).

Assuming this minimal basis, then, Carnap proceeds to construct larger objects by means of definition; that is, a new object is constructed by demonstrating that statements about the new object can be transformed into statements either about the basic elements in the system or else into statements about objects that have already been constructed from the basic elements themselves. Such definitions are called explicit. If, however, a concept is introduced that cannot be specified by means of explicit definition, then a process of implicit definition is required which permits ascension to a new constructional level.[20] Consequently, the various constructional levels (which are ultimately determined by the extralogical basis) largely determine the structure of the system created. Therefore, as suggested earlier, the problem of system form is directly related to the problem of the basis, and the precise nature of this relationship was explored at length by certain of Carnap's immediate successors, including Quine.

Quine appears to have encountered Carnap's *LCW* for the first time in the early 1930s when the book was discovered by one of his fellow Harvard graduate students. Although Quine's Ph.D. research, which was supervised by Whitehead himself, had been devoted to simplifying the methodology of *PM*, his interest in the work of the Vienna Circle in general, and of Carnap in particular, was sufficient to prompt him to take the joint advice of two associates and apply for a scholarship that would enable him to spend some time in Vienna. His application was successful and he arrived in the city in September 1932. As a result of this expedition, Quine became one of the conduits through which the work of the Vienna Circle was conveyed to North America; a development that was (eventually) to have significant consequences for syntactic theory.

Quine remained in Vienna until May 1933 (his stay punctuated by frequent trips to other European cities) and during this period he came into close contact with various members of Schlick's Circle. With his rapidly improving German, he attended the group's weekly meetings and even presented a paper outlining his own doctoral research. On arriving in the city, he had been disappointed to find that Carnap had recently left for Prague, but a meeting between the two men was arranged to coincide with Carnap's trip to Vienna in 1933. So began a relationship that Quine was later to describe as a 'sustained intellectual engagement' (Quine 1985: 98). In February of the same year, Quine travelled to Prague and was entertained by the Carnaps for several weeks, during which time he attended Carnap's lectures on his yet-to-be-published *The Logical Syntax of Language* (from henceforth *LSL*). Carnap encouraged Quine to read the typescript of the book, which was then in the process of preparation, and, as a result, Quine acquired a detailed knowledge of Carnap's most recent work.[21]

Back at Harvard, Quine was keen to communicate some of the ideas he had encountered in Europe to his colleagues. Consequently, he lectured on Carnap's latest work in November 1934, and in 1935 he led a series of 'informal seminars' concerning the *LSL* of which 'the participants were a professor, [David] Prall, an instructor, Henry Leonard, and some graduate students, including Nelson Goodman, Charles Stevenson and John Cooley' (Quine 1985: 122).[22]

Carnap himself was able to join the group in December 1935, since he was in America to spend the winter in Chicago. During his stay at Harvard he lectured on the *LSL*, with Goodman and Quine (along with Prall and Leonard) functioning as his intellectual bodyguards: 'we moved with Carnap as henchmen through the metaphysicians' camp' (Quine 1985: 122). These interactions appear to have been mutually rewarding, and, to some extent, they determined the course of the research undertaken by all the main participants for the next few years. In particular, Quine became increasingly concerned with technical difficulties associated with the syntax of formal languages. His syntactic interests are apparent both in his pedagogic publications from this time (especially *Mathematical Logic* (Quine 1940), which was discussed in 2.8) and certain journal papers. For instance, inspired by the work of Tarski and Hans Hermes (b. 1912), Quine devoted a whole paper to an exploration of the role of concatenation in formal language theory, suggesting that the concatenation relation could provide a viable foundation for the whole of arithmetic (Quine 1946). As shown in section 5.4, some of these ideas would later resurface in TGG.

It was during these seminars devoted to the *LSL*, therefore, that Goodman and Quine first came into regular contact, and, given their respective philosophical predilections, it is no surprise that they quickly became friends and collaborators. Although two years older than Quine, Goodman's academic career advanced more slowly, but, by the time the two men met, his intellectual interests had already begun to coalesce. Indeed, he was already actively working with Henry Leonard on a research project that explored aspects of Carnapian logical epistemology and which would ultimately provide material for his 1941 Ph.D. thesis. Appropriately, Goodman and Leonard first confessed their secret project to Quine while the three men were travelling back from Cambridge (where they had just left Carnap) to Baltimore, and Quine's recollection of the conversation indicates that the context of the research was clear to him even at the time:

> We talked in our hotel room until four in the morning. They were concerned with constructing a systematic theory of sense qualities, and their effort had

much in common with Carnap's *Logische Aufbau der Welt*. As an auxiliary they had developed a logic of the part–whole relation, which I recognised as Leśniewski's so-called mereology. They had been meeting fortnightly on the project, and I happily joined them in subsequent meetings. Leonard was called away but Goodman and I continued to meet. This project flowered in Nelson's dissertation, which he revised and published as *The Structure of Appearance*. (Quine 1985: 124)

Leśniewski's 'mereology' was discussed in section 3.4, and the nominalistic nature of this work was emphasised there. Although Goodman (in conjunction with Leonard) had developed his notion of the part–whole relation without being aware of Leśniewski's research, as will be shown later, there is no doubt that both approaches share the same kind of preoccupation with nominalism. In general, though, Quine's observation that Goodman and Leonard's project was directly inspired by *LCW* was entirely accurate. Indeed, when Goodman's Ph.D. thesis, *A Study of Qualities*, was eventually submitted, it was generally perceived to constitute an attempt to improve upon the type of constructional system that Carnap had developed in *LCW*. In fact, in later years Carnap himself came to recognise Goodman as one of the first philosophers to have responded directly to some of the issues he had raised in his early work.[23] Further, the extent of Goodman's appreciation of Carnap's *LCW* reveals itself in the frequent references to this text in his publications which appeared during the 1940s and 1950s. For instance, chapter 5 of his book *The Structure of Appearance* (from henceforth *SA*), published in 1951, comprises an extended summary and critique of *LCW*, and this fusion of admiration and dissatisfaction is typical of Goodman's attitude towards Carnap's work since, as he claimed in *SA*, 'the purpose of my critical scrutiny is not to disparage [Carnap's] accomplishments but to determine just where the remaining problems lie and perhaps pave the way for their solution' (Goodman 1951: 114). Twelve years later, writing in his 1963 essay 'The Significance of *Der logische Aufbau der Welt*', Goodman was still keen to defend the work from critical attacks, even attacks from Carnap himself, and, accordingly, the paper articulates a robust defence of Carnapian logical epistemology.

There is no doubt, then, that the research project undertaken by Goodman and Leonard, and which eventually involved Quine, was directly inspired by Carnap's *LCW*. Equally, there is no doubt that this project provided the main focus for Goodman's academic work during the late 1930s, since it resulted in his first published paper, 'The Calculus of Individuals and its Uses', which appeared in 1940 and which was co-authored with Leonard. The main purpose of this paper was to facilitate the use of multigrade relations in constructional systems.

Multigrade relations are predicates that take classes of various magnitudes for their arguments and which cannot therefore be analysed in terms of, say, dyadic relations which ultimately define the association between primitive elements in the system. For instance, as Goodman and Leonard demonstrate, the predicate 'met with' is a multigrade relation since any number of people could meet with any number of other people, and the event of meeting cannot accurately be analysed as the sum of individual meetings which involve only two people. For these reasons, and partly motivated by what Goodman and Leonard refer to as 'considerations of economy' (Goodman and Leonard 1940: 51), philosophers working within a broadly logical-epistemic framework had been forced to reject multigrade relations as primitives in their constructional systems. Accordingly, Goodman and Leonard were keen to encourage the use of such relations by introducing the 'part–whole' relation, '$x \mid y$', indicating 'x and y have no part in common', and by demonstrating that this relation can be used to analyse these relations more intuitively. As indicated previously, this is the aspect of Goodman and Leonard's work that Quine recognised as an independent reformulation of Leśniewski's mereology. It is of particular interest that Goodman and Leonard cite 'consideration of economy' as one of the reasons why multigrade relations had been rejected as appropriate predicates for extralogical bases of constructional systems, since such considerations of economy were increasingly to dominate Goodman's academic research for the next two decades. More specifically, partly motivated by his exploration of the part–whole relation defined in his first paper, Goodman came to believe that 'simplicity' and 'economy' were crucial aspects of system construction. However, he also recognised that these related notions were currently being used inconsistently, and that their precise meaning needed to be clarified. Consequently, during the 1940s and 1950s he endeavoured to provide this clarification.

Although the term 'simplicity' has intuitive appeal, Goodman realised that a formal definition was required if the centrality of basal simplicity in constructional system theory was to be fully acknowledged. He also perceived that the existing definitions were conspicuously inadequate. The intuitive assumption underlying his own approach was that a constructional system possessing a simpler, more economical, basis was preferable to an alternative system that utilised a more complex basis. Initially, the easiest way of determining the relative simplicity of two given bases appeared to involve merely counting the number of extralogical primitives, and, certainly, with this end in view, Goodman was keen to develop ways of reducing the number of such primitives. For instance, in his 1940 paper 'Elimination of Extra-Logical Postulates', which was written with Quine, Goodman devised a definitional methodology that effected the elimination of basal relations. For example, if a given basis contains the primitive transitive relation 'Pt', which indicates 'is a spatial part of', then 'x Pt y' states that 'x is a spatial part of y', and this relation can be determined by the extralogical postulate

$$\forall x \forall y \forall z [x \text{ Pt } y \wedge y \text{ Pt } z \rightarrow x \text{ Pt } z] \tag{3.14}$$

In this case, rather than taking 'Pt' as a primitive element in the basis, the more general relation 'O', which indicates spatial overlapping, could be introduced instead with the result that the transitivity of the relation 'Pt' becomes a theorem rather than a primitive notion:

$$x \text{ Pt } y =_{df} \forall z [x \text{ O } z \rightarrow y \text{ O } z] \tag{3.15}$$

In other words, (3.14) has become unnecessary since it is merely an abbreviation, according to (3.15), which can be derived using the logical component of the system. In this manner various extralogical primitives in the basis can be replaced by 'mere definition' (Goodman and Quine 1940: 104), and, consequently, their number can be reduced. Indeed, Goodman and Quine go on to demonstrate that such primitives are 'ordinarily eliminable' (Goodman and Quine 1940: 109), and this prompts them to suggest that existing ideas concerning the relative economy of constructional system bases should be reassessed. In particular, they argue that a distinction must be made between 'real and apparent economy' (Goodman and Quine 1940: 109), and in subsequent work they both went on to explore this distinction further. Quine returns to the notion of theory-internal simplicity, for instance, throughout his 1953 book *From a Logical Point of View* (from henceforth *LPV*), and distinguishes consistently between the 'economy of practical expressions', which is merely a notational convenience, and 'economy in grammar and vocabulary', which actively 'simplifies theoretical discourse' (Quine 1953: 26). Using the terminology introduced above, the former concern here is 'apparent', while the latter is 'real'. In a similar fashion, Goodman argued that only apparent economy is achieved if, for example, one simply concatenates all extralogical primitives in a given basis, for the basis of any system could easily be reduced to one in this manner, thus invalidating this method of counting the number of extralogical primitives as a means of determining the relative simplicity of various systems. Clearly, a more subtle approach to the problem of basal economy was required. Goodman's musings concerning this topic are revealing and so are worth quoting in full.

> What we apparently need is a way of gauging the relative simplicity and complexity of ideas ... We do not need to be able to determine whether a given idea is simpler than another in every way, but only whether it is simpler in those respects which are relevant to economy. Naturally, any criterion of simplicity must, within announced limitations, conform to our stronger and justifiable intuitions concerning simplicity in general. But beyond this, the crucial test for our present purposes will be whether the replacement of a given idea by one that is simpler does generally require – and therefore signify – the application of some special knowledge concerning the ideas involved. It is this that makes an economy significant or genuine. If, through the application of some purely automatic procedure like that by which the number of extralogical primitives in a basis can always be reduced to one, an idea that is less simple by the criterion in question can always or even usually be replaced by another that is more simple, then that criterion in unsatisfactory for our purposes. (Goodman 1943: 108)

A number of the issues raised here are worth highlighting. For instance, it is important to recognise that, for Goodman, simplicity considerations are only valid if they involve the replacement of one idea by another, and if the replacement is motivated by 'some special knowledge concerning the ideas involved'. Consequently, some kind of simplicity criterion is required that would be able to quantify the degrees of genuine economy associated with the extralogical primitives in the respective bases of two given constructional systems and, in his 1949 paper 'The Logical Simplicity of Predicates' Goodman proposed one possible criterion for nominalistic constructional systems. He begins by introducing a complexity measure that assigns a value to the predicates in the basis of a given system. Initially, the measure merely computes the complexity value for an n-place predicate using the formula $2n - 1$. For instance, a 2-place predicate, a 3-place predicate, and a 5-place predicate are associated with the values 3, 5, and 9 respectively. This complexity measure reveals that a basis containing a single 5-place predicate is more complex than a basis that contains a 2-place predicate and a 3-place predicate, since, in this case, the bases have the complexity values 8 and 9 respectively. Goodman proceeds to consider other aspects of predicate structure, including the number of joints and segments, and, ultimately, the complexity value for a given predicate is determined by computing the value of the initial complexity measure and adding the number of joints and segments.[24] He also emphasises that these numbers are dependent upon the available information: if it is not known how many joints and segments are associated with a given predicate, then (obviously) these values cannot be incorporated into a measure of complexity.

Goodman elaborated his approach to complexity measurement in several later papers as well as in *SA*. For instance, in 1950 he proposed a superior way of counting the joints associated with a predicate (Goodman 1950), and in 1955 modified his whole approach to the problem by attempting to place the task of complexity measurement on an axiomatic foundation (Goodman 1955). In addition, in his 1952 paper 'New Notes on Simplicity' he considered the issue of choosing between two extralogical bases that have the same complexity value, and his heuristic decision criteria are specified as follows (see Goodman 1952: 190):

> If *A* and *B* are alternate bases of equal computed complexity, we choose *A* rather than *B* if:
>
> (i) each consists of one predicate, and *A* has fewer places; or
> (ii) *A*, in number of predicates and of places in each, is exactly like some basis that consists of some but not all the predicates of *B*; or
> (iii) after the above rules have been applied, *A* and *B* have the same total number of places but *A* has the more predicates and thus the lower ratio of places to predicates.

These criteria enable one basis to be preferred in cases of equal complexity and they contribute to the task of reducing basis analysis and selection to an essentially mechanical procedure.

Despite his own conviction that basal economy and complexity measures were crucial to the task of constructional system creation, Goodman recognised that the importance of this aspect of system theory was not necessarily immediately apparent. One obvious counter-argument was that the inherent simplicity of the basis of a constructional system was merely an aesthetic consideration that had no significant consequences for the resultant system itself. In his 1943 paper 'On the Simplicity of Ideas', Goodman explicitly refuted this argument.

> The motives for seeking economy in the basis of a system are much the same as the motives for constructing the system itself. A given idea *A* need be left as primitive in a system only so long as we have discovered between *A* and the other primitives no relationship intimate enough to permit defining *A* in terms of them; hence the more the set of primitives can be reduced without becoming inadequate, the more comprehensively will the system exhibit the network of interrelationships that comprise its subject-matter. Of course we are often concerned less with an explicit effort to reduce our basis than with particular problems as to how to define certain ideas from others. But such special problems of derivation, such problems of rendering certain ideas eliminable

> in favor of others, are merely instances of the general problem of economy. Thus it is quite wrong to think of the search for economy as a sort of game, inspired by an abnormal love of superficial neatness. Some economies may be relatively unimportant, but the inevitable result of regarding all economy as trivial would be a willingness to accept all ideas as primitive at the outset, making a system both unnecessary and impossible. (Goodman 1943: 107)

As it is presented here, far from being a manifestation of 'an abnormal love of superficial neatness', the general theory of simplicity is a metalogical concern which impinges upon the validity of a given constructional system. In essence, a 'simpler' system is a better system, so long as it does not become 'inadequate'; and 'better' in this context means a more economical system, since such systems are understood to provide more profound insights into the phenomena analysed. By 1955 Goodman apparently sensed that he had managed to win this particular battle, since he felt able to declare:

> No longer do we need to take seriously the idea that simplicity is something to be sought only if there is time after truth has been attained. To seek truth is to seek a true system, and to seek such system [sic] at all is to seek simplicity. (Goodman 1955: 709)

Theory-internal simplicity is here unequivocally associated with some kind of philosophical truth, and as will be shown later, it is significant that Goodman was exploring these ideas and engaging in this kind of inspiring polemic in the late 1940s, around the time he began to teach philosophy at the University of Pennsylvania to a promising young undergraduate called Noam Chomsky. The precise nature of the influence of simplicity considerations and other aspects of constructional system theory upon TGG is explored at length in sections 4.3, 4.4, and 5.4.

3.6   Constructive nominalism

As indicated in the preceding section, Goodman began his philosophical career as a logical empiricist in the *LCW* tradition, and, during the 1940s, his empirical stance became even stricter. Once again Carnap's influence was significant, for he returned to Harvard during the academic year 1940/1941 and was involved in discussions with both Goodman and Quine concerning various aspects of logic. Ever since completing the *LSL*, Carnap's academic work had focused on problems associated with formal language theory and, as he later recalled, the discussions at Harvard enabled him to refine some of his ideas.

> My thinking on these problems received fruitful stimulation from a series of conversations which I had with Tarski and Quine... when I was at Harvard: later Nelson Goodman participated in these talks. We considered especially the question of which form the basic language, i.e., the observation language. must have in order to fulfil the requirement of complete understandability. We agreed that the language must be nominalistic, i.e., its terms must not refer tc abstract entities but only to observable objects or events. (Carnap 1963: 79)

The ideas promulgated and debated in these meetings clearly influenced the thinking of all the participants, and Goodman and Quine eventually articulated their response in their 1947 paper 'Steps Towards a Constructive Nominalism' (from henceforth 'SCN'). The basic purpose of this work was to implement precisely the type of nominalistic formal language that had been proposed during the Harvard discussions, and this project was pursued within the broad framework of constructional system theory. The polemically nominalistic stance of the paper is declared in its notorious opening sentence ('We do not believe in abstract entities' (Goodman and Quine 1947: 105)), and this declaration provided the philosophical foundation for the entire scheme. In order to motivate their extreme stance, Goodman and Quine explain their refusal to tolerate such notions as follows:

> Fundamentally this refusal is based on a philosophical intuition that cannot be justified by appeal to anything more ultimate. It is fortified, however, by certain *a posteriori* considerations. What seems to be the most natural principle for abstracting classes or properties leads to paradoxes. Escape from these paradoxes can apparently be effected only by recourse to alternative rules whose artificiality and arbitrariness arouse suspicion that we are lost in a world of make-believe. (Goodman and Quine 1947: 105)

This statement indicates that, for Goodman and Quine (as for Leśniewski before them) the main motivation for a nominalistic approach to constructional system theory was the belief that, by rejecting abstract entities, the infamous paradoxes that had disrupted all attempts to place mathematics on a secure (set-theoretical) foundation might be avoided. Consequently, in this paper, Goodman and Quine make a clear distinction between 'platonistic logic' (i.e., logic that admits abstract entities such as sets) and 'nominalistic logic' (i.e., logic that does not admit abstract entities such as sets), and the first sections of the paper are devoted to outlining some of the strategies that must be employed in order to convert platonistic statements into nominalistic statements. For instance, the platonistic statement 'Class A has three members' assumes the existence of a finite class (i.e., set), which is an abstract entity. However, if there are three distinct objects x, y, and z, such that an object is in A if and only if it is x

or y or z, then this abstract set-theoretical statement can be converted into the nominalistic statement

$$\exists x \exists y \exists z [x \neq y \wedge y \neq z \wedge x \neq z \wedge \forall w [w \in A \\ \equiv w = x \vee w = y \vee w = z]] \qquad (3.16)$$

Clearly, (3.16) assumes the existence of nothing other than concrete individuals in addition to the basic logical operators.

Having outlined their basic approach in this fashion, Goodman and Quine proceed to develop in detail the nominalistic syntax they require in order to remove all 'taint' of platonism from their system (Goodman and Quine 1947: 107). The syntax they create is inscriptional by design since it is ultimately concerned with strings of physical marks rather than with abstract entities of any kind. Consequently, as the foundation of the extralogical basis of their system, Goodman and Quine define six so-called 'shape-predicates'. These are predicates that take concrete individuals as arguments and which specify the shape of a particular character. For instance, the predicate 'Vee x' means 'the object x is a vee (i.e., a v-shaped inscription)' (Goodman and Quine 1947: 112). The other characters defined in this way are: ', (,), |, and ϵ. In addition, a concatenation relation, C, is assumed where 'x C yz' is understood to mean that 'x and y are composed of various characters of the language ... and that the inscription x consists of y followed by z' (Goodman and Quine 1947: 112). The role of concatenation is crucial in this system. As mentioned in section 3.5, Quine had already explored the idea that the whole of arithmetic could be founded upon the basis of concatenation alone, and, the inclusion of the C predicate in 'SCN' suggests that the notion of concatenation was considered to be fundamental also to the formal syntax of a nominalistic object language. The final two predicates used are introduced as 'Part' and 'Bgr', and are taken to mean 'is part of' and 'is bigger than' respectively. More precisely, 'x Part y' means 'x, whether or not it is identical with y, is contained entirely within y', while 'x Bgr y' means 'x is spatially bigger than y' (Goodman and Quine 1947: 112–113).

Having presented the basic syntax of their object language, Goodman and Quine then provide definitions of auxiliary predicates that are constructed in a purely nominalistic manner from their initial predicate set. For instance, a four-part predicate can be defined using the existential operator, logical conjunction, and the concatenation operator:

$$xy \ C \ zw = \exists t [x \ C \ yt \wedge t \ C \ zw] \qquad (3.17)$$

Ultimately, it is demonstrated that variables, quantification, formulae, and (ultimately) proofs can all be obtained within the unremittingly nominalistic framework outlined in the paper.

Interestingly, their joint work on constructive nominalism eventually led Goodman and Quine in very different directions. Goodman continued to advocate the strict, individual-based type of logical epistemology associated with nominalistic constructional system theory, and, as was mentioned earlier, he revised his ideas concerning simplicity measures for extralogical bases so that the methods he devised could be used in the more extreme nominalist framework presented in 'SCN'. Further, in his 1954 book *Fact, Fiction and Forecast*, Goodman highlighted some of the problems that had bedevilled traditional justifications of the inductive processes required by logical epistemology of the *LCW* variety, before attempting to resolve some of these problems by developing a 'theory of projection' that was designed to distinguish between valid and invalid inductive procedures. By contrast, during the late 1940s Quine began increasingly to reject the type of logical epistemology that had so entranced him previously. His most perceptive rebuttal of this whole philosophical movement was succinctly articulated in 'Two Dogmas of Empiricism' (1953), which remains a seminal text of North American analytic philosophy. In this artful paper, Quine endeavoured to demonstrate that two basic assumptions that have often characterised 'modern empiricism' (Quine 1953: 20), as manifest in Carnapian logical epistemology, were essentially invalid. These two assumptions can be summarised as (i) the Kantian belief that there is a qualitative difference between analytic and synthetic truths,[25] and (ii) the reductionist belief that each meaningful statement can be exhaustively analysed as a logical construct ultimately derived from sensory experience. It is essential to note here that consideration (i) was a topic of much discussion in the 1950s. For instance, this particular issue was considered at length by Morton White (b. 1917) in his paper 'The Analytic and the Synthetic: an Untenable Dualism' (1952). In this article, White referred to 'a revolt' against the general acceptance of the conventional Kantian distinction, and he indicated that this revolt was led by himself and certain 'fellow revolutionaries' (White 1952: 272) – namely, Goodman and Quine. Presumably in order to further the cause of the revolution, White indicated that his purpose in the paper was to 'present some of the reasons for this decline of faith' (White 1952: 272). While the specific details of White's argument are not necessary here, it is crucial to recognise that his attempt to destabilise the analytic-synthetic distinction depended upon problems inherent in the notion of meaning in natural language. For instance, (following Quine) White considered the sentence

88 *Mathematical linguistics*

$$\text{Every man is a man} \tag{3.18}$$

and argued (with some justification) that (3.18) embodies a tautology and therefore can be classified as an analytic truth. He then presents the sentence

$$\text{Every man is a rational animal} \tag{3.19}$$

and suggests that sentence (3.19) can only be classified as analytical if the synonymy of 'man' and 'rational animal' can be irrefutably established. In the ensuing assessment of synonymy, White acknowledges that artificial languages (e.g., L_1) could be created that would resolve all problems of synonymy, but he goes on to declare that

> these languages are the creatures of formal fancy; they are dreamed up by a logician. If I ask: 'Is "All men are rational animals" analytic in L_1?', I am rightly told to look up the rule-book of language L_1. But natural languages have no rule-books and the question of whether a given statement is analytic in them is much more difficult. (White 1952: 277)

Clearly the implication here is that natural languages and logical languages differ considerably, at least as far as considerations of meaning are concerned, and this view should be situated in the context of the general move towards the further integration of natural and logical languages that has already been discussed with reference to the work of Bloomfield, Ajdukiewicz, Harwood, and Bar-Hillel. More specifically, White argues that issues of meaning are fundamentally problematic in natural languages, though they can (usually) be resolved in logical languages. As will be shown in sections 4.4 and 4.5, Quine's assault upon, and Goodman's defence of, logical empiricism, along with Quine and White's questioning of the analytic–synthetic dualism, all stimulated Chomsky while he was in the process of developing TGG, and it is crucial to recognise that these developments were largely provoked by the constructive nominalist research programme that Goodman and Quine had propounded in the 1940s.

3.7 Formal linguistic theory

In the previous section the influence of Carnap's *LCW* upon North American philosophy was discussed and in chapters 4 and 5 it will be shown that the work of Goodman and Quine directly inspired various aspects of TGG. However, Carnap's later work concerning logical syntax (particularly *LSL*) also fascinated linguists during the first half of the twentieth century. Consequently, in this section, some distinctive features of formal syntactic theory are considered, and their influence upon linguistics is assessed.

As indicated in section 3.4, the fact that a formal syntactic theory devised by a logician (i.e., Ajdukiewicz) was later extended by a linguist (i.e., Bar-Hillel) in the 1950s indicates that, by the middle of the twentieth century, symbolic logic had begun to influence certain areas of linguistics directly. However, during the 1930s and 1940s other developments in the theory of logical syntax occurred, which were ultimately to have profound implications for linguistic research, and the starting point was usually Hilbert's proof theory, which seemed to imply that meaning-less syntactic manipulations could suffice to resolve a whole range of epistemological problems. As mentioned in section 2.6, Hilbert's work had influenced the Vienna Circle directly, and one of the most distinctive developments associated with Vienna-based research into the nature of logical systems in the 1930s was the shift of focus away from the structure of logic itself towards a concentration upon the structure of the language in which logical arguments are expressed. As mentioned previously, the most influential work of this type was due to Carnap, whose *LSL* appeared in 1934, with an English translation of the German original following in 1937, and it should be recalled that this is the text which had fascinated both Goodman and Quine, and which had ultimately pushed them towards constructive nominalism. However, Carnap's own agenda, as expressed in *LSL*, was not explicitly nominalistic, and his main intention was simply to explore the nature of logical syntax with greater precision. In particular, he emphasised the fact that all logical arguments, as expressed in conventional publications, usually consist of various formal deductions that are connected by sentences written in a natural language. Since these natural languages are external to the formal logical system being used, sentences written in them are not precisely defined, and therefore constitute weak links in any logical argument. Consequently, Carnap's intention was to provide a coherent logical system that could be used to analyse these sentences about sentences. In other words, just as Hilbert had created metamathematics (mathematics about mathematics), so Carnap was keen to construct a more general metalanguage that could be used to define and describe any given language.

Given the importance of Carnap's undertaking, it is essential to determine precisely what he meant by the term 'language'. In parts 1, 2, and 3 of *LSL* Carnap develops two artificial formal languages in an attempt to clarify the relationship between logic and the language of science, and he states his central aim as follows:

90 *Mathematical linguistics*

> The aim of the logical syntax is to provide a system of concepts, a language, by the help of which the results of logical analysis will be exactly formulable. *Philosophy is to be replaced by the logic of science* – that is to say, by the logical analysis of the concepts and sentences of the science, for *the logic of science is nothing other than the logical syntax of the language of science.* (Carnap 1937[1934]: xiii)

This passage suggests that, at this stage in his career, Carnap was convinced that philosophy could be replaced by the systematic study of logical syntax. However, in part 4 he broadens his basic approach and attempts to outline the formal syntactic structure of language in general. It is crucial to note that Carnap consistently views artificial languages as forming a well-defined subset of natural languages, though he makes it clear that his intention is *not* to describe the syntax of natural language.

> In consequence of the idiosyncrasies and logically imperfect structure of the natural world-languages (such as German or Latin), the statement of their formal rules of formation and transformation would be so complicated that it would be hardly feasible in practice... Owing to the deficiencies of the world-languages, the logical structure of a language of this kind will not be developed. (Carnap 1937[1934]: 2)

The types of rules that Carnap refers to as 'formation' and 'transformation' rules will be discussed at some length below, but it is necessary to stress that the above passage reveals the domain of Carnap's enquiry: instead of focusing on natural languages, he concentrates on the task of defining and constructing formal artificial languages, and, in order to accomplish this, he utilises assumptions and techniques derived from (Hilbertian) Formalism. Despite this emphasis, Carnap does not entirely preclude the possibility that the techniques he develops in *LSL* may be of relevance for theories of natural language. Indeed, he states explicitly that

> The method of syntax which will be developed in the following pages will not only prove useful in the logical analysis of scientific theories – it will also help in the *logical analysis of the world-languages*. Although here, for the reasons indicated above, we shall be dealing with symbolic languages, the syntactical concepts and rules – not in detail but in their general character - may also be applied to the analysis of the incredibly complicated world-languages. (Carnap 1937[1934]: 8)

As will be shown in chapters 4 and 5, this basic belief that 'symbolic' and 'world' languages could (in principle) be analysed using the same fundamental techniques exerted a potent influence over certain linguists during the following years.

It was suggested above that *LSL* reveals the influence of (Hilbertian) Formalism, and Carnap's indebtedness to Formalism is explicitly acknowledged several times; indeed, the influence of Hilbert pervades the entire book. For instance, Carnap specifically credits Hilbert with developing the theory of formal languages, observing that '[t]he point of view of the formal theory of languages (known as 'syntax' in our terminology) was first developed for mathematics by Hilbert' (Carnap 1937[1934]: 1), and he utilises Hilbert's notion of a formal system extensively. For instance, at the very beginning of part 1 Carnap offers the following definition of the term 'formal':

> A theory, a rule, a definition, or the like is to be called *formal systems* when no reference is made in it either to the meaning of the symbols (for example, the words) or to the sense of the expressions (e.g., the sentences), but simply and solely to the kinds and order of the symbols from which the expressions are constructed. (Carnap 1937[1934]: 1)

and, obviously, this quotation evinces the same concern for meaning-less symbol manipulation as the various pedagogic texts considered in 2.8, with the result that Carnap's formal languages consist of meaning-less formulae derived ultimately from primitive symbols by means of rules in a characteristically Formalist manner; that is, the formal languages are defined solely in terms of the syntactic structure of the sentences they produce, and the meanings of the resulting formulae and primitive symbols are not considered. In order to emphasise this point, Carnap considers the sentence 'Pirots karulize elatically' and states that this sentence can be parsed accurately as a Noun+Verb+Adverb sequence even though the words are all unfamiliar (Carnap 1937[1934]: 2), thus demonstrating that sentences can be exhaustively analysed solely in terms of their formal syntactic structure even if the meaning of the individual words is not known. This type of argument, which (according to Carnap) affirms the separation of meaning and syntax, proved to be influential, and it will reappear when TGG is discussed in section 5.7.

There is another aspect of the theory Carnap develops in *LSL* that is relevant to the development of TGG. As mentioned above, Carnap distinguishes between formation rules and transformation rules, and he introduces these terms in a passage that considers the possibility of reducing logic to 'syntax':

> Logic will become syntax, provided that the latter is conceived in a sufficiently wide sense and formulated with exactitude. The difference between syntactical rules in the narrower sense and the logical rules of deduction is only the

> difference between formation rules and transformation rules, both of which are completely formulable in syntactical terms. Thus we are justified in designating as 'logical syntax' the system which comprises the rules of formation and transformation. (Carnap 1937[1934]: 2)

As this passage indicates, in the framework Carnap outlines in *LSL*, a distinction can be made between rules that are used to construct strings of symbols from (ultimately) primitive elements, and the rules of inference that enable one string of symbols to be inferred from another string of symbols. Specifically, the former are classified as formation rules, while the latter are referred to as transformation rules. For example, in part 1 of *LSL*, logical conjunction is categorised as a formation rule since it enables a sentence to be constructed from smaller units. In this case, the sentences $\mathfrak{S}_1$ and $\mathfrak{S}_2$ can be conjoined to create the sequence

$$\mathfrak{S}_1 \vee \mathfrak{S}_2 \qquad (3.20)$$

where '$\vee$' is a two-termed junction symbol (Carnap 1937[1934]: 19), and this type of conjoining is classified as a formation process. By contrast, the rule of implication is categorised as a transformation rule in Carnap's system, since it enables sentences to be inferred from other sentences. Therefore, given the premises $\mathfrak{S}_1$ and $\mathfrak{S}_2$, the rule of implication is stated as follows (Carnap 1937[1934]: 32)

$$\mathfrak{S}_2, \mathfrak{S}_1 \supset \mathfrak{S}_3 \qquad (3.21)$$

where '$\supset$' is the symbol Carnap uses to indicate implication. This rule states that sentence $\mathfrak{S}_3$ can be obtained from the sentences $\mathfrak{S}_1$ and $\mathfrak{S}_2$ by means of implication, although $\mathfrak{S}_3$ does not constitute a simple combination of $\mathfrak{S}_1$ and $\mathfrak{S}_2$. Consequently, (3.21) constitutes a transformation rule, and it should be obvious that this rule is simply a restatement of Hilbert's proof-theoretical schema, given as (2.10) above.

Transformation rules are used extensively in *LSL*, and Carnap repeatedly emphasises their centrality. The following passage is typical:

> For the construction of a calculus the statement of the transformation rules, as well as of the formation rules, as given for language I, is essential. By means of the former we determine under what conditions a sentence is a *consequence* of another sentence or sentences (the *premises*). But the fact that $\mathfrak{S}_2$ is a consequence of $\mathfrak{S}_1$ does not mean that the thought of $\mathfrak{S}_1$ would be accompanied by the thought of $\mathfrak{S}_2$. It is not a question of psychological but of a logical relation between sentences. (Carnap 1937[1934]: 27)

Once again, this passages stresses the fact that in Carnap's framework transformation rules are purely rules of logical inference that indicate a 'logical relation' between particular sentences, with one sentence following as a consequence of another sentence (or group of sentences). In case this summary gives the impression that Carnap was devoid of any qualms concerning the nature of logical inference, it is necessary to indicate that he was fully cognizant of the many difficulties that beset his methodology. Indeed, Carnap was happy to acknowledge that the notion of 'consequence' had to remain undefined in his system, though the more restrictive notion of derivability could be established.

> It is impossible by the aid of simple methods to frame a definition for the term 'consequence' in its full comprehension. Such a definition has never yet been achieved in modern logic (or, of course, in the older logic)... At present, we shall determine for Language I, instead of the term 'consequence', the somewhat narrower term '*derivable*'... For this purpose, the term '*directly derivable*' will be defined, or – as it is more commonly expressed – *rules of inference* will be laid down. (Carnap 1937[1934]: 27)

As will be demonstrated in section 5.5, Carnap's presentation of his formation and transformation rules, with their associated terminology and philosophical preoccupations, were subsequently adapted in different ways by several linguists during the years following the publication of *LSL*, and, as will be shown, the nature of these rules was debated in various discussions and disputes that were sustained while TGG was being developed.

There is no doubt that formal approaches to syntax, such as that outlined by Carnap in *LSL*, captured the imagination of many linguists during the first half of the twentieth century, and once again Bloomfield emerges (perhaps unexpectedly) as a prophetic figure. Bloomfield's interest in the axiomatic-deductive method was discussed in section 3.2, and it was shown there that he was familiar with recent developments in modern mathematics. Indeed, during the 1930s Bloomfield seems to have become preoccupied with the nature of the relationship between mathematics and linguistics, and his understanding of this topic was directly influenced by the work of the Vienna Circle. The full extent of Bloomfield's familiarity with the main publications associated with the leading member of Schlick's Circle can be gauged from his 1936 paper 'Language or Ideas?' In this paper, Bloomfield cites five works written by Neurath and seven by Carnap, including *LSL*. This suggests that Bloomfield was entirely familiar with Carnap's provocative ideas concerning logical syntax, and, as will become apparent, this fact is of some significance. In this context, then, Bloomfield pursued his interest in the relationship between mathematics and linguistics, and his most extended consideration of this subject was contained in a long essay which he contributed to the *International Encyclopedia of Unified Science* in 1939 (five years after *LSL* appeared). The *Encyclopedia* was a forum for assessing the methodology of scientific research, and many of the contributors were associated either directly or indirectly with the Vienna Circle. In particular, Carnap was on the board of editors that read and assessed the contributions, including Bloomfield's paper. This paper, 'Linguistic Aspects of Science', was based on a 1935 article that he had published, and it served several purposes. For instance, it summarised various ideas and techniques employed in linguistic research in the early decades of the twentieth century, and, in this respect, it can be viewed in part as a brief informal summary of Bloomfield's 1933 book *Language*. However, in addition, the essay considers the relationship between linguistics and mathematics, or, as Bloomfield puts it himself, 'the relation of linguistics to logic and mathematics' (Bloomfield 1955[1939]: 273). In the light of the foundations debates (and given Bloomfield's knowledge of the same), this statement should be read very carefully, since it appears to imply that, for Bloomfield, mathematics and logic were separate fields of research. In other words, by stating his interest in this way, Bloomfield may be consciously avoiding the extreme Logicist viewpoint that would consider mathematics to be entirely derivable from logic. Whether this is so or not, having outlined his basic intention, Bloomfield then considers various aspects of the broad topic he has broached. For example, he declares that 'logic is a branch of science closely related to linguistics, since it observes how people conduct a certain type of discourse' (Bloomfield 1955[1939]: 273–274), and this leads him to suggest in turn that logical arguments can be analysed specifically as linguistic discourses. Such statements certainly imply a close correspondence between linguistics and logic, and they reinforce the suggestion (made in section 3.2) that during the 1930s Bloomfield had started to think of mathematics as a form of language that would be amenable to linguistic analysis.

Clearly, then, Bloomfield was fascinated by the relationship between logic and natural language, and one of the most revealing aspects of the discussion he offered in his 1939 paper was his enthusiastic acceptance of Hilbert's basic Formalist creed; the very creed that had inspired Carnap's *LSL*. For example, Bloomfield makes a clear distinction between formal and informal scientific discourse, describing the former as a manner of communication that 'uses a rigidly limited vocabulary and syntax and moves from sentence to sentence only within the range of conventional rules' (Bloomfield 1955[1939]: 261), and he later argues that, in considering the 'characters' (i.e., symbols) used in logical and mathematical discourse, he has not 'left the domain of language' since

> In general, to be sure, the separate characters have been agreed upon as substitutes for specific words or phrases. In many cases, however, we manage best by ignoring the values and confining ourselves to the manipulation of the written symbols; systems of symbolic logic, especially, may be viewed, in a formal way, as systems of marks and conventions for the arrangement of these marks... our formal systems serve merely as written or mechanical mediations between utterances of language. (Bloomfield 1955[1939]: 262)

This passage, which could easily have come from one of the textbooks discussed in 2.8, suggests that Bloomfield was essentially convinced of the validity of the Formalist approach to mathematics. At the very least, it implies that Bloomfield accepted the Formalist dictum that 'we manage best' (to use his own words) if we focus on syntactic manipulation and ignore considerations of meaning. The implications of this aspect of Bloomfield's work are considerable and have never been adequately discussed. Indeed, an exhaustive exploration of Bloomfield's appreciation of Formalism could well help to explain why so many young linguists in the 1950s found that the techniques of structural linguistics appeared to be compatible with the techniques employed by the formal sciences. In essence, as the above passage demonstrates, Bloomfieldian linguistics and the formal sciences were both shaped by Formalism during the 1930s, and the effects of this influence are readily apparent in Bloomfield's work. For instance, to consider one example, it is well known that Bloomfield repeatedly expressed scepticism concerning the role of meaning in linguistic theory. A standard expression of this mistrust, taken from *Language*, runs as follows: 'The statement of meaning is... the weak point in language-study, and will remain so until human knowledge advances very far beyond its present state' (Bloomfield 1933: 140). In the past, attempts to account for this scepticism have focused upon ideas concerning syntax and semantics within linguistics, and upon the relationship between linguistics and psychology.[26] While there is no doubt that linguistics and psychology were both responsible for determining the direction of Bloomfield's thought in many ways, it is certainly possible that some of his ideas concerning the role of meaning in linguistic theory were directly influenced by his knowledge of Formalism (and/or vice versa), which appeared to advocate the manipulation of meaning-less symbols extracted from their semantic context. While it would be needlessly excessive to claim that Bloomfield mistrusted linguistic meaning primarily because he was intrigued by the methodology of Formalism, it might well have been the case that his understanding of the foundational debates within mathematics confirmed his initial misgivings about semantics in linguistic research, causing him to marginalise the role of meaning in his own work, and therefore unwittingly to pave the way for the type of 'formal' syntactic theories that began to emerge in the late 1940s and early 1950s.

Although Bloomfield's 1939 essay is detailed and authoritative, it was not his most extensive discussion of the relationship between linguistics and mathematics, for, two years previously, he had submitted a 300-page manuscript on the topic to the Committee on Research of the Linguistic Society. The proposed monograph was called *The Language of Science* and it constituted an elaborate attempt to analyse large portions of modern mathematics from a linguistic perspective.[27] Indeed, this extraordinary document appears to have constituted an attempt to resolve the foundations crisis by approaching the paradoxes of set theory from the perspective of linguistic theory. With becoming humility, the linguists on the committee considered themselves to be unequal to the task of assessing the value of the manuscript, so it was passed on to several professional mathematicians, including the prominent Formalist Haskell Curry (1900–1982). Since the manuscript contained a few mathematical errors, Curry advised against publication, but, despite his technical reservations, he was impressed by Bloomfield's approach and offered general advice as to how the manuscript could be improved. However, Bloomfield decided that he would not be able to revise the text so as to make it acceptable either to mathematicians or to linguists, and, instead, he used the reverse sides of the pages as scrap paper. Consequently, only a few fragments survive, but (fortunately) enough remains to reveal the ambitious nature of the work. For instance, it is known that there were chapters dealing with such topics as infinite classes, recursion, logical vocabulary and syntax, and many other topics from (then) modern mathematics. These glimpses of Bloomfield's text hint at the full extent of his familiarity with issues concerning the nature and function of logical syntax, and it is particularly tantalising that several of the techniques he considered (i.e., those associated with recursive function theory and logical syntax) were to be incorporated into TGG in the 1950s.

Despite Bloomfield's discussion of the various topics mentioned above, though, his main intention was not simply to provide an expository overview of contemporaneous mathematics, but rather to solve some of the problems of self-reference that had undermined set theory. His interest in the problem of self-reference had been signalled in his 1935 paper when he had discussed the differences between natural and mathematical languages. In particular, in that paper he had identified two stages in the process of scientific activity which he characterises as follows:

> The linguist naturally divides scientific activity into two phases: the scientist performs 'handling' actions (observation, collecting of specimens, experiment) and utters speech (report, classification, hypothesis, prediction). The speech-forms which the scientist utters are peculiar both in their form and in their effect upon hearers. (Bloomfield 1935: 499)

He later clarifies the nature of this peculiarity by observing that the language of mathematics can only be understood after 'severe supplementary training', and that utterances in such a language have the curious effect of causing the hearers to 'respond uniformly and in a predictable way' (Bloomfield 1935: 499). Clearly, therefore, the language of science differs significantly from natural language, and the speech-forms of scientific language appear to constitute 'a highly specialized linguistic phenomenon' (Bloomfield 1935: 500). It is at this point that Bloomfield's ambitious agenda starts to reveal itself. The following passage is crucial:

> To describe and evaluate this phenomenon is first and foremost a problem for linguistics. The linguist may fail to go very far towards the solution of this problem, especially if he lacks competence in the branches of science other than his own. It is with the greatest diffidence that the present writer dares to touch upon it. But it is the linguist and only the linguist who can take the first steps towards its solution; to attack this problem without competence in linguistics is to court disaster. The endless confusion of what is written about the foundations of science or of mathematics is due very largely to the author's lack of linguistic information. (Bloomfield 1935: 500)

The central idea here is transparent: the complex and acrimonious arguments that had come to characterise the mathematical foundations crisis debates in the 1920s and 1930s could be resolved if only the participants were able to view the problem from a linguistic perspective. Indeed, in Bloomfield's words, 'the linguist and only the linguist' can intervene in order to resolve the disputes. Obviously, this is a bold and startling claim, hence Bloomfield's self-confessed 'diffidence', but the proposal is serious nonetheless. Since (infuriatingly) Bloomfield does not cite specific sources in his discussion, the precise causes of his dissatisfaction with existing proposed solutions to the foundations crisis can only be guessed. It should be recalled, though, that, as mentioned previously, introductory texts such as Young's *Lectures on the Fundamental Concepts of Algebra and Geometry* predated the main foundational debates, and consequently did not contain detailed discussions of the main disagreements, suggesting that Bloomfield acquired his knowledge of these debates from primary sources. As mentioned in section 3.5, some foundational issues were addressed in certain works produced by the members of the Vienna Circle, and Bloomfield certainly knew some of these publications. However, questions concerning specifics inevitably remain. Had Bloomfield read the main publications associated with Hilbert or Russell? If so, precisely which publications had he read? Certainly, references in Carnap's *Logische Syntax der Sprache* (which Bloomfield *had* read) would have provided him with information concerning Hilbert's most significant pre-1934 articles, and, by the mid-1930s, Russell and Whitehead's work, especially *Principia Mathematica*, had already become a common starting point for most contemporary work in symbolic logic, and was therefore hardly an obscure and unobtainable text. Whatever the precise sources of his knowledge, though, it is clear that Bloomfield was well aware of the fact that the paradoxes which had provoked the foundations crisis in the early decades of the twentieth century were associated with specific kinds of self-reference.[28] Indeed, it is this aspect of the whole foundations debate that seems to have intrigued Bloomfield most, since, as he was keen to demonstrate, the basic problem of self-reference can be approached from a linguistic perspective. His particular concerns are manifest in the following footnote in which he reflects upon Kurt Grelling's (1886–1942) well-known heterological paradox.[29]

> An adjective which describes itself is *autological* (e.g., *short* is autological, since the adjective *short* is actually a short word). An adjective which is not autological is *heterological* (e.g., *long* is not a long word). Is the adjective *heterological* heterological? If it is heterological, it describes itself and is therefore autological. If it autological, it does not describe itself and is therefore heterological. (Bloomfield 1935: 500.n3)

Before continuing with the footnote it is worth pausing to clarify the discussion. As should be apparent, Grelling's heterological paradox is closely related to Russell's paradox (discussed in section 3.4 above), the main difference being that, rather than being situated in the context of set theory, Grelling's paradox enables Bloomfield to view the problem from the perspective of natural language so that it can be assessed from a different standpoint. However, a mere restatement of a known difficulty is one thing, while a specific proposal for its resolution is quite another, yet, as the footnote continues, this is precisely what Bloomfield attempts:

> The fallacy is due to misuse of linguistic terms: the phrase 'an adjective which describes itself' makes no sense in any usable terminology of linguistics; the example of *short* illustrates a situation which could be described only in a different discourse. E.g.: We may set up, without very rigid boundaries, as to meaning, various classes of adjectives. An adjective which describes a phonetic feature of words is *morphonymic* (e.g., *short, long, monosyllabic*). A

> morphonymic adjective which describes a phonetic feature of itself is *autological*. A morphonymic adjective which is not autological is *heterological*. The adjectives *autological* and *heterological* designate meanings of adjectives and not phonetic features; hence they are not morphonymic. – Contrast the following sensible discourse: A *hakab* is a word that ends in a bilabial stop (p, b). A word that is not a hakab is a *cowp*. The word *hakab* and *cowp* are hakabs. (Bloomfield 1935: 500.n2)

Although this discussion is necessarily sketchy, constituting as it does a brief footnote, the basic outline of Bloomfield's proposal is clear: his intention was to avoid the problem of direct self-reference by reanalysing the categorical allocation of the words involved. In this simple example, by introducing the notion of morphonymic adjectives, Bloomfield suggests that linguistic categories can be redefined in order to exclude the type of direct self-reference that engenders paradox. It is important to note that, for Bloomfield, this was specifically a linguistic solution for a pervasive problem.

The radical stance of the unpublished 1937 MS is clear from the observation that it could be characterised as 'contradicting the beliefs of mathematicians', though Bloomfield's self-doubt is also apparent. Ultimately, his doubts seem to have predominated, since, as mentioned above, he did not resubmit the manuscript, and only fragments now survive. Thankfully, though, Bloomfield's basic motivation for writing the text is clearly articulated in one of the surviving passages. For instance, after observing that no 'student of human speech' has ever made an extensive study of mathematics, he continues:

> Having made the attempt, the present writer has reached the conclusion that such a study, apart from its linguistic interest, leads to the solution of certain problems that have baffled non-linguistic attack – the problems which concern the foundations of mathematics. If this conclusion is justified, the following pages should be of wider than linguistic interest. (Bloomfield 1970a[1937]: 335)

This is an extraordinary statement. As indicated above, in his 1935 article Bloomfield had observed that certain problems of self-reference within mathematics could be avoided if a linguistic approach were adopted. In the light of this remark it becomes apparent that the now lost 1937 MS constituted an extended attempt actually to provide a linguistic-based solution to the foundations crisis. Although it is no longer possible to reconstruct Bloomfield's arguments in exhaustive detail, some kind of revivification can be accomplished. For instance, as mentioned previously, a partial chapter list has survived, and, consequently, it is known that the MS contained sections dealing with such topics as 'infinite classes', 'recursion', 'logical vocabulary and syntax', and other subjects that were active areas of contemporaneous mathematical research. The reference to a chapter concerning 'infinite classes' is of especial interest since Bloomfield delivered an (unpublished) paper on this topic to the Annual Meeting of the Linguistic Society in 1936, and it was clearly a subject that preoccupied him at the time.[30] Given his familiarity with the foundations debates, this preoccupation is not surprising since, as mentioned in section 2.4, many of the paradoxes of mathematics were understood to be associated with the notion of an infinite set, and, therefore, any valid solution to the foundations crisis must either reconsider the implications of such sets, or else must reformulate this aspect of set theory in such a way that such sets were precluded.[31] Indeed, the extant MS fragments suggest that, in his 1937 text Bloomfield focused primarily upon the task of *naming* infinite sets. For instance, he considers various methods that can be used to define irrational numbers, and criticises the use of summation series.

> The members of the summation series can be obtained one by one, but we have no finite formula for the direct naming or recognition of these members. To prescribe the naming, in this form, of an irrational number, is to insist that our hearers *complete the recitation* of an infinite class of speech-forms. This fallacy is still current among mathematicians; we shall return to it in Chapter 22. (Bloomfield 1970a[1937]: 337)

Unfortunately, Chapter 22 no longer exists, so Bloomfield's discussion of this perceived fallacy cannot be completely revived. However, his analysis of the use of limits as a means of defining irrational numbers has survived, as has a short section of his discussion of the Φ class. Bloomfield defines the Φ class using linguistic notions associated with naming. He defines three activities:

(1) Say *decimal point*
(2) recite any sequence of digits or none
(3) name a second sequence of digits, not all zeros as a circulating sequence

where a 'circulating sequence' is any sequence of numbers that repeats itself, and Bloomfield concludes by asserting that 'any speech-form of the shape (1)-(2)-(3) or of the shape (1)-(3) is a member of the class Φ' (Bloomfield 1970a[1937]: 338). With this definition in place, Bloomfield proceeds to consider the implications of naming infinite sets.

> Given the class Φ, together with a formula for well-ordering it... we can define, *as functions of* Φ, infinite classes of speech-forms of the type **N**. For instance, we add 1 to the kth digit of the kth **R** [**R**s are defined earlier as 'thing-nouns'], except that when the sum is 10 we replace it by 1. We thus obtain the infinite class of speech-forms $\mathbf{N}^1$, the non-circulating decimals whose first

ten digits are .5471111117. This formula for naming $\mathbf{N}^1$, is stated in terms of Φ and its well-ordering: a digit of $\mathbf{N}^1$ can be named only if one first names k digits of the kth **R**. Hence to calculate and recite digits of $\mathbf{N}^1$ to the end of one's patience is not to name a number: it is only the formula $\mathbf{N}^1$, interpreted as above, which names a number. (Bloomfield 1970a[1937]: 338)

Although this remnant of a larger discussion is opaque in places, the basic thrust of the passage is clear: the act of enumerating the members of an infinite class (i.e., set) is not the same as naming the set, and, presumably, in the remaining chapters of the MS, Bloomfield sought to demonstrate that the paradoxes of set theory could be obviated if this kind of linguistic distinction were systematically observed.

When the remaining MS fragments were collected by Hockett in 1970 for inclusion in *A Leonard Bloomfield Anthology* (which he was then editing), he commented concerning the destruction of the manuscript:

> I cannot refrain from expressing my regret at this loss. Had he [i.e., Bloomfield] lived to rework the topic, benefiting from Professor Curry's suggestions (even if not accepting them all), some of his successors, who have concerned themselves with the inter-relations of language and mathematics, might have been helped to avoid various stupid errors. (Bloomfield 1970b: 334)

Unfortunately, Hockett does not name the linguists who had been guilty of making 'stupid errors', nor does he indicate which particular mistakes he has in mind. There can be little doubt, though, that some of the names that feature prominently in the remaining chapters of this book may well have been Hockett's intended targets.

Bloomfield's ideas concerning the relationship between mathematics and linguistics and, in particular, his Formalist tendencies (whether overtly or covertly expressed) which emphasised the primacy of syntactic (rather than semantic) considerations, exerted a profound influence over a whole generation of linguists that came to maturity in the 1940s and 1950s. It is important to recognise, though, that this desire for a more mathematical approach to linguistic analysis was not solely confined to North America. For instance, to consider just one European example, Bloomfield's interest in recent advances in mathematics was shared by the heterogeneous group of researchers that constituted the Copenhagen Circle, and especially by Louis Hjelmslev (1899–1965). In his 1943 book *Prolegomena to a Theory of Language,* for example, Hjelmslev cited Bloomfield's 1926 paper in a footnote when he refers to 'transcendent kinds of linguists' who have attempted to construct 'systems of axioms' (Hjelmslev 1961[1943]: 6). Hjelmslev not only shared Bloomfield's interest in axioms and deduction, though, he was also inspired by the methodology of Formalism, with its emphasis on syntactic manipulation. In particular, according to Hjelmslev, a description of a language should be 'free of contradiction (self-consistent), exhaustive, and as simple as possible', linguists should assume 'as few premisses as possible', and all definitions constructed should be 'strictly formal' (Hjelmslev 1961[1943]: 20). This explicit injunction to avoid contradictions, along with the emphasis placed on formal structure, imply an informed awareness of Hilbert's proof theory, and Hjelmslev later explicitly discusses Hilbert's work in relation to the Lvov-Warsaw school, Carnap, and Saussurian linguistics.

> The logistic theory of signs finds its starting-point in the metamathematics of Hilbert, whose idea was to consider the system of mathematical symbols as a system of expression-figurae with complete disregard of their content, and to describe its transformation rules in the same way as one can describe the rules of a game, without considering possible interpretations. This method is carried over by the Polish logicians into their 'metalanguage' and is brought to its conclusion by Carnap in a sign-theory where, in principle, any semiotic is considered as a meaning expression system without regard for the content... The sign-theory of linguistics, on the other hand, has deep roots in the tradition according to which a sign is defined by its meaning. It is within this tradition that Saussure struggles with the problem. (Hjelmslev 1961[1943]: 110–111)

This passage indicates that, for Hjelmslev, there was a clear difference between the concerns of metamathematics and linguistics. The two disciplines were associated by their status as sub-branches of semiotics, but linguistics could never be subsumed by metamathematics because semantic considerations dominate in the former while they are non-existent in the latter. Nevertheless, the above passage clearly indicates that Hilbertian Formalism passed from the realm of mathematics into the realm of linguistics in Europe as well as North America, and that, for Hjelmslev (at least), the transmission of ideas was mediated by 'the Polish logicians' and Carnap.

While certain European linguists, such as Hjelmslev, were gradually developing a more formal approach to linguistic theory during the 1930s and 1940s, similar developments were occurring in North America, and since TGG is part of the story of North American linguistics, the focus of this discussion must once again fall upon the United States. As already indicated, the influence of Formalism is perhaps most apparent in the work of the post-Bloomfieldians – a disparate group of linguists that included Bloch, Hockett, Yuen Ren Chao (1892–1982), Rulon Wells (b. 1919), Martin Joos (1902–1978) and, of course, Harris[32] - who were, in many different ways, directing their research towards the task of formalising the discovery procedures that were believed to be required for the sort of distributional linguistic analysis that had developed in the tradition of Edward Sapir (1884–1939) and Bloomfield. Increasingly, during the 1940s, the researchers working in this general area began to emphasise the desirability of greater formal clarity. For instance, as partial justification for his 1947 development of Immediate Constituent analysis, Wells stated that his aim was 'to replace by a unified, systematic theory the heterogeneous and incomplete methods hitherto offered' (Wells 1947: 81). Similarly, in the previous year, Harris had claimed that the techniques introduced in his paper 'From Morpheme to Utterance' constituted a 'formalised procedure for describing utterances distinctly in terms of sequences of morphemes rather than of single morphemes' (Harris 1946: 161). Indeed, the notion of a 'formalised procedure' was still sufficiently new in 1946 to prompt the following footnote *apologia* from Harris:

> In view of the fact that methods as mathematical as the one proposed here have not yet become accepted in linguistics, some apology is due for introducing the procedure. However, the advantage which may be gained in explicitness, and in comparability of morphologies, may offset the trouble of manipulating the symbols of this procedure. (Harris 1946: 161.n1)

The phrase 'manipulating the symbols' suggests the Formalist tendency of Harris' thinking (i.e., morphemic analysis is essentially viewed as an exploration of symbol permutations), and Harris' apology for using this kind of 'mathematical' procedure suggests that he himself believed that the nature of linguistic research had begun to change. In the same way, many of the post-Bloomfieldian papers written during the 1940s and 1950s reveal fragments of their intellectual heritage which serve to illuminate the various influences that were prompting these changes. However, it was only with hindsight that Harris himself comprehensively acknowledged the multifarious influences that had inspired his own research during this period:

> The expectation of useful mathematical description of the data of language stems from developments in logic and the foundations of mathematics during the first half of the twentieth century. One main source was the growth of syntactic methods to analyse the structure of formulas, as in Skolem normal form and Löwenheim's theorem, and in the Polish School of logic (as in the treatment of sentential calculus in J. Lukasiewicz, and the categorial grammar of S. Leśniewski, and later K. Ajdukiewicz...), and in W. V. O. Quine's *Mathematical Logic* (Norton, New York) of 1940. Another source is in the post-Cantor paradoxes constructionist views of L. E. J. Brouwer and the Intuitionist mathematicians, and in the specific constructionist techniques of Emil

> Post and Kurt Gödel, in recursive function theory, and from a somewhat different direction in the Turing machine and automata theory... In linguistics, the 'distributional' (combinatorial) methods of Edward Sapir and Leonard Bloomfield were hospitable to this approach. Cf. also Nelson Goodman, *The Structure of Appearance*... (Harris 1991: 145)

This catalogue of influences indicates that Harris was well aware of the major developments in the philosophy of mathematics that had dominated the first decades of the twentieth century, and that he believed these ideas had directly influenced his own approach to the study of language. Also, once again we encounter the claim that techniques derived from the formal sciences were considered to be compatible with the distributional methods employed by the post-Bloomfieldians. For Harris, the 'distributional methods' used in linguistics, and originally associated with Bloomfield and Sapir, seemed to be 'hospitable' to the techniques of logical analysis, and this recalls Bar-Hillel's assertion that Ajdukiewicz's system of logical syntax could be combined with mechanical discovery procedures; and, as suggested above, Bloomfield's Formalist tendencies may well have been responsible for preparing the ground for this compatibility. In addition, it is worth noting that, in the same paragraph as that partly quoted above, Harris goes on to refer explicitly to two contemporaneous textbooks, Kleene's *Introduction to Metamathematics* and Church's *Introduction to Mathematical Logic*, citing them as sources that were used by linguists at the time. Once again, therefore, the influence of these pedagogic texts upon the linguistics community is apparent. Indeed, the relationship between logicians and linguists was growing closer during the 1940s, and, in the context of this rapprochement, it is significant that the manuscript of Church's book was proofread by the philosopher-cum-linguist Rulon Wells (Church 1944: vi).

Since a consideration of Carnap's *LSL* has already occupied part of this section, and since the text was to influence the development of TGG directly, it is worth emphasising the fact that, although Carnap is not one of the authors Harris cited explicitly in his 1991 reflections, several publications from the 1950s reveal the extent of Harris' knowledge of *LSL*. For instance, in *MSL*, Harris considers the general problem of linguistic analysis and observes in a footnote:

> It is widely recognised that forbidding complexities would attend any attempt to construct in one science a detailed description and investigation of all the regularities of language. Cf. Rudolf Carnap, Logical Syntax of Language 8, 'Direct analysis of (languages) must fail [...]'. Linguists meet this problem differently than do Carnap and his school. Whereas the logicians have avoided the analysis of existing languages, linguists study them; but instead of taking

parts of the actual speech occurrences as their elements, they set up very simple elements which are merely associated with features of speech occurrences. (Harris 1951: 16.n17)

Obviously, this passage indicates that Harris was familiar with Carnap's work. However, more than this, the content of the passage indicates that, far from wholeheartedly advocating the adoption of techniques from logic for the purposes of analysing natural languages, Harris was keen to stress the differences that distinguish linguistics and logic. Essentially, the main difference appears to be that linguists deal with natural languages, while logicians create artificial languages. Nevertheless, this does not imply that, for Harris, logical languages and natural languages were entirely different kinds of systems, rather that different types of researchers (i.e., linguists and logicians) focus on different aspects of the problem.

As suggested above, formal syntactic theories (especially the theory outlined by Carnap in his *LSL*) exerted an influence on Bloomfield, Hjelmslev, Wells, Harris, and many other linguists, particularly during the 1940s and 1950s. However, perhaps the most enthusiastic adherent of Carnapian syntactic theory in linguistic circles was the irrepressible Bar-Hillel. Bar-Hillel's undergraduate training had been in mathematics and philosophy (not an uncommon route to the theoretical study of language in the days when there were few undergraduate linguistics courses on offer) and, in his preface to *Language and Information* (1964), he provided a detailed overview of his own intellectual development. Once again there is a polymathic cascade of names – Quine, Tarski, Bloomfield, Reichenbach, Ajdukiewicz, and so on – but, in particular, he recalls the influence of Carnap. He first encountered *LSL* during the academic year 1936/1937 and,

> For the next couple of years, I was seldom seen without a copy of this book under my arm. My fellow students dubbed it 'Bar-Hillel's Bible'. It was doubtless the most influential book I read in my life, and a good part of my work is directly or indirectly related to it. (Bar-Hillel 1964: 2)

Clearly, then, Bar-Hillel's peers considered his devotion to *LSL* to have been equivalent to a religious conviction, and some of the main tenets of Bar-Hillel's logico-syntactic faith are discussed in relation to TGG in section 4.5. It is of interest, though, that Bar-Hillel had also encountered Bloomfield's 1939 essay concerning the scientific status of linguistics, and that this text too influenced the development of his thinking. Once again his own comments are illuminating:

> I think that the only work by a modern professional linguist I had studied in some depth before these talks [i.e., talks with Harris in the early 1950s] was Bloomfield's little contribution to the Encyclopedia of Unified Science, published in 1939. This booklet showed a surprising convergence between ways of thinking of at least certain circles of American linguists and those of say, Carnap, and I made a mental note to pursue this issue further sometime. But only in 1951 did I find the time to do so. (Bar-Hillel 1964: 4)

This passage indicates that, for Bar-Hillel at least, Bloomfield's work suggested the possibility of integrating techniques from Carnapian logical syntax with the methodology of linguistics. As already indicated, this kind of project was certainly not unique since, by the early 1950s, there was a general tendency in certain linguistic circles to seek formal linguistic theories (particularly syntactic theories) which advocated meaning-less symbol manipulation rather than contentual, semantics-based analysis, and, as discussed above, Carnap's *LSL* was a prominent text that appeared to provide formal analytic techniques that could be usefully transferred from the realm of logical syntax into the sphere of linguistics.

3.8 New directions

To summarise the discussion so far, the topics considered in this chapter have included the use of the axiomatic-deductive method in linguistic research, the use of recursive definitions to analyse sentences in natural languages, the use of logical categories to analyse the notion of grammaticality and to construct syntactic descriptions, the creation of constructional system theory as an extension of logical analysis, the need for simplicity measures, the development of formal linguistic theories, and the influence of such theories upon syntactic research. The various connections between mathematics, metamathematics, logic, and linguistics implied by the research discussed in the preceding sections largely motivated the interest in formal analytical procedures that became such a characteristic feature of syntactic research in the 1950s, and, not surprisingly, these developments did not go unnoticed. In 1949, for instance, Carl Borgström (1909–1986) acknowledged that there had been a recent shift away from the analysis of particular linguistic phenomena towards a preoccupation with the general analytical discovery procedures themselves, and he made an explicit distinction between 'basic-research', which concerned itself with the analysis of language, and 'meta-research', which concerned itself with the analysis of the analysis of language:

> Meta-research is a kind of research in which the processes (secondary experiences) of previous research are turned into objects of research (primary experiences) by being subjected to new processes (e.g., by being named and described); the previous research is the basic research. (Borgström 1949: 4)

The strongly Hilbertian character of this terminology is immediately apparent. In discussing this recent shift, though, Borgström did not fail to recognise the similarities between the work of the post-Bloomfieldians and the work of the Copenhagen Circle, particularly Hjelmslev, and he opined that both traditions were becoming interested in 'form' over 'substance' (Borgström 1949: 9). By the early 1950s the similarities between the two movements were so conspicuous that they were being discussed in detail. In 1951, for example, Einar Haugen (1906–1994) noted the recent interest in 'metalanguage' amongst linguists, indicating that it had its roots in Formalist-inspired logical analysis, and commenting that the post-Bloomfieldians and the Copenhagen Circle were

> both attempting to give a mathematical formulation to linguistic statements. Harris has described his syntactic analyses as 'mathematical'; Hjelmslev declares his purpose is the creation of a 'linguistic algebra'. Harris expressly points out that his analysis is purely formal; Hjelmslev describes his theory as being based on 'an exclusively formal set of postulates'. (Haugen 1951: 213–214)

Haugen concludes by claiming that the formal procedures advocated by the post-Bloomfieldians do not constitute 'a linguistics as we have known it, but rather a metalinguistics' (Haugen 1951: 212). Linguistics papers now 'bristle like a page of symbolic logic', and Haugen admits that, although he would not change the current emphasis, he misses 'the leisurely, even charming quality of the traditional grammars' (Haugen 1951: 222). Nevertheless, the charming traditional grammars were never to return since, as will be demonstrated in chapters 4 and 5, it was this new, complex, interdisciplinary, intellectual culture, with its drive towards ever-increasing rigour and precision of formal exposition, that directly inspired the creation of TGG.

4   Systems of syntax: 1951–1955

4.1   Chapter overview

The main purpose of this chapter is to consider Chomsky's research from the years 1951–1955 in the light of the topics presented in the previous chapters, and, to renew the words of warning in the introduction, it is at this stage of the discussion that the convenient abbreviation 'TGG' ceases to be especially helpful. As indicated previously, the main problem is that, during this period, Chomsky explored a number of different approaches to syntactic theory and, though various aspects of these approaches were maintained and further developed, others were swiftly discarded. As a result, it is not possible simply to use the term 'TGG' with reference to Chomsky's work of the early 1950s as if it denoted a clear and consistently identifiable grammatical theory. Consequently, it is necessary either to accept that TGG must be viewed as a fluid concept that altered continually during this period, or else to avoid using the term altogether (whenever possible). In this chapter and the next the latter course is adopted, since it necessitates more specific reference to the various ideas that Chomsky explored during this period and so avoids confusion.

The main sections of this chapter focus upon the influences that shaped Chomsky's earliest work. The basic approach is to identify the presence of a particular influence, and then to trace its development as his research gradually matured during the 1950s. Consequently, the intention is not simply to provide a strict, consistently chronological study of the gradual evolution of TGG as a whole. Rather, a number of distinct (but fundamentally related) themes are considered, with the result that, as the various topics are presented, a more complete picture of the overall development of TGG starts to emerge. This type of approach enables the continuities and discontinuities to be revealed more clearly. It should be noted, incidentally, that the task is not only to identify those techniques and ideas that Chomsky actually adapted and used in his own linguistic research, but also to consider some of the techniques that he rejected, since a negative assessment can often be as informative as a positive advocation. With this in mind, the basic chapter plan can be summarised as follows. In section 4.2 some biographical information about Chomsky is presented, with particular attention given to his contact with some of the individuals mentioned in chapter 3. This enables direct connections between his work and that of his most influential predecessors to be established. In section 4.3 the influence of Goodman is explored by examining the way in which Chomsky reformulated the notion of simplicity in syntactic terms. This consideration of simplicity naturally invites an assessment of other aspects of Goodman's influence upon the young Chomsky, and section 4.4 explores his brief flirtation with constructive nominalism. Finally, in section 4.5 some of the arguments concerning the relationship between syntactic theory and the formal sciences are considered. In particular, the debate between Bar-Hillel and Chomsky concerning the relationship between logic and linguistic theory that took place during the years 1954–1955 is assessed, since it provides valuable insights into Chomsky's whole approach to syntactic theory.

4.2 Biography and influences

The basic facts concerning Chomsky's early life and intellectual development are well known and a comprehensive account will not be attempted here. Instead, the following discussion will focus on Chomsky's relationships with those linguists and philosophers who appear to have exerted the greatest influence over his early work. More information concerning the issues considered in the following discussion can easily be found in the standard texts.[1]

Chomsky was born on 7 December 1928 and the whole of his early life was centred in Philadelphia, Pennsylvania. His father, William Zav Chomsky (1897–1977), a Hebrew teacher, had left Russia with his wife for the United States in 1913 and, in time, he became a noted scholar, publishing numerous books on a range of topics including linguistics and education policy. He specialised in medieval Hebrew and one of his most important publications, *Hebrew, the Eternal Language*, appeared in 1957. Chomsky's mother, Elsie Simonofsky (1903–1972) also taught Hebrew and is believed to have been instrumental in inculcating a strong sociopolitical conscience in her eldest son. Whatever the exact nature of his mother's influence upon his intellectual development, from 1930 to 1940 Chomsky attended Oak Lane County Day School, an experimental institution that eschewed the more formal aspects of conventional education. Consequently, it was not until he began to attend the Central High School in Philadelphia that he experienced traditional teaching methods for the first time. In 1945, at the age of 16, he enrolled in a general undergraduate programme at the University of Pennsylvania, but disliked the experience and considered leaving in order to join one of the flourishing kibbutzim in Israel. However, in 1947 he encountered Zellig Harris, who encouraged him to continue with his formal education, and there is no doubt that Harris was instrumental in encouraging Chomsky's interest in theoretical linguistics. Indeed, Chomsky would claim later that his introduction to linguistics occurred when Harris asked him to proofread the manuscript of *MSL*. Chomsky submitted his B.A. thesis, *The Morphophonemics of Modern Hebrew* in 1947, and, in the same year, entered the Graduate School at Pennsylvania. Two years later he completed his M.A. thesis, which (curiously) was simply a revised version of his B.A thesis, and, during this period, prompted by Harris, he began to study philosophy with Goodman and White, as well as mathematics with Nathan Fine (1916–1994). The association with Goodman in particular proved to be advantageous for, in 1951, Goodman helped Chomsky secure a Junior Fellowship in the Society of Friends at Harvard. The fellowship lasted until 1955 and, during this period, Chomsky came into close contact with Quine and the other members of the Harvard intellectual elite. The Society was instituted in 1933 by Abbott Lawrence Lowell (1856–1943), who was President Emeritus of Harvard at the time. When Chomsky joined in 1951, the fellowship included (amongst others) Kuhn and Marvin Minsky (b. 1927), in addition (of course) to Goodman and Quine, and, in general, the Harvard community was strongly influenced by James Bryant Conant (1893–1978), who was president from 1933 to 1953. Despite the attractions of this environment, the fellowship did not come with tenure, and in 1955 Chomsky left Harvard for the Massachusetts Institute of Technology, and he has remained on the academic staff there ever since.

Some of Chomsky's later observations concerning his education and his former teachers merit consideration here, since they constitute his own reflections upon some of the issues considered in the main chapters of this book. For instance, he has suggested that Harris was never particularly interested in linguistic theory *per se*, concerning himself instead with practical methods:

> [Harris] thought of linguistics as a set of procedures for organising texts, and was strongly opposed to the idea that there might be anything real to discover. He did think that the methods of linguistic analysis could be used for analysis of ideology, and most of my actual graduate courses were devoted to that ...
> (quoted in Barsky 1997: 52)

This perception of Harris' work seems to have been commonplace. For example, in the 1960s Hockett had referred to Harris' 'theoretical nihilism' (Hockett 1968: 35). However, despite Harris' early interest in Chomsky, the two men drifted apart as Chomsky matured. To quote a portion of Barsky's rather sycophantic summary (which is useful mainly because it draws heavily upon Chomsky's own recollections),

> even at this early stage [i.e., early 1950s], Chomsky was producing highly original work, which diverged fundamentally from Harris'. In his B.A. thesis he was doing things that were, in his own words, 'radically at odds with everything in structural linguistics... which is why [both the thesis and *The Logical Structure of Linguistic Theory*] were published only 30 years later'. The thesis was 'as different from structural linguistics as anything could be', which was why 'Harris never looked at it and no one in the field reacted to it'. (Barsky 1997: 53)

In a later passage Chomsky suggests that Harris considered the nascent theory of TGG to be 'crazy' (Barsky 1997: 54), although no evidence to support this claim is provided. Strangely, the basic pattern of Chomsky's relationship with Harris (or at least Chomsky's own account of it) is identical to the basic pattern of his relationship with Goodman. At first Goodman encouraged and supported Chomsky, helping him to obtain a Junior Fellowship at Harvard, but then the association turned sour. The following passage is also taken from Barsky's account, mainly because (once again) it weaves together some of Chomsky's own words. After mentioning (with no details) that Chomsky began to study the work of Carnap, Frege, Whitehead, and Wittgenstein (no mention of Russell?), Barsky continues,

> the readings Chomsky now undertook gave him a fresh perspective that his teacher Nelson Goodman considered to be 'completely mad'. When Goodman found out about Chomsky's work in the mid-1960s, he apparently ended their friendship, even though, as Chomsky says, they'd 'been quite good friends until he learned about this, which he regarded somehow as a personal betrayal'. (Barsky 1997: 54)

There are various problems with this account. First, it is not at all clear why Goodman would have been offended by any ideas Chomsky might have gleaned from Carnap, Whitehead, and Wittgenstein (or even Russell). Second, as will be shown in section 5.3, if anything caused Chomsky to find a 'fresh perspective' during the early 1950s, it was Goodman's own work. Third, it is not clear why it took Goodman ten years to find out about Chomsky's research into syntactic theory. By the mid-1960s Chomsky's name was already well known and Goodman must have been living as a hermit not to have heard something about TGG before *c.* 1965. Curiously, though, Chomsky's memories of his friendship with Quine outline a similar pattern: at first Quine had encouraged him (for instance, by reading his 1953 paper before it was submitted), but then 'lost interest' (quoted in Barsky 1997: 93) in Chomsky's work.

This general pattern of initial closeness followed by sudden separation is clearly of interest and it raises various questions: why did Chomsky come to be spurned by his early mentors, and precisely which aspects of his work offended them? Whatever the truth of Chomsky's recollections, though, as will be shown in the next two chapters, there can be no doubt that, during the early 1950s, Chomsky was working closely with Harris, Goodman, Quine, and others, and that he was directly influenced by some of their ideas. Accordingly, the task of revealing traces of these influences in his work from the 1950s is accomplished in the following sections, and it may be the case that an exploration of this kind proves to be of greater interest than a protracted attempt at retrospective psychological analysis.

4.3   Simplicity and grammar

As indicated in the introduction, the importance of the notion of 'simplicity' in Chomsky's early syntactic research has never really been adequately discussed, even though Chomsky himself frequently acknowledged the source of his ideas at the time, and even though he has recently suggested that this aspect of his early work has been revived (albeit in a different form) in his most recent research.[2]

In this instance, even the arduous nature of the requisite intellectual archaeology cannot truthfully be cited as a valid reason for the neglect, since, as was shown in section 3.5, the task of devising a simplicity measure for extralogical bases in constructional systems was an abiding preoccupation for Goodman throughout the 1940s and 1950s, during which time he was lecturing both at Pennsylvania and Harvard; and since it is known that Chomsky studied under Goodman directly during this time, it is no real surprise that similar considerations figure prominently in Chomsky's earliest known research. Indeed, there are many traces of Goodman's thinking in Chomsky's work from the 1950s, but, as will become apparent below, even at this early stage Chomsky was not simply borrowing techniques from one field and mindlessly employing them, unmodified, in another area. Rather, he was keen to shape and adapt the methods he had encountered in an attempt to facilitate the specific task of syntactic analysis, and this process of adaptation can be identified in his 1951 Master's thesis *The Morphophonemics of Modern Hebrew* (hereafter *MMH*).

In the introduction to *MMH*, Chomsky states that a grammar constructed for a given language must meet two kinds of adequacy criteria. First, it must 'correctly describe the "structure" of the language'; that is, it must 'isolate the basic linguistic units and, in particular, must distinguish and characterise just those utterances which are considered "grammatical" or "possible" by the informant' (Chomsky 1979b[1951]: 1). Second, the grammar must either meet criteria that are imposed by the 'special purpose' for which the grammar was created (e.g., pedagogic utility), or else, if there is no such purpose, it must meet requirements of 'simplicity, economy, compactness, etc.' (Chomsky 1979b[1951]: 1). From the very beginning, then, Chomsky seems to have been persuaded that considerations of simplicity were intimately involved in the processes of grammar construction, and the task of unearthing the sources of these ideas is fairly simple, mainly because Chomsky never attempted to conceal his intellectual debts. For instance, in *MMH* he explicitly cites Goodman's 1943 paper, 'On the Simplicity of Ideas', and paraphrases Goodman's argument against simplicity being considered merely an aesthetic luxury in a constructional system (quoted in full in section 3.5 above). With particular reference to syntactic theory, one of the implications of Goodman's views concerning the critical importance of simplicity criteria in constructional systems is that the reasons for wanting a grammar to be as simple as possible are the same as for wanting a grammar at all. Crucially, though, it should be noted that this focus upon theory-internal economy considerations was not encouraged by Harris, who was the other main influence upon the form and content of *MMH*. For instance, in *MSL* Harris had clearly stated that 'it is a matter of other than descriptive purpose how compact and convenient the formulation is, or what other qualities it may have' (Harris 1951: 9), and he had gone on to claim that

> It therefore does not matter for basic descriptive methods whether the system for a particular language is so devised as to have the least number of elements (e.g., phonemes) or the least number of statements about them, or the greatest over-all compactness, etc. These different formulations differ not linguistically but logically. They differ not in validity but in their usefulness for one purpose or another (e.g., for teaching the language, for describing its structure, for comparing it with genetically related languages). (Harris 1951: 9.n8)

For Harris, then, practical utility, rather than considerations such as simplicity, was the guiding principle of grammar construction, and this may well be a good example of Harris' aforementioned 'theoretical nihilism' (Hockett 1968: 35). Whether this is the case or not, the clear implication of the above passage is that Harris deemed issues such as grammatical 'compactness' to be extraneous to the task of linguistic analysis, or, at the very least, he was convinced that such considerations should only be assessed with reference to the utility of the grammar. In other words, if simplifications facilitate the use of the grammar as a pedagogic tool, then they are valuable; if not, then they are of no real interest. The clear juxtaposition of Goodman's repeated emphasis on the importance of theory-internal economy and Harris' apparent indifference to the same must have intrigued Chomsky at the time, and, indeed, *MMH* can be viewed partly as an attempt to introduce Goodman-style simplicity criteria into a Harris-style analytic framework. Already, therefore, Chomsky's remarkable ability to reconcile and synthesise existing techniques is clearly apparent in the perceived analogy between syntactic analysis and constructional system theory.

Having outlined the basic problem in this general fashion, Chomsky goes on to distinguish between 'discovery' processes (e.g., Harris' distributional procedures) and processes of 'description'. The distinction between these processes is clear: discovery processes can be used to determine the set of grammatical sentences in a corpus, while processes of description can be used to analyse the form of those utterances. In this context, it is worth recalling that Bar-Hillel's revival of Ajdukiewicz's system of syntactic analysis (discussed in section 3.4) was intended to provide a method of 'description' (Bar-Hillel 1953b: 47) and was not intended to constitute a discovery procedure. In the early 1950s, then, the distinction that Chomsky's draws was certainly not unique. However, he proceeds to extend the argument by suggesting that, although this distinction might be easy to make when a grammar is constructed for a 'special purpose', it is less useful when it is created without a particular use in mind, for, in this case, there are no arbitrary constraints imposed upon the grammar. Consequently, in the latter case, the grammar must be constructed 'solely in accordance with considerations of elegance' (Chomsky 1979b[1951]: 2). Indeed, Chomsky goes on to suggest that the very notion of 'elegance' itself threatens to undermine the basic distinction between discovery and description processes, since such considerations are fundamental to the task of discovery *and* to the task of description. In the light of this observation, it is worth emphasising that, from the very beginning, Chomsky's focus was upon syntactic analysis for the sake of syntactic analysis. He appears never to have been especially interested in the practical (i.e., pedagogical) applications of the sort that so preoccupied Harris.

Despite the fact that Chomsky explicitly places the issue of grammatical simplicity at the core of the theoretical framework he outlines in *MMH*, he does not provide an exhaustive discussion of the topic. He observes that merely counting the number of rules in the grammar is an inadequate way of measuring simplicity, and he refers somewhat obliquely to an unpublished paper of his own that considers the topic, but he does not summarise the contents of that paper in his thesis.[3] Nevertheless, Chomsky maintained his interest in simplicity measures long after his M.A. thesis was submitted, and the most comprehensive discussion of the subject was offered in chapter 4 of his manuscript *The Logical Structure of Linguistic Theory* (hereafter *LSLT*), the first draft of which was completed by early 1955.[4] In this work the importance of grammatical simplicity is stressed repeatedly and (once again) it is considered to play a fundamental role in the task of grammar construction.

> In linguistic theory we face the problem of constructing this system of levels in an abstract manner, in such a way that a simple grammar will result when this complex of abstract structures is given an interpretation in actual linguistic material. (Chomsky 1975[1955]: 100)

In other words, it is desirable that a general theory of linguistic structure is designed so as to permit the creation of simple grammars for given languages. As Chomsky puts it later in the same chapter, the 'reduction of the complexity of grammar is one of the major motivations behind level construction' (Chomsky 1975[1955]: 100).[5] Given this general goal of grammatical complexity reduction, it is obvious that the notion of 'simplicity' requires adequate elucidation in the specific context of linguistic theory. However, before attempting to clarify these terms, Chomsky is keen to demonstrate why the notion of simplicity is of considerable importance when a general theory of linguistics is being devised. In particular, he argues that grammatical simplicity is significant primarily because it can provide a way of choosing between various competing grammars. In other words, if the degree of grammatical simplicity could be measured consistently, then, given a corpus and various grammars all of which exhaustively generate all the grammatical utterances in the corpus, a simplicity measure of some kind could provide a viable evaluation procedure that would enable one grammar to be preferred above all the others, and the centrality of decision criteria that can be used to select one from amongst several competing grammars is stressed throughout *LSLT*.[6]

> Linguistic theory must enable us to choose among proposed grammars, and every consideration relevant to the choice must be built into the theory. So far, the only consideration we have placed on the grammar is that the system of levels it determines ... must be of the form required by linguistic theory. But this feature of grammatical construction leaves out one of the most important and characteristic features of grammar construction. In careful descriptive work, one almost always finds that one of the considerations involved in choosing among alternative analyses is the simplicity of the resulting grammar. If we can set up elements in such a way that very few rules need to be given about their distribution, or that the rules are very similar to the rules for other elements, this fact certainly seems to be a valid support for the analysis in question. It seems reasonable, then, to inquire into the possibility of defining

linguistic notions in the general theory partly in terms of such properties of grammar as simplicity. (Chomsky 1975[1955]: 114)

This passage neatly summarises the core motivation for an assessment of simplicity in the context of linguistic theory: simpler grammars are preferred because they capture more general linguistic patterns than more complex grammars. Clearly, this assumption echoes Goodman's pro-simplicity arguments, which were discussed in detail in section 3.5. For instance, Goodman had asserted that 'the more the set of postulates can be reduced without becoming inadequate, the more comprehensively will the system exhibit the network of interconnections that comprises its subject matter' (Goodman 1943: 107), and this observation is clearly related to various passages in *LSLT* such as that quoted above. Specifically, in linguistic terms, a measure of grammatical simplicity is required in order to permit the 'best' grammar for a given corpus to be selected from among all other possible grammars, and the task of creating such a simplicity measure is precisely the one that Chomsky sets for himself in chapter 4 of *LSLT*. Before discussing his treatment of this topic in detail, though, it is worth highlighting his belief (already expressed in *MMH*) that the technical issue of grammatical simplicity is not merely a superficial adjunct to linguistic theory. Indeed, Chomsky bluntly asserts that the notion of simplicity is of fundamental importance, and he admits that his thinking concerning this issue has been guided by the work of both Goodman and Quine.

> It is important, incidentally, to recognise that considerations of simplicity are not trivial or 'merely esthetic'. It has been remarked in the case of philosophical systems that the motives for the demand for economy are in many ways the same as those behind the demand that there is a system at all. See Goodman, 'On the simplicity of ideas', where the reference is to economy in the basis of primitives. It seems to me that the same is true of grammatical systems, and of the special sense of simplicity that will concern us directly. See Quine, *From a Logical Point of View* for recent discussion of the role of simplicity in the choice of scientific theories. (Chomsky 1975[1955]: 114.n2)

This footnote is actually an extended, more specific version of footnote 1 in *MMH* and the main difference between the two notes is that in the 1951 version only Goodman's work is cited, while in the above version Quine's recent arguments concerning the role of simplicity in scientific theories in general are enlisted as additional support. Clearly, the basic thrust of Chomsky's argument is that, since simplicity plays a crucial role in the creation of any theoretical system, it is necessarily involved in the task of grammar construction. Consequently, it is expedient to assess the way in which the notion of simplicity is presented in *LSLT* in some detail, since it reveals the manner in which Chomsky modified some of Goodman's and Quine's ideas so that they could be used to facilitate the specific task of syntactic analysis.

At the outset of his discussion of grammatical simplicity in chapter 4 of *LSLT* Chomsky openly confesses that his current thinking on this topic is still at a preliminary stage and that, therefore, it is 'sketchy and incomplete' (Chomsky 1975[1955]: 116). Despite this, he is sufficiently confident about the issues involved to be able to propose a series of consolidation rules that converts a given grammar into a maximally condensed form. Once again, this emphasis on rule-driven processes recalls Harris' interest in automatic discovery procedures (mentioned in section 3.7), as well as Bar-Hillel's enthusiasm for syntactic categories that enable a sentence to be analysed 'mechanically' (discussed in section 3.4). In the present context, then, Chomsky's desire for an algorithmic approach to simplicity measures is in keeping with the general drift of syntactic research in the 1950s. In addition, though, the search for a mechanical procedure that would permit an *automatic* measurement of grammatical simplicity again echoes Goodman who, in his 1943 paper, advocated the avoidance of intuition when determining the respective simplicity of various bases, favouring instead an 'automatic procedure' (Goodman 1943: 108). Given the fact (discussed at length in section 5.4) that the definition of a linguistic level offered in *LSLT* draws heavily upon constructional system theory, it would be reasonable to suspect that, following Goodman, Chomsky would focus on the task of reducing the number of primitive relations associated with a particular syntactic level. However, since each level of the general system outlined in *LSLT* uses concatenation as its sole primitive relation, reducing the number of such relations was not a feasible option. Consequently, Chomsky realised that, if a measure of grammatical simplicity were ever to function as a valid evaluation procedure, it must operate upon something other than the extralogical bases of the linguistic levels.

Accordingly, developing the scheme outlined in *MMH*, Chomsky argued that the basic formal components of the grammatical theory developed in *LSLT* that must be involved in any technical definition of simplicity are the rewrite rules, called 'conversions' in the early TGG literature. In the standard TGG notation, rewrite rules take the form '$X \rightarrow Y$', and they are used to permit the analysis of larger syntactic units into smaller sub-components. For instance, a standard **P**-level (i.e., phrase-level) conversion is 'Sentence $\rightarrow$ NP VP', which states (obviously) that a sentence can be rewritten as a noun phrase followed by a verb phrase. It is reasonable that such rules should be involved in the technical definition of a simplicity measure, since a measure of any kind necessarily involves some sort of quantification, and the conversions in a given grammar can be counted easily. Indeed, the assumption that conversions could provide a viable foundation for a simplicity measure underlies Chomsky's whole discussion of the subject in *LSLT*, and he states clearly that 'it is tempting... to consider the possibility of devising a notational system which converts considerations of simplicity into considerations of length' (Chomsky 1975[1955]: 177). In other words, as an initial proposal, Chomsky felt that it was reasonable to assume that grammars containing fewer conversions (i.e., shorter grammars) should be preferred over grammars containing a larger number of conversions. This basic approach, with its emphasis on the trivial enumeration of key components, is reminiscent of Goodman's preliminary statements concerning the relative simplicity of extralogical bases in constructional systems: systems with fewer extralogical predicates are preferred over systems with a larger number of predicates. However just as Goodman swiftly realised that such a trivial measure was too crude, so Chomsky quickly rejected the trivial approach to grammatical simplicity outlined above (just as he had done in *MMH*), and the motivation for the modifications he goes on to propose comes from the insight (again related to Goodman's work on constructional systems) that prioritising shorter grammars indirectly prioritises grammars that attain greater generality; and such generality is highly valued: if a particular sub-sequence of conversions can be replaced by a single conversion, then the grammar more accurately captures a general fact about the corpus being analysed. It should be noted that, while stressing the importance of generality and the relationship between generalising and enumerating conversions, Chomsky was keen to avoid the misconception that generality and length are *exactly* equivalent concepts in this context. Consequently, he drew a clear distinction between 'real' simplicity and all other kinds. As an example, he observed that a complex grammar, represented schematically as $Q(a_1, \ldots, a_n)$, could be defined as $f(x_1, \ldots, x_n)$, with the result that $f(a_1, \ldots, a_n)$ provides a concise (i.e., one-line) representation of the complex initial grammar (Chomsky 1975[1955]: 118). However, as Chomsky demonstrated, this modification is nothing more than a notational sleight of hand that effects no actual simplification of the grammar, and this type of argument recalls Goodman and Quine's distinction between the 'real' and 'apparent' economy of extralogical bases (discussed in section 3.5). For Chomsky then, following Goodman and Quine, the task is to avoid superficial simplifications that do not actually contribute to the reduction of system complexity.

In order, therefore, for a coherent simplicity measure to be constructed, it is necessary to ensure that a given grammar is maximally 'consolidated', and that the consolidation constitutes a real reduction in the complexity of the grammar. Accordingly, Chomsky introduces a number of 'notational transformations' (Chomsky 1975[1955]: 118) which essentially define a normal form for the grammar. In other words, given the set of notational transformations, any grammar can be reduced to a maximally condensed format, which permits the direct comparison of competing grammars. For instance, adopting the notation '{}' to indicate positional equivalence and '−' to indicate the null element, it follows that the three strings

$$a \frown d \frown e \frown g \tag{4.1}$$

$$b \frown d \frown g \tag{4.2}$$

$$c \frown d \frown f \frown g \tag{4.3}$$

can be replaced by the single consolidated string

$$\{a, b, c\}d\{e, -, f\}g \tag{4.4}$$

It is clear that (4.4) is more general than the separate strings in (4.1)–(4.3), and that it is not simply a vacuous tautological restatement of pre-existing facts, since it makes more particular claims about the distributional properties of the formal language used in the example. As Chomsky observes, since this kind of consolidation can be applied to both sides of a given conversion rule, these notational manipulations enable a maximally consolidated grammar to be constructed in such a manner that real complexity reduction is assured.

> The notational devices we have introduced permit certain selected features of similarity among statements of the grammar (i.e., each type of partial generalisation) to effect a decrease in length, so that grammars whose rules have these features are more highly valued. Thus these constructions can be understood as offering an analysis for certain aspects of simplicity. (Chomsky 1975[1955]: 123)

Having devised, in this fashion, a coherent measure of simplicity based upon conversion consolidation, Chomsky goes on to discuss the issue of conversion ordering. It is obvious that conversions in a formal grammar cannot simply be listed in an *ad hoc* fashion: rules converting phrases into morphemes, for example, must apply before morphemes can be converted into phonemes. Indeed, it is this observation that causes Chomsky to refer to the conversions in a given grammar as constituting a 'sequence' rather than a set, since the order of elements in a set is irrelevant, while a sequence is determined precisely by the order of its elements. Consequently, the issue of conversion ordering is considered to be sufficiently important to merit explicit specification within a general theory of linguistic structure.

> There is a great advantage in giving the principle of ordering once and for all in the general theory. Otherwise, the gain in economy resulting from ordering of rules in a particular grammar will be much reduced because of the need to specify, within that grammar, the order of application of rules. The most favourable situation is one in which we can linearly order the conversions in such a way that all derivations can be formed by running through this sequence from beginning to end. (Chomsky 1975[1955]: 125)

The implication here is that the conversions that constitute the grammar should be so arranged that all grammatical utterances in a given corpus can be correctly derived simply by applying the various conversions in sequence. This observation leads Chomsky to propose certain 'optimality conditions', which he introduces as follows:

> Putting it roughly, a grammar will meet these conditions if, when the rules are given in a maximally condensed form, it is possible to arrange the resulting statements in a sequence in such a way that:
>
> (i) we can form all derivations by running through the sequence of rules from beginning to end;
> (ii) no conversion $X \to Y$ will appear twice in the sequence (i.e., no rule need be repeated in several forms at various places in the grammar);
> (iii) each conditioning context is developed to exactly the extent relevant for the application of the rule in which it appears. (Chomsky 1975[1955]: 125)

These practical conditions define a heuristic procedure similar to that proposed by Goodman for extralogical bases in his 1952 paper 'New Notes on Simplicity' discussed in section 3.5. In practice, these optimality conditions should be applied at each linguistic level and they are designed to ensure (i) the linearity of the grammar, (ii) the avoidance of redundancy, and (iii) the validity of context-dependent rules. Given this set of conditions, it becomes possible to resolve the problem of choosing between formal grammars: given two grammars, both of which generate all the grammatical sentences in a given language, choose the grammar that is simpler in accordance to the optimality conditions stated above. As is obvious, this concentration on simplicity necessitates a detailed consideration of the formal properties of the proposed grammars, and therefore motivates many of the innovations associated with the development of TGG. For example, as shown in section 5.5, grammars that used transformational rules were generally perceived to be 'simpler' than phrase structure grammars, and this perception was of crucial importance since in the 1950s it was not known whether the formal machinery of a phrase structure grammar was actually insufficient to enable it to generate all the sentences of a language.[7] However, as was claimed at the time, the difference between standard phrase structure grammars and transformational grammars was that the latter were able to deal with unbounded dependencies more successfully than the former, while being able to generate complex sentences, such as active–passive constructions, more economically, and considerations such as these emphasised the centrality of simplicity criteria in the earliest TGG research.

4.4 Constructive nominalist syntax

As the preceding section has emphasised, the influence of Goodman is clearly manifest (and explicitly acknowledged) in Chomsky's earliest work. However, Chomsky borrowed more from Goodman than merely some of his ideas concerning simplicity measures for constructional systems. Indeed, the extent of Chomsky's preoccupation with Goodman's work can be gauged most accurately by assessing the contents of his first published paper, 'Systems of Syntactic Analysis' (hereafter 'SSA'), which appeared in 1953.[8] Once again, this paper demonstrates that, at an early stage, Chomsky was concerned with the non-trivial task of combining various existing techniques in order to develop a more 'mechanical' approach to linguistic analysis.

It was shown above that in both *MMH* and *LSLT* Chomsky had sought to reconcile Harris' distributional techniques with some of Goodman's ideas concerning theory-internal simplicity criteria. In 'SSA' a different kind of synthesis was attempted which involved reconciling the methodology of nominalistic constructional system theory, as expounded by Goodman and Quine in 'SCN', with the sort of syntactic discovery procedures advocated by Harris. Consequently, 'SSA' constitutes an initial attempt to develop a constructional system that can automatically assign morphemes in a given corpus of utterances to syntactic categories using distributional information. It is essential to stress that, as usual, the intellectual origins of this research are freely acknowledged by Chomsky throughout the paper itself. For instance, having observed the recent trend in syntactic theory to develop formal methods of analysis that do not require reference to semantic information, Chomsky outlines his own particular project as follows:

> It is of interest to inquire seriously into the formality of linguistic method and the adequacy of whatever part of it can be made purely formal, and to examine the possibilities of applying it... to a wider range of problems. In order to pursue these aims it is first necessary to reconstruct carefully the set of procedures by which the linguist derives the statements of a linguistic grammar from the behavior of the language users, distinguishing clearly between formal and experimental in such a way that grammatical notions,

> appearing as definienda in a constructional system, will be formally derivable for any language from a fixed sample of linguistic material upon which the primitives of the system are experimentally defined. (Chomsky 1953: 242)

This passage clearly demonstrates that Chomsky considered 'SSA' to be as much an exercise in applied constructional system theory as a contribution to linguistics, and it should be noted that the paper appeared in the *Journal of Symbolic Logic* rather than in an established linguistics journal, such as *Language* or *Word*. The Formalist emphasis of Chomsky's paper is clear from the stated desire to make syntactic analysis (or at least part of it) 'purely formal', and the basic methodology of the paper is indicated in the above quotation: 'grammatical notions' are created by means of a process of iterated definition within a constructional system, thereby associating each created grammatical object with a definitional genealogy. In the footnotes that accompany the above passage, Chomsky reveals the sources of his ideas and he explicitly cites Harris' *MSL*, Goodman's *SA*, and Goodman and Quine's 'SCN' as particular influences. In addition, Chomsky thanks the three aforementioned individuals personally for their offered suggestions and criticisms, indicating that he had discussed his research with them before publishing his paper. The precise nature of the relationship between the proposed method of syntactic analysis and the type of constructive nominalism adopted in 'SCN' is further clarified when Chomsky explains why he considers an 'inscriptional nominalistic framework' to be of value when performing syntactic analysis:

> The inscriptional approach seems natural for linguistics, particularly in view of the fact that an adequate extension of the results of this paper will have to deal with the problem of homonymity ... It will appear below that the calculus of individuals can often supply quite simple solutions to constructional problems that seem on the surface to require a set-theoretic solution, thus removing all necessity for an involved hierarchy of types and increasing the overall workability of the system. (Chomsky 1953: 243)

This passage suggests that the main advantage of a constructive nominalist approach to syntactic analysis is that it obviates the need for set-theoretical assumptions, and consequently avoids the sort of type hierarchies (i.e., artificial approaches such as Whitehead and Russell's theory of logical types) which had fallen into disrepute in the realm of mathematical logic. It is no coincidence, of course, that these kinds of set-theoretical constructs are precisely those that had been rejected by Goodman and Quine in 'SCN', since, as discussed in section 3.6, the need to reject such entities largely motivated their whole constructive nominalist project. The influence of Goodman in particular is revealed in the passage quoted above, since the 'calculus of individuals' mentioned there is that developed by Goodman and Leonard during the mid-1930s, and Chomsky makes direct use of this system throughout his own paper, employing the particular version of the calculus that appeared in Goodman's *SA*. The implications of using this type of constructional system for the purposes of syntactic analysis are many. In particular, the 'inscriptional' emphasis determines that the sentences in a language must be manipulated as finite strings of symbols, as in Formalist mathematics. Also, the rejection of such abstract entities as sets ensures that all larger structures must be exhaustively analysed in terms of their constituent elements.

Given the above, and given the freely confessed nominalist agenda of 'SSA', Chomsky's claim that a constructional approach to syntactic analysis could help to resolve certain fundamental problems associated with the phenomenon of homonymity is intriguing, if somewhat premature, since (as he himself acknowledges) such problems do not manifest themselves in the simple formal languages discussed in the paper, and (so far) he has never explored these issues in subsequent work.[9] Indeed, it is important to emphasise that throughout 'SSA' Chomsky is solely concerned with formal languages, and openly declares that 'the present system as given here is not adequate for the analysis of natural languages' (Chomsky 1953: 243). The particular language he uses in order to illustrate his theoretical points consists merely of 'utterances' such as 'ab' and 'axd', where each alphabetic character represents a morpheme in the language. Obviously, this focus on such simple languages is in marked contrast to Chomsky's later work, which was predominantly concerned with problems of natural language analysis; an issue that is further discussed in section 4.5.

As indicated above, in the details of its structure, the type of nominalistic constructional system that Chomsky develops in sections 2 and 3 of 'SSA' is merely an implementation of the system presented by Goodman in *SA*, with the majority of the definitions, axioms, and theorems presented being borrowed unaltered. The paper's main contribution, in fact, is simply the attempt to apply constructional system theory to the task of syntactic analysis. Accordingly, following Goodman, the core of the system outlined in the paper contains a logical basis (i.e., standard symbolic logic of the *PM* variety) and an extralogical basis consisting of primitive elements (i.e., inscriptions which are the basic morphemes) and five primitive relations. It should be remembered that (as mentioned above) the primitive elements are all considered to be 'experimentally defined', thus revealing the strong empirical nature of the proposed analytic method.[10] The primitive relations include such predicates as 'O', where '$a \, O \, b$' means a 'overlaps' b (i.e., there exists an inscription that is part of both a and b), and these relations are all taken, unmodified, from *SA*, as Chomsky readily admits. He then proceeds to construct a set of 'elementary notions' such as 'SEG', where '*a* SEG *b*' means '*a* is a segment of *b*', and is defined in terms of the logical and extralogical bases as

$$a \text{ SEG } b = \forall x [x \text{ O } a \rightarrow x \text{ O } b] \tag{4.5}$$

which indicates that *a* is a segment of *b* if, for all *x*, *x* overlaps both *a* and *b*. Once again these definitions are Goodman's (indeed, (4.5) is identical with Goodman's definition of his 'Part' relation, given as (3.15) above), and they enable further axioms and theorems to be constructed. Finally, in section 3 the manner in which Goodman's constructional system can be utilised for the task of syntactic analysis is outlined. The basic methodology is to construct 'an indefinite series of similarity relations' of the form 'S_n' (Chomsky 1953: 249), where the subscript *n* ranges over numerals and indicates the length of the morpheme sequence. These similarity relations can be used to group the morphemes encountered in a given corpus into syntactic classes. To illustrate how the process works, Chomsky uses a corpus of six sentences, *ab*, *cb*, *de*, *fe*, *axd*, and *cyf*, and he shows that the morphemes *a* and *c* would be related by the similarity relation S_1, as would the morphemes *d* and *f*, while *a..d* and *c..f* would be related by S_2, with *x* and *y* being related by S_3.

As the above summary indicates, the general methodology offered in 'SSA' suggests that the nominalistic constructional system presented by Goodman in *SA* could be used in the context of syntactic theory as a discovery procedure that would reduce the task of syntactic class assignment to an automatic process, thus illustrating the potential correspondence between Harris' discovery procedures and constructional system theory. As mentioned in the introduction, though, Chomsky's 1953 paper has generally been neglected by linguistic historiographers, and, given the above summary, it is not difficult to see why it has been forgotten (or perhaps intentionally ignored?). When viewed in a cursory manner, the paper appears to be only tenuously connected to the type of syntactic theory Chomsky was soon to develop in *LSLT* and which would eventually become known as TGG. For a start, as mentioned above, 'SAA' is solely concerned with simple formal languages, and, as shown in the next section, Chomsky was soon to question the validity of arguments involving such languages when used in the context of linguistic theory (as opposed to pure logical research). Also, drawing as it does upon Goodman's work in constructional system theory, 'SA' appears to have a strong empiricist bias (though Hiorth, for one, has doubted this (Hiorth 1974: 35)), since it focuses upon the automatic assignment of morphemes in a specific corpus using distributional information.

Nevertheless, despite these clear differences, various aspects of the approach to syntactic analysis proposed in 'SSA' were to manifest themselves in the mature theory of TGG, although often in subtly different guises. For instance, as discussed in section 5.4, the machinery of constructional system theory was *not* entirely discarded after 1953; rather, parts of it were included in the definition of a linguistic level expounded in *LSLT*. Similarly, Chomsky's preoccupation with mechanical axiomatic-deductive analytic methods did not wane during the mid-1950s; rather, it remained constant, eventually manifesting itself in terms of conversion-based deductions in mature TGG. However, this is not to suggest that significant aspects of the stance adopted in 'SSA' were not rejected later. Indeed, it is clear that this was the case. For instance, 'SSA' clearly constitutes yet another attempt to automate Harris-style discovery procedures, and there is no doubt that by the mid-1950s Chomsky had started to question the validity of such procedures, favouring instead evaluation procedures, as discussed in section 5.3. The purpose of the above discussion, therefore, has been to argue neither for complete uniformity nor for complete disseverance, but rather to illustrate the full complexity of the situation. It is crucial, though, to emphasise that 'SSA' is not merely of marginal interest to the history of TGG, and that it is completely mistaken to view it as a bizarre, isolated, and self-evidently immature foray into the realm of empiricist philosophy. Rather, the paper is absolutely central to the genesis of TGG, since it reveals the course of Chomsky's intellectual development, and so provides an early insight into several analytical techniques and preoccupations that would later become standard features of TGG.

4.5 Logic and linguistic theory

The previous sections of this chapter have demonstrated that, from the very beginning, Chomsky was involved in the task of combining the methodology of structural linguistics with techniques derived from constructional system theory, and his emphasis on the role of simplicity criteria in the creation of formal grammars, along with his attempt to adapt Goodman's 'calculus of individuals' for the purposes of syntactic analysis, reveals the extent of his preoccupation with these issues. However, it is not the case that Chomsky recommended this kind of interdisciplinary approach indiscriminately, and the complexity of his views can best be explored by considering his attitude towards the relationship between linguistics and logic. His most explicit statements concerning this topic are contained in a 1955 paper that was written in response to an article by Bar-Hillel in which the latter had advocated the further integration of linguistics and logic. It is not remarkable that such a subject should have been debated in a leading linguistics journal of the time for, as chapter 3 and the earlier sections of this chapter have demonstrated, during the 1940s and 1950s the precise nature of the relationship between logic and natural language was being reassessed by various logicians and linguists, and certainly Bar-Hillel and Chomsky were both active participants in this process of reassessment. Their exchange in the mid-1950s began with the publication of Bar-Hillel's paper 'Logical Syntax and Semantics' (1954) in *Language* and continued when Chomsky published 'Logical Syntax and Semantics: Their Linguistic Relevance' (1955) (hereafter 'LSS') in the same journal. While considering the various arguments put forward by Bar-Hillel, it is essential to remember that, as discussed in section 3.4, he had recently revived the work of Ajdukiewicz, and had suggested that techniques adapted from logical syntax and logical semantics could be used to analyse natural language, thus laying the foundations for the function-based syntactic theory now known as Categorial Grammar. Clearly, therefore, Bar-Hillel was fully persuaded that logic could provide valuable insights into the nature of linguistic structure and, though he later confessed that these ideas were 'deplorably naïve' (Bar-Hillel 1964: 3), they certainly inspired his 1954 paper, which must now be considered at length.

In general terms, Bar-Hillel's paper constitutes a 'plea for the reintroduction of semantics into the theatre of operations of descriptive linguistics' (Bar-Hillel 1954: 235–236), and his primary motivation seems to have been a profound dissatisfaction with the type of analytical methodology advocated by Harris in his *MSL*. Revealingly, in order to articulate his frustration with distributional procedures more precisely, Bar-Hillel quotes a lengthy passage from the 1937 English translation of Carnap's *LSL*, a book with which he had become obsessed.[11] The quoted passage is taken from the general introduction in which Carnap considers the relationship between syntax and logic, and in which he distinguishes between formation and transformation rules. Carnap observes that 'the prevalent opinion' (i.e., in 1934) was that syntax and logic are 'fundamentally theories of a very different type', yet he goes on to challenge this presupposition by asserting that both disciplines are 'equally concerned with the relation of meaning between sentences', which in turn leads him to prophesy that 'logic will become part of syntax' (Carnap 1937[1934]: 1–2). By means of this conviction, Carnap is able to speak coherently of 'logical syntax', a hybrid term that gestures towards the interrelation of the two disciplines.

Having presented Carnap's views in this direct manner, Bar-Hillel then considers the way in which these ideas had been (and could be) developed by linguists. He emphasises the fact that formation rules (in the Carnapian sense) had been explored in some detail, citing Harris' *MSL* and Fries' *The Structure of English* (1952) as key examples of works in the broad tradition of distributional structural linguistics (just as he had cited them in his 1953 paper in which he had revived Ajdukiewicz's work), but he bewails the corresponding neglect of transformation rules (again in the Carnapian sense).[12] In other words, in Bar-Hillel's view, structuralist linguistic theories are solely concerned with constructional grammatical processes that enable larger linguistic complexes to be analysed in terms of smaller constituent elements (e.g., phonemes or morphemes), and such theories pay insufficient regard to the logical relations that exist between linguistic expressions.[13] Bar-Hillel attributes this neglect partly to the fact that logicians (such as Carnap) devote their time primarily to the task of creating and analysing artificial formal languages that are much simpler than natural languages. Indeed, as shown in section 3.7, Carnap's pessimism concerning the possibility of analysing natural languages in detail using the formation and transformation rules that he developed was clearly stated in *LSL* and certainly Bar-Hillel was aware of Carnap's opinion on this matter (see Bar-Hillel 1954: 231). However, Bar-Hillel points out that linguists, not logicians, are the people that concern themselves most directly with natural language, and that, therefore, the burden of responsibility for exploring the applicability of transformation rules in this context falls upon them. Indeed, he claims that (in his view) Carnap's ideas might be 'linguistically sound', but, since Carnap himself is not 'a linguist proper', he concludes that it behoves practising linguists carefully to scrutinise and assess the implications of these ideas (Bar-Hillel 1954: 231).

Having identified a lack of interest in Carnapian transformation rules on the part of linguists, Bar-Hillel then considers the sort of rules that are neglected in standard structuralist distributional analyses, but which could prove to be of value to linguistics, and, as an example, he discusses the problem of synonymy. The starting point for his discussion is Harris' claim in *MSL* that distributional procedures can provide a cogent analysis of linguistic meaning. In particular, Harris had stated that

> distributional procedures, once established, permit, with no extra trouble, the definite treatment of those marginal cases which meaning considerations leave indeterminate or open to conflicting opinions. (Harris 1951: 8.n7)

and Bar-Hillel interpreted this to mean that linguistic units associated with different distributions inevitably have different meanings. Consequently, he concludes that, for Harris, units with identical distributions are considered to be synonymous. This is admittedly a rather strong interpretation of Harris' statement, but the inference is not entirely unreasonable. However, Bar-Hillel rejects the idea that synonymy can be fully analysed in terms of distribution, arguing that, while a distributional analysis might be able show that (i) 'oculist', (ii) 'eye-doctor', and (iii) 'dentist' can all appear in the same syntactic positions, it can never indicate that (i) and (ii) have identical meanings, while this is not the case either for (i) and (iii) or (ii) and (iii). This failure, according to Bar-Hillel, is caused by the neglect of the truth-conditions that would provide information about the meaning of the words. Consequently, since distributional procedures ignore such semantic considerations, they provide an incomplete basis for linguistic analysis.

Bar-Hillel's conviction that semantic considerations can be incorporated into syntactic analyses without the latter succumbing to 'an infestation by meaning' (Bar-Hillel 1954: 234) clearly has its roots in his well-attested interest in the work of Carnap and the Lvov-Warsaw school of logicians. As discussed in section 3.7, Carnap's research into logical syntax had been influenced by Hilbert's proof theory and consequently, he had defined a number of formal languages that would enable him to create logical systems that were free from semantic considerations. However, in turn (and rather ironically), this work caused Carnap to reflect upon the relationship between formal linguistic systems of the type presented in the *LSL* and the external world. In other words, his interest in formal syntactic systems that attempted to avoid semantic considerations inculcated a profound interest in semantics, and for the next twenty years Carnap focused his research upon this broad topic. In 1942 he published his *Introduction to Semantics* while, in the following year, his *Formalization of Logic* appeared, and both books explored various aspects of semantics in relation to formal systems. The main emphasis in both texts is upon truth-conditional interpretations. In other words, given a statement in a formal language, in order to explore its meaning, Carnap argued that it was first necessary to know how the universe would have to be configured in order for the statement to be true. In Carnap's treatment, the rules for semantic interpretation constitute a separate and isolated part of the full linguistic system he develops: the syntactic component outputs sentences in a formal language that are subsequently subjected to semantic interpretation. In order to clarify his position, Carnap offers the following definition of a semantic system:

> A *semantical system* is a system of rules which states *truth-conditions* for the sentences of an object language and thereby determine [*sic*] the meaning of these sentences. A semantical system S may consist of *rules of formation* defining 'sentence in S', *rules of designation* defining 'designation in S', and *rules of truth* defining 'truth in S'. The sentence in the metalanguage '$\mathfrak{S}_i$ is true in S' means the same as the sentence $\mathfrak{S}_i$ itself. This characteristic constitutes a condition for the *adequacy* of definitions of truth. (Carnap 1942: 22)

As this passage indicates, Carnap's basic approach to logical semantics was truth-conditional, and his thinking in this respect had been influenced by Tarski, one of the members of the Lvov-Warsaw school. Appropriately, Carnap explicitly acknowledged his debt to his younger contemporary.[14] Tarski had studied with Ajdukiewicz, and since the latter considered syntax and semantics to be closely related, it is not surprising that Tarski should have been convinced that formal languages required a system of semantic interpretation in order to be complete. In a 1931 paper,[15] Tarski emphasised the relationship between truth and meaning, and, while seeking an adequate definition of truth, he introduced the schema, (T), which takes the form

(T) X is true if, and only if, p (4.6)

The basic idea behind this schema is that any sentence will be classified as an 'equivalence' of the form (T) if the letter 'p' above can be replaced by a sentence, and the letter 'X' by the name of the sentence. Once again, the Hilbertian notion of a metalanguage is dominant here since there is a clear distinction between metalanguage and object language. The most famous example of a sentence-name pair that is equivalent to (T) is the sentence 'Snow is white if and only if snow is white', and it is the concept of a metalanguage alone that rescues this statement from tautology: 'X' (i.e., 'snow is white') is true if and only if it is actually the case that p holds (i.e., snow is white). In a paper written several years later,[16] Tarski again emphasised the relationship that exists between statements in a formal language and the external world:

> We shall understand by semantics the totality of considerations concerning those concepts which, roughly speaking, express certain connexions between the expressions of a language and the objects and states of affairs referred to by these expressions. (Tarski 1956b[1936]: 401)

Consequently, his understanding of meaning was based upon his understanding of the extension of a predicate expression. Essentially, the extension of such an expression constitutes the class denoted by the expression, while the intension of the expression constitutes the property (or properties) that distinguishes the members of the class denoted by the expression. As he expressed it in a later paper, 'A sentence is true if it designates an existing state of affairs' (Tarski 1944: 343).

As mentioned in section 3.6, during the early 1950s some of these developments in the theory of logical semantics caused various philosophers to explore aspects of the traditional (Kantian) distinction between analytic and synthetic truths. For instance, in 1952 Carnap published a paper in which he attempted to provide a new 'way of explicating the concept of analyticity' (Carnap 1952: 66). The basic approach outlined in the paper involved sentences of the type 'If Jack is a bachelor, then he is not married' being formally represented using meaning postulates of the type

$$B(a) \to \neg M(a) \tag{4.7}$$

where, in this case, 'B' and 'M' indicate 'is a bachelor' and 'is married' respectively. Since this implication is necessarily valid, Carnap suggested that the following meaning postulate could be adopted

$$P_1 : \forall x [B(x) \to \neg M(x)] \tag{4.8}$$

and the rest of the paper considered the ways in which adopting such postulates can simplify the task of semantic analysis. As already implied above, this revival of logical semantics in the 1930s and 1940s, which was largely engineered by Ajdukiewicz, Tarski, and Carnap, can be viewed as a reaction against the more extreme varieties of Formalism that attempted to exclude meaning entirely from logical syntax.

To return to Bar-Hillel's paper in the light of this summary, it is clear that he was entirely familiar with the developments sketched above. For instance, he refers to 'the Warsaw-Lvov school' explicitly, and mentions Ajdukiewicz and Tarski by name. In addition, while considering these topics, he points to similarities between the work of Bloomfield and Carnap concerning the role of meaning. Since the relevant passage appears not to be well known, it merits being quoted in full.

> It is an interesting fact, deserving the attention of sociologists of science, that at approximately the same time, but in complete independence of each other, Bloomfield and Carnap were fighting the psychologism that dominated their respective fields, linguistics and logic. They both deplored the mentalistic mud into which the study of meaning had fallen, and tried to reconstruct their fields on a purely formal-structural basis. I think it is correct to say that the difference between the structural linguist and the formal logician is one of stress and degree rather than of kind. Both are essentially attempting to construct language systems that stand in some correspondence to natural languages – though most linguists would say that they are just describing the latter. But whereas for the linguist the closeness of the correspondence is the criterion by which he will judge the adequacy of the language system he is setting up, which alone entitles him to consider himself as describing a given natural language, the logician will look primarily for other features of his system, such as simplicity of handling, fruitfulness for science, and ease of deduction and computation, with close correspondence to a natural

language as only a secondary desideratum. Constructed language systems are judged by the linguist according to the degree to which they approximate a natural language; natural languages are judged by the logician according to the degree to which they approximate efficient, well-constructed language systems. (Bar-Hillel 1954: 234–235)

There are several issues here that merit comment. For instance, the parallel between Bloomfield and Carnap is yet another instance of the association that was felt to hold between logic and linguistics in the 1950s, and this helps to explain why certain syntacticians borrowed techniques from formal logic (and related disciplines) and used them to facilitate (or so they hoped) the analysis of natural language. Bar-Hillel's own advocation of logical syntax and recursive definitions has already been considered, as has Chomsky's adaptation of constructional system theory. As Bar-Hillel acknowledges, one of the reasons for this perceived closeness was the rejection of meaning that had characterised Bloomfield's and Carnap's early work – an association that has already been mentioned several times in earlier chapters (especially section 3.7). In the context of this observation, it should be noted, though, that Bar-Hillel's claim that Bloomfield and Carnap worked 'in complete independence' is not entirely true. As mentioned in section 3.7, Bloomfield had read *LSL* and in 1939 he wrote an article for an *Encyclopedia* of which Carnap was one of the editors, though admittedly it is difficult to gauge the full extent of their contact during this period. Whatever the precise nature of their interaction, though, there is no doubt that Bloomfield's work seemed to make certain assumptions that were similar to those made by Carnap in his pre-1935 publications, and, as noted previously, to a later generation of linguists this apparent similarity appeared to provide a basis for future developments. At the very least, it seemed to licence a free borrowing of the techniques of formal logic for the task of linguistic analysis.

While the picture painted by Bar-Hillel gives the impression of being clear and comprehensive, it is (not surprisingly) rather too simplistic as an account of the real situation. For instance, not all linguists shared his perception of this close correspondence. As already indicated, Harris, for one, was convinced that logicians and linguists did different things, and he was not forced into this conclusion by ignorance of recent developments, for his familiarity with *LSL* (at least) is well attested by the various references to Carnap's book in *MSL* (as discussed in section 3.7). Indeed, the difference between Harris' and Bar-Hillel's views concerning logic and natural language could not be more striking, since, according to the latter, linguists and logicians differ in 'degree' rather than in 'kind', while the former had stated that 'linguists meet the problem [i.e., that of describing the structure of language] differently than do Carnap and his school' (Harris 1952: 16.n17). The main difference between linguists and logicians from Bar-Hillel's perspective was that the latter were often more concerned with the form of the systems they created than with the task of validating said systems by means of empirical investigation. By contrast, linguists were forced to compare the results of their theoretical investigations with utterances in actual corpora. Therefore, issues such as 'simplicity of handling' (whatever that might be exactly) and 'ease of deduction and computation' are primarily a concern for logicians. However, as was shown in section 4.3, the notion of theory-internal simplicity had already begun to infiltrate Chomsky's conception of syntactic theory largely due to his interest in Goodman's work. Also, around this time, Chomsky was starting to reconsider the usefulness of corpus-based discovery procedures, and would eventually introduce a different kind of research method that was not so deeply rooted in empirical validation. In both these respects, then, Bar-Hillel's description of linguistic investigation was soon to become outdated. Nevertheless, the conception of linguistics and logic that he develops in his paper is fundamental to Bar-Hillel's view of their potential inter-connectivity.

As indicated above, Chomsky's response to Bar-Hillel's paper is of considerable interest for various reasons. His primary intention is to refute Bar-Hillel's suggestion that advances in the theory of logical syntax and semantics can facilitate the analysis of meaning in natural language, a task of real significance since, by the mid-1950s, Chomsky was fully persuaded that considerations of meaning had no place in the study of syntax. For instance, to take just one quotation from his other 1955 paper, 'Semantic Considerations in Grammar', which also considers the role of meaning in linguistic theory, Chomsky had plainly stated (in true Bloomfieldian fashion) that

> Meaning is a notoriously difficult notion to pin down. If it can be shown that meaning and related notions do play a central role in linguistic analysis, then its results and conclusions become subject to all the doubts and obscurities that plague the study of meaning, and a serious blow is struck at the foundations of linguistic analysis. (Chomsky 1955b: 141)

The implication here is clear: meaning is a pernicious, troublesome aspect of natural language that should be excluded (if possible) from linguistic analysis. In the light of this observation, and before considering in some detail the argument Chomsky constructed to refute Bar-Hillel, it is worth outlining the sources upon which he drew. As ever, this task is fairly easy to accomplish due to Chomsky's willingness to specify both the nature and extent of his indebtedness. In this case, he openly confesses that, in preparing his response, he has 'borrowed freely from various critical accounts of the theory of meaning' (Chomsky 1955a: 36). More specifically, he explicitly names Quine's *LPV* (especially chapters 2, 7, and 8), as well as White's paper 'The Analytic and the Synthetic: An Untenable Dualism', which first appeared in 1950 (while Chomsky was still attending White's lectures?), but which was later published in the collection *Semantics and the Philosophy of Language* edited by Leonard Linsky. The appearance of this book in 1952 seems to have been partly responsible for provoking Bar-Hillel's and Chomsky's exchange in the mid-1950s, since it is referred to in both papers and raises many questions about the status of meaning in philosophical theories of language. In particular, Quine's and White's attacks upon the traditional Kantian distinction between analytic and synthetic truths, which were briefly summarised in section 3.6, appear to have persuaded Chomsky, and his use of their ideas in his own arguments implies his acceptance of their views. In this context, the details of his argument will now be considered below.

Appropriately enough, Chomsky begins his paper by summarising Bar-Hillel's main points and immediately attacks the idea that Carnapian transformations can be profitably used by linguists in order to analyse natural language. His central argument is that, since Carnap assumes such relations as 'formal consequence' and 'synonymy' as primitives in the logical systems he creates, his work offers no means of explaining or clarifying these notions, and therefore the use of such relations cannot benefit linguistics except in a 'trivial' fashion. If such relations were adopted in a linguistic theory, Chomsky claims, the validity of the resulting inferences could only be assessed by listing all possible options as postulates of the given language system, an argument that Chomsky had borrowed directly from White's paper since, as mentioned in section 3.6, White had argued that a 'rule-book' (White 1952: 277) of synonyms would be required in order to deal with analytic truths in natural language, and (of course) no such book exists. With considerable scorn, then, Chomsky declares that this constitutes nothing more than 'an ad-hoc approach to the problem of classification and characterisation of elements in particular languages' (Chomsky 1955a: 38), and (in his opinion) the apparent failure of Carnap's transformation rules to contribute anything of substance to the task of analysing natural language phenomena such as synonymy entirely undermines Bar-Hillel's trumpeted belief in the efficaciousness of such rules in a linguistic context.

Having proceeded thus far in his demolition of Bar-Hillel's argument, Chomsky pauses to consider the term 'formal', which 'has played a rather crucial role in this discussion' (Chomsky 1955a: 39). In particular, Chomsky is keen to reconsider the consequences of using such terminology while discussing linguistic systems. For instance, Bar-Hillel had claimed in his paper that the active–passive relation that converts 'plays' into 'is played by' is a relation of formal consequence. Chomsky does not accept this, since the meaning of the term 'formal' has 'misleading connotations' in this context. Consequently, he offers a (somewhat opaque) definition of 'formal' in which a relation is so classified if 'it holds between linguistic expressions' (Chomsky 1955a: 39), and while agreeing with Bar-Hillel's statement concerning the active–passive relation, he adds that the relation 'longer by three words' is also formal (in the above sense), since it too holds for the expression pair 'John did not come home' and 'John came'. Since logical syntax of the Carnapian variety is unable to determine which of these examples is an instance of formal consequence, Chomsky is forced to conclude that relations of formal consequence are of no use when analysing a natural language. Rather, the 'systematic investigation of linguistic expressions alone' (Chomsky 1955a: 39) is required in order to specify the sets of expressions for which such relations hold. Presumably, in this context, the phrase 'systematic investigation' denotes some kind of Harris-style distributional procedure that can be used to group expressions in a given language, or possibly the type of constructional system-based approach developed in 'SSA'. It is crucial to recognise, though, that such a procedure would still be 'formal', since no semantic considerations would be permitted in such a scheme. Chomsky concludes this section of his discussion with the unambiguous declaration that 'logical syntax and semantics provide no grounds for determining synonyms and consequence relations' (Chomsky 1955a: 39).

The various arguments (summarised above) that Chomsky marshals in the first part of his paper are partly designed to undermine Bar-Hillel's claim that linguistics could benefit from those aspects of Carnap's work in logical systems that deal with logical syntax. However, Chomsky is not convinced that logical semantics has much to offer either, and, by rejecting this possibility, he reveals the full extent of his dissatisfaction with contemporaneous accounts of linguistic meaning. The causes of his dissatisfaction are established when he goes on to assess the difference between logical implication and similar phenomena in natural language. He considers several examples (including one borrowed from Goodman) and easily demonstrates that natural language inferences are unexpectedly complex, and therefore cannot be glibly analysed in terms of the standard logical implication operator. Once again this provides him with an ideal opportunity to stress the divide that separates natural language and the type of artificial languages that Carnap creates in his 'logical laboratory'.

> The question as to the nature of inference in natural languages can scarcely be intelligibly put now, since we have almost no systematic knowledge about

inference or meaning in ordinary linguistic behavior, and no study of new and deeper foundations for mathematics can be expected to tell us more about this. (Chomsky 1955a: 40)

The advice here (directed towards Bar-Hillel and like-minded logician-linguists, no doubt) is to resist the temptation unthinkingly to appropriate techniques developed in the course of research into the foundations of mathematics, since it does not follow that they will *necessarily* facilitate the analysis of natural language. As is shown below, towards the end of the paper Chomsky does not exclude the possibility that such techniques *could* prove to be useful tools in the context of linguistic research; his point is simply that the utility of such methods is not guaranteed. Nevertheless, it is fascinating to juxtapose statements of this kind with the sort of optimism encountered in 'SSA', written just two years before. As mentioned in section 4.4, in his 1953 paper, Chomsky actively used Goodman's 'calculus of individuals' (a logico-philosophical system) to analyse linguistic structures. More to the point, the language he analysed in that paper was a simple formal language, and he openly stated that the methodology presented could not be used to analyse natural language. Clearly, sometime during the years 1953–1955, Chomsky had changed his mind concerning the feasibility, and perhaps the validity, of the type of project attempted in 'SSA'. It is important to note, therefore, in the light of his exchange with Bar-Hillel, that Chomsky was not discussing these matters solely from the perspective of abstract linguistic theory, since, in addition to his pronounced theoretical concerns, he had considerable practical experience of working both with logical systems and with artificial languages.

Not content, however, with having undermined Bar-Hillel's statements concerning the usefulness of logical syntax and semantics, Chomsky also questions Bar-Hillel's understanding of these topics, and he does this by focusing on the theory of meaning. After asserting that Tarski's main contributions were to the theory of reference and not to the theory of meaning (Bar-Hillel had claimed the latter), Chomsky considers the recent work of Quine and concludes that, far from extending Carnap's notion of intension (as Bar-Hillel had argued), Quine had actively sought to demonstrate the parlous state of meaning in logical systems theory. In particular, Chomsky cites Quine's celebrated paper 'Two Dogmas of Empiricism', referring to it as 'Quine's most trenchant attack on current formulations of the theory of meaning' (Chomsky 1955a: 41), and he goes on to suggest that, for Quine, this theory 'remains in pretty much the state that repelled Bloomfield' (Chomsky 1955a: 40). In addition to Quine's, White's influence can also be detected here, since his discussion of analytic and synthetic truths (cited explicitly by Chomsky at the start of his paper) also served to destabilise logical semantics. It is apparent, therefore, that Chomsky's main intention in this passage is twofold. First, he is keen to correct Bar-Hillel's alleged misreading of recent developments in logical semantics. However, second, he is also eager to demonstrate that none of the recent advances cited by Bar-Hillel had enabled meaning to be considered as a viable foundation for linguistic theory. Consequently, as far as Chomsky is concerned, the post-Bloomfieldian emphasis on the manipulation of meaning-less linguistic forms still provides the most secure basis for syntactic theory, and, although this conclusion is not new, Chomsky's argument certainly demonstrates the extent to which his thinking on this issue had been influenced by contemporaneous discussions in the field of analytic philosophy, an influence that has not been adequately recognised in the past.

With his basic position now established, Chomsky seeks to render it more secure by dismissing Carnap's suggestion (endorsed by Bar-Hillel) that the study of artificial languages can provide insights into the nature of natural language. Consequently, Bar-Hillel's assertion that logicians and linguists differ only in 'degree' is shown to be mistaken: if one draws conclusions about natural language from logical systems constructed to explore the foundations of mathematics 'one might as well argue that a science-fiction writer or an artist is doing roughly the same thing as a physicist' (Chomsky 1955a: 42). The analogy is polemical, but Chomsky is able to conclude that 'artificial languages are neither special cases nor idealised versions of natural language' (Chomsky 1955a: 42), and yet again the purpose here is to convey the impression that a significant divide separates the disciplines of logic and linguistics, an attitude that has already been identified in the work of Harris, suggesting that Chomsky was here dutifully following Harris' lead. In general, Chomsky's aim is to acknowledge and emphasise the independence of linguistics as an intellectual discipline. If the association between it and logic were accepted too rapidly and too extremely, the former would simply be annexed to the latter, with (presumably) dire consequences. Once again, though, it is worth emphasising that Chomsky himself had attempted to develop a system of linguistic analysis in 'SSA' that had concentrated on simple artificial languages, and the above pronouncements must have been influenced to some extent by his own personal experience of this type of approach.

In characteristic fashion, having arrived at the strident position outlined in the above paragraph, Chomsky then immediately proceeds to reveal the full complexity of his views. Although he remains adamant that 'logical syntax and semantics can bring the linguist no nearer to an adequate conception of synonymy and transformations' (Chomsky 1955a: 41), he does not rule out the possibility that logic *can* be fruitfully employed in a linguistic context, and he specifically mentions Bar-Hillel's work involving recursive definitions as a recent positive example. Aware that such pronouncements could seem paradoxical when juxtaposed with the previously articulated scepticism, Chomsky seeks to clarify his position:

> The correct way to use the insights and techniques of logic is in formulating a general theory of linguistic structure. But this does not tell us what sort of systems form the subject matter for linguistics, or how the linguist may find it profitable to describe them. To apply logic in constructing a clear and rigorous linguistic theory is different from expecting logic or any other formal system to be a model for linguistic behavior. (Chomsky 1955a: 45)

This single passage reveals the full intricacy of Chomsky's attitude towards the use of techniques derived from formal symbolic logic in linguistic analyses, and, despite some of the more extreme comments quoted above, it emerges that he is neither simply for, nor simply against, the use of logic in linguistic research. Rather, he is opposed to the unthinking assumption that logic will necessarily provide insights into the structure of natural language. In the event, some techniques derived from logic may prove to be useful when a linguistic theory is being constructed, while others may offer no benefits. The task of the linguist is sensibly to assess the validity of the various techniques in the context of natural language analysis. As indicated above, Chomsky is seemingly convinced that the methods of logic can certainly be usefully employed when 'a general theory of linguistic structure' is developed, and, as with his remarks concerning the use of artificial languages in linguistic research, his comments here are not abstract musings since, during early 1955, Chomsky was busy completing the first draft of *LSLT*, the main text in which he outlined his own general theory of linguistic structure. The full title of this work alone emphasises the point made at length above: *The Logical Structure of Linguistic Theory*, with its conscious nod towards (the English translation of) Carnap's *The Logical Structure of Language*,[17] implies that the structure of linguistic *theory* must be logical. However, it does not follow from this that the task of analysing natural language can be reduced in a trivial fashion to an exercise in logical manipulation. In choosing his title, therefore, Chomsky seems simultaneously to be aligning himself with, and distancing himself from, Carnap's work. Consequently, it is appropriate that many of the insights into the nature of the relationship between logic and linguistics, which can be gleaned from his 1955 paper, can be considered in relation to various aspects of *LSLT*, some of which will be explored in detail in chapter 5.

As a coda to the above discussion, it is worth mentioning that, eight years after Chomsky's paper appeared, some of the issues raised in the exchange were reconsidered by Bar-Hillel and (even more intriguingly) by Carnap himself. Bar-Hillel contributed an essay entitled 'Remarks on Carnap's Logical Syntax of Language' to the 1963 volume of Schilpp's *Library of Living Philosophers*, which was devoted to an assessment of Carnap's work. This paper shows that Bar-Hillel's basic views had changed little over the intervening years, though he did acknowledge that Chomsky's 1955 defence of Harris had been 'well taken' (Bar-Hillel 1963: 542). Responding to Bar-Hillel's paper, Carnap himself considers the relationship between linguistics and logic and declares that he has 'full sympathy' with the suggestion that the former could profit from the techniques borrowed from the latter, although he does advise caution when applying them. With specific reference to the Bar-Hillel *versus* Chomsky exchange in the mid-1950s, Carnap observes,

> It is always difficult to build a bridge between two fields of knowledge which have developed their methods and techniques separately, so that even elementary connections are not easy. Bar-Hillel's paper of 1954 ... seems to have found little echo among linguists so far, although his paper, in contrast to my publications, is written in a generally comprehensible language, is published in a linguistics periodical, and makes direct reference to the work of the structural linguists. I am not surprised to find that Chomsky in his reply to Bar-Hillel's article does not agree with Bar-Hillel's views; I think that Chomsky is to some extent right, because Bar-Hillel claims too much when he speaks about the *immediate* importance of my investigations for linguistics. But, on the other hand, I have the impression that Chomsky failed to grasp the meaning of Bar-Hillel's appeal and also the aims and nature of my theories of syntax and semantics, and this shows the great difficulty of communication between the two fields. (Carnap 1963: 941)

Unfortunately, Carnap does not go on to discuss the precise nature of Chomsky's perceived misunderstanding either of Bar-Hillel's proposals or of his own work, and it is no real surprise to find that a discussion which partly concerns the role of meaning in linguistic theory should conclude with the suggestion that certain lines of reasoning had been misinterpreted. Nevertheless, the issues raised by Bar-Hillel, Chomsky, and Carnap concerning the relationship between natural and logical languages, and, in particular, the role of semantics in linguistic analysis, remained topics of debate throughout the 1960s. Indeed, as is well known, the more extreme integrationist position adopted by Bar-Hillel reached its apotheosis in the late 1960s and early 1970s in the work of Richard Montague (1930–1971). Although the large body of work devoted to 'Montague Semantics' is (alas) outside the scope of this book, it is worth emphasising that, for Montague, natural and logical languages were identical, or, as he expressed it in the trenchant beginning of his 1970 paper 'English as a Formal Language', 'I reject the contention that an important theoretical difference exists between formal and natural language' (Montague 1970: 188). Consequently, Montague was able to develop a detailed formalism for a truth-theoretical analysis of natural language which was explicitly intended to provide an alternative to generative grammar, indicating that the old divisions of the 1950s were still clearly motivating research twenty years later.[18]

5 Transforming generative grammar: 1955–1957

5.1 Chapter overview

The main purpose of this chapter is to continue to reassess the development of TGG in the light of advances in the formal sciences. Consequently, Chomsky's writings from the years 1955–1957 will be the focus of the discussion, although, as previously, connections will be made between Chomsky's work and that of both his predecessors and his contemporaries. To this end, in section 5.2 Chomsky's rejection of stochastic grammars is considered as part of his assertion that syntax can be studied autonomously. In section 5.3 his redefinition of syntactic research is assessed, particularly the recommended shift away from discovery procedures and towards evaluation procedures. Since certain of the arguments that caused Chomsky to reconsider the role of discovery procedures in linguistic research were initially articulated by Goodman and Quine, it is necessary to explore the influence of constructional system theory upon the approach to syntactic analysis outlined in *LSLT* and *Syntactic Structures* (hereafter *SS*), and this is achieved in section 5.4 where it is shown that Chomsky's definition of a linguistic level is derived from constructional system theory. Given the name of the syntactic theory discussed in this book, 'Transformational Generative Grammar', it is necessary to discuss both the concept of 'transformation' and the process of 'generation'. Accordingly, the complex evolution of grammatical transformations in syntactic theory is traced in section 5.5, while in section 5.6 the generative role of recursive definitions in TGG is considered. In both these sections the connections that exist between Chomsky's work and that of Bar-Hillel and others are emphasised. Finally, in section 5.7, the influence of Formalism upon TGG is considered, and the proof-theoretical character of the theory is discussed.

5.2 Stochastic processes and autonomous grammar

Before considering the type of syntactic theory that Chomsky developed during the years 1955–1957, it is first necessary to assess his reasons for claiming that the grammar of a language could be considered in isolation from all other aspects of language (especially semantics). In section 4.5 the various arguments that Chomsky developed in the mid-1950s to justify his rejection of logical semantics were discussed at length, and one consequence of this was that, following the tradition of Bloomfield and Harris, Chomsky became convinced that syntax could be studied separately from semantics. In fact, he claimed specifically that syntax provides a basis for semantics.[1] However, Chomsky not only felt compelled to rescue syntax from the hands of the logicians, but he was also keen to preserve it from the clutches of statisticians. In particular, he responded negatively to the concept of a stochastic grammar, which had been proposed by Shannon and Weaver in the 1940s, and which had been enthusiastically welcomed by certain post-Bloomfieldian syntacticians. Consequently, before discussing Chomsky's rejection of these ideas, it is necessary to summarise them in some detail.

In the first decades of the twentieth century the statistical properties of natural language became an active area of research. For instance, Andrei Markov (1856–1922) introduced stochastic processes, called finite state automata, and used them to model letter frequencies in Russian poetry (see Sheynin 1988). Also, George Zipf (1902–1950) published two books, *The Psycho-Biology of Language* (1935) and *Human Behavior and the Principle of Least Effort* (1949), in which he explored frequency counts for linguistic units such as phonemes, syllables, and words, observing that they were invariably distributed in a characteristic fashion, with a small group of frequently occurring units and a long tail of infrequent units. This type of distribution, which can be represented as a linear plot when the natural logarithm of the frequency is plotted against the natural logarithm of the unit number, was later called a Zipfian distribution, and research of this kind suggested that there were patterns hidden in natural language that could best be revealed by detailed statistical analysis. In turn, this implied that stochastic models of linguistic behaviour constituted a branch of statistical theory that was well worth exploring. This general project was given significant impetus by the publication of Claude Shannon (1916–2001) and Warren Weaver's (1894–1978) *The Mathematical Theory of Communication* in 1949.[2] This text, which became one of the seminal works of information theory, provided a clear introduction to a number of comparatively recent advances in the theory of stochastic processes, thus making these techniques available to a wide, non-specialist audience for the first time.

From the viewpoint of linguistic theory, the most significant mathematical model discussed by Shannon was the finite state machine; that is, the stochastic process introduced by Markov which, by the 1940s, had come to be known as a Markov model. Assuming the existence of a finite set of discrete symbols (i.e., an alphabet), a Markov model is a stochastic process that generates a string of symbols in a probabilistic fashion. Each symbol, S_i, can be associated with a probability, $p(S_i)$, and the probability of symbol S_i being followed by symbol S_j is given by the transition probability $p(S_i, S_j)$. If the history of the symbol sequence is taken into account, then conditional probabilities of the form $p(S_j \mid S_1, S_2, \ldots, S_{j-1})$ can be defined which consider the probability of the current symbol to be conditionally related to the preceding sequence of symbols. With these probabilities established, a Markov model can generate a string of symbols in an automatic fashion, and it is important to note that, in Shannon and Weaver's discussion of the topic, they explicitly state that Markov models can be used to approximate natural languages such as English. More precisely, they define an ordered series of such approximations which can be summarised as follows:

- zero-order approximation: all symbols are independent and equi-probable.
- first-order approximation: all symbols are independent and associated with their respective frequencies in English.
- second-order approximation: the symbol probabilities are dependent upon the previous two symbols (i.e., $p(S_j \mid S_{j-2}, S_{j-1})$)
- n^{th}-order approximation: the symbol probabilities are dependent upon the previous n symbols (i.e., $p(S_j \mid S_{j-n+1}, \ldots, S_{j-1})$).

The potential benefit of Markov modelling to the task of grammar construction is explicitly emphasised by Weaver later in the book, though it is made clear that the approach recommended is far from idealistic since, when dealing with natural language, one can only hope to achieve approximate results.

> Language must be designed (or developed) with a view to the totality of things that man may wish to say; but not being able to accomplish everything, it too should do as well as possible, as often as possible. This is to say, it too should deal with its task statistically. (Shannon and Weaver 1949: 117)

Accepting that to do 'as well as possible, as often as possible' is all that syntactic theory can hope to achieve, the suggestion here is that language *must* be studied as some kind of stochastic information source, since only a model of this type will permit the sort of approximations which (it is supposed) are required when natural language is modelled mathematically. However, as will be discussed below, this humble desire was not shared by the more idealistic members of the current generation of linguists, who wanted to accomplish something more than mere approximation.

In the years immediately following the publication of Shannon and Weaver's text, there was a flurry of books and papers that explored some of the implications of finite state grammars and stochastic processes, and the general response was one of interest and enthusiasm. For instance, George Miller (b. 1920) devoted a whole chapter of *Language and Communication* (1951) to 'The Statistical Approach'. In this chapter he summarises Shannon's use of stochastic approximations as a model of linguistic behaviour, and emphasises that 'the question under consideration is the extent to which any particular verbal unit is determined by the other verbal units that surround it' (Miller 1951: 81). It is important to note that Miller did not only see possible value in Shannon's approximations for the modelling of syntax, but was keen also to suggest that stochastic processes could be used to model any aspect of natural language structure, including phonetic and phonological structure. The use of stochastic techniques to analyse the phonetic structure of language was further explored by Colin Cherry (1928–1981), Morris Halle (b. 1923), and Roman Jakobson (1896–1982) in their joint 1953 paper 'Toward the Logical Description of Languages in their Phonemic Aspect', in which it was unambiguously stated that the main purpose of the research presented there was to 'contribute to a logical description of the phonemic structure of language, employing some of the elementary concepts of statistical communication theory' (Cherry, Halle, and Jakobson 1953: 34). In a footnote the authors explicitly cite Shannon and Weaver's text, and state clearly that 'in the description that follows, language will be treated as a Markoff [*sic*] process' (Cherry, Halle, and Jakobson 1953: 36). However, perhaps the most enthusiastic advocate of finite state process for the modelling of syntactic phenomena was Hockett, who at that time was one of the leading post-Bloomfieldians. In 1953, for instance, he reviewed Shannon and Weaver's book in the journal *Language*, and responded positively, stating that Shannon's ideas 'must be investigated' (Hockett 1953: 70). Further, he felt that some of the techniques associated with stochastic theories of language shared similarities with the sort of methods standardly employed by structural linguists (yet another example of the commonly mooted mathematics-linguistics correspondence), and, after his discussion of Shannon's ideas in relation to linguistic theory, he declared that 'we have demonstrated that a certain number of problems of concern to linguists can be phrased in the terminology of information theory' (Hockett 1953: 89). As indicated above, this belief in the compatibility of linguistics and statistics can be compared with Bar-Hillel's conviction that the methodology of language-based structural analysis could be combined with certain types of logical systems, as well as with Chomsky's attempt to fuse Harris-style discovery procedures and constructional system theory. Clearly these perceived connections were exciting at the time and, for Hockett, his perception of this apparent compatibility was associated with a sense of 'exhilaration', although he was quick to warn against the unthinking acceptance of a 'misleading analogy' (Hockett 1953: 89).

Hockett's 1953 review of Shannon and Weaver's book was followed two years later by a detailed statement of his belief in the utility of statistical methods in linguistic analysis which appeared in his *A Manual of Phonology* (1955). In this work, Hockett uses engineering-style flow diagrams to represent the way in which information is communicated by the speaker to the hearer in a conversational situation. In order to clarify the stages in the process, he posits the existence of a 'Grammatical Headquarters' (or 'G.H.Q'), which is responsible for generating the sentences that are spoken, and his description of this stage of the process indicates the extent to which he had come to accept Shannon's basic approach to syntax.

> A unit regarded as purely a source of a discrete flow of signals can be mathematically characterized in a complete fashion on the basis of the statistics of the signal-flows which it emits; the technique for doing this was developed by Claude Shannon. We imagine that G.H.Q. can be in any number of a very large number of different *states*. At a given moment it is necessarily in one or another of these states. Associated with each state is an array of probabilities for the emission of various morphemes of the language: a certain relative probability that the morpheme *and* will next be emitted, a certain relative probability that the morpheme *tackle* will next be emitted, and so on. When some morpheme is actually emitted, G.H.Q. shifts to a new state. Which state the new one is depends in *a determinate way* (not just probabilistically) on both the preceding states and on what morpheme has actually been emitted. (Hockett 1955: 7)

This is a strong statement of the stochastic grammar creed: the sequence of linguistic units emitted by the G.H.Q can be determined 'in a complete fashion' by the Markov process. The basic assumption appears to be that finite state machines are *entirely* adequate for the task of modelling the grammar of natural language. Hockett's belief in the theoretical validity of this assumption (even though he recognises that such an approach could entail practical difficulties) is indicated when he states that

> By making an enormous count of relative frequencies of occurrence of all the morphemes and many morpheme-sequences in natural English, followed by an enormous amount of computation, and by writing very small entries on an

enormous sheet of paper, the entire grammatical structure of English could be portrayed ... (Hockett 1955: 10)

Once again, therefore, Hockett stresses his conviction that stochastic processes, at least in theory, provide an adequate model for the grammar of a natural language, since, as indicated above, he believed that 'the entire grammatical structure of English' could be analysed using statistical techniques.

In the light of this support for stochastic techniques amongst certain linguists, particularly Hockett, it is revealing to consider Chomsky's assessment of these techniques,[3] and the most complete presentation of his ideas concerning stochastic grammars can be found in his 1956 paper 'Three Models for the Description of Language' (hereafter 'TMDL') which (it should be noted) appeared in the I.R.E. Transactions for Information Theory. In fact, the paper was delivered as part of a series that focused on various aspects of information theory, and the event took the form of a conference at MIT in 1956. Such a gathering was hardly a conventional forum for a discussion of the syntax of natural language, and it is revealing that this particular conference should be considered by some to indicate the emergence of fully-fledged cognitive science.[4] As the title of his 1956 paper suggests, Chomsky's main purpose was to explore three different models (i.e., grammars) that provided different descriptions of a given language. Specifically, the three types of model he considers are finite state grammars, phrase structure grammars, and transformational grammars. Various aspects of his presentation of the latter two types will be considered in the other sections of this chapter, therefore, for now, the emphasis will be exclusively upon his assessment of finite state grammars.

As expected, Chomsky's presentation of finite state machines was derived primarily from Shannon and Weaver's 1949 book. Consequently, following them, he states that a finite state grammar, **G**, for a given language, **L** consists of

- a finite number of states, $s_0, \ldots, s_q$
- a set, A, of transition symbols where $A = \{a_{ij} \mid 0 \leq i, j \leq q\}$
- a set, C, of connected state pairs where $C = \{(s_i, s_j)\}$

In order to clarify the nature of the set C, it is best to consider an example: if state s_j can be reached from state s_i, then the pair of states (s_i, s_j) constitutes a connected pair. Sentences are formed from the grammar by concatenating the symbols that are generated. Consequently, a sentence, S, in **L** takes the form $S = a_1 \frown a_2 \frown \ldots \frown a_n$, where $a_i \in A$ for $1 \leq i \leq n$.

Having summarised Shannon and Weaver's Markov process formalism in this fashion, Chomsky then states that he intends to consider 'the absolute limits' (Chomsky 1956: 115) of the type of finite state languages he has just defined. In other words, he is keen to determine precisely which languages can be generated by finite state grammars, and which cannot be generated by such machines. In order to accomplish this, he introduces the concept of 'dependency'. Assuming that language **L** and a sentence S are defined as above, then (i, j)-dependency for sentence S with respect to **L** can be said to hold only if the following conditions are met:

1. $1 \leq i < j \leq n$
2. there are symbols $b_i, b_j \in A$ with the property that S_1 is not a sentence of **L**, and S_2 is a sentence of **L**, where S_1 is formed from sentence S by replacing the ith symbol of S (namely, a_i) by b_i, and S_2 is formed from S_1 by replacing the jth symbol of S_1 (namely, a_j) by b_j.

The above conditions rely upon the concept of replacement, which, though not defined, is understood to correspond to substitution. In this way, the type of technique Chomsky uses in order to investigate 'the absolute limits' of finite state grammars, which exploit the distributional properties of symbol pairs, are closely related to some of the methods employed by Harris and other post-Bloomfieldians. The basic idea behind replacement is that two symbols, a_i and a_j, are dependent if, when a_i is replaced by b_i (where $a_i \neq b_i$), a_j must also be replaced, this time by the symbol b_j (where $a_j \neq b_j$). To consider a specific example, given the sentence $S = a_1 \frown a_2 \frown a_3 \frown a_4$, where $S \in \mathbf{L}$, if the following sentences can be obtained by means of replacement,

$$S_1 = b_1 \frown a_2 \frown a_3 \frown a_4 \tag{5.1}$$
$$S_2 = b_1 \frown a_2 \frown a_3 \frown b_4 \tag{5.2}$$

where $S_1 \notin \mathbf{L}$ and $S_2 \in \mathbf{L}$, then a_1 and a_4 are dependent and the sentence S has (1,4)-dependency. Armed with this technical definition, Chomsky then proceeds to define a dependency set, **D**, such that $\mathbf{D} = \{(\alpha_1, \beta_1), \ldots, (\alpha_m, \beta_m)\}$. The set **D** is a dependency set if and only if the following conditions are met:

- (i) for $1 \leq i \leq m$, S has a (α_i, β_i)-dependency with respect to **L**
- (ii) for each $i, j, \alpha_i < \beta_j$
- (iii) for each i, j such that $i \neq j, \alpha_i \neq \alpha_j$ and $\beta_i \neq \beta_j$

If the first element in a connected pair is referred to as a 'determining' element and the second element as a 'determined' element, then the above conditions ensure that all determining elements precede all determined elements and that no two determiners and no two determined elements are identical. In short, the conditions guarantee that every two dependencies are distinct. Since the number of elements in **D** is m, it follows that, for a given sentence S, the corresponding finite state grammar must contain at least 2^m states. This conclusion leads Chomsky to state a necessary condition for any language, **L**, generated by a finite state grammar:

- Condition 1: There is an m such that no sentence S of **L** has a dependency set of more than m terms in **L**

The crucial function of this condition is to delimit the range of languages that can be generated by a finite state grammar. It achieves this by indicating that, for any such grammar, there must be an upper bound on the number of terms contained in the dependency set. This condition then enables Chomsky to create three simple languages (an infinite number are possible) that cannot be generated by a finite state grammar. For instance, if the language **L** uses a two-letter alphabet (i.e., $A = \{a, b\}$), then some typical grammatical sentences in **L** might be

$$S_1 = a \frown a \qquad (5.3)$$
$$S_2 = a \frown b \frown b \frown a$$
$$S_3 = a \frown a \frown b \frown b \frown a \frown a$$

The dependency set for **L** can be given as $\mathbf{D} = \{(1, 2m), (2, 2m - 1), \ldots, (m, m + 1)\}$ for any m, and since **D** can contain more than any fixed number, m, of terms, it violates condition 1 above.

In the light of Chomsky's doubts concerning the usefulness of artificial languages when analysing natural language (discussed in section 4.5), it is of interest that, as in 'SSA', he here makes full use of simple toy languages in order to determine the limitations of finite state grammars. However, having determined these limits, Chomsky is eager to explore these findings in relation to natural language. Consequently, in order to prove that finite state grammars are not sufficiently powerful to provide a valid grammatical model for a given natural language, he simply needs to demonstrate that natural languages contain mirror-image structures (for instance) such as those presented in (5.3) above. He accomplishes this by considering structures of the type

$$\text{if } S_1, \text{ then } S_2 \qquad (5.4)$$

and by observing that there is a dependency between 'if' and 'then' in (5.4), since the clause indicated by S_1 could itself contain structures of the form 'if ... then', thus producing an English sentence with the mirror-image property assessed previously. Consequently, Chomsky concludes that English fails condition 1 above and that therefore 'no finite-state Markov process that produces symbols with transitions from state to state can serve as an English grammar' (Chomsky 1956: 113).

Having demonstrated that finite state grammars are not sufficiently powerful to generate all the possible sentences of English, Chomsky then dismisses the idea that n^{th} order approximations, of the type proposed by Shannon and Weaver, can ever be used to generate the set of grammatical sentences in English. The thrust of his argument is that grammaticality and frequency are not related notions, and to indicate that this is so he considers the sentences

Colorless green ideas sleep furiously (5.5)

Furiously sleep ideas green colorless (5.6)

Chomsky claims that these sentences (which were later made famous in *SS*), occur equally infrequently in English, yet sentence (5.5) is grammatical while sentence (5.6) is not. Therefore, he is obliged to conclude that frequency reveals nothing about grammaticality. The only possible conclusion, therefore, is that n^{th} order approximations must be rejected since 'as n increases, an nth order approximation to English will exclude (as more and more improbable) an ever-increasing number of grammatical sentences, while it still contains vast numbers of completely ungrammatical strings' (Chomsky 1956: 116).

As ever, it is essential to emphasise the full complexity of Chomsky's argument. Indeed, there are, in fact, general parallels between his rejection of stochastic techniques in 'TMDL' and his rejection of certain tools from logic in 'LSS'. In particular, just as Chomsky had advised linguists not to apply blindly the methodology of logic while attempting to analyse the structure of natural language, but rather to select and adapt specific techniques if they seem to be useful, so his advice to statistically minded linguists was actually expressed as caution rather than prohibition. Certainly, as indicated above, he was convinced that the grammar of natural language simply cannot be comprehensively modelled as a stochastic process (despite the initial claims of Hockett and others), but this did not lead him to advocate banishing statistical methods from linguistics entirely. Indeed, on the contrary, he freely confessed that the form and structure of natural language could be usefully explored using statistics, but his scepticism concerning syntactic modelling remained.

> Given the grammar of a language, one can study the use of the language statistically in various ways; and the development of probabilistic models for the use of language (as distinct from the syntactic structure of language) can be quite rewarding ... One might seek to develop a more elaborate relation between statistical and syntactic structure than the simple order of approximation model we have rejected. I would certainly not care to argue that any such relation is unthinkable, but I know of no suggestion to this effect that does not have serious flaws. (Chomsky 1957b: 17.n4)

In the excised section above, Chomsky cites recent work by Herbert A. Simon (1916–2001) (specifically, Simon 1955) and Benoit Mandelbrot (b. 1924) (specifically, Mandelbrot 1954) as specific examples of revealing statistical studies, and, as the above passage indicates, he is willing to accept that statistical analyses of linguistic structure can highlight significant patterns. However, he emphasises that these studies are primarily descriptive in intention and do not make elaborate claims about the actual mechanisms of language. For Chomsky, these sorts of concerns must be left for the linguists to discuss, since linguists are more inclined (than statisticians) to focus upon the actual properties of natural language, and therefore they are better able to resist the temptation to become obsessed with peripheral non-linguistic considerations.

5.3 From discovery to evaluation

As mentioned in the previous section, Chomsky's repeated assertion that grammar is autonomous was at least partly motivated by his belief that semantics and statistical considerations should not be involved in the definition of grammaticality, and it is this belief that enabled him to focus his attention exclusively upon syntactic phenomena during the 1950s. In this respect, Chomsky's work cannot really be distinguished from that of certain post-Bloomfieldians since, as discussed at length in section 3.7, several generations of linguists, from Bloomfield to Harris, had sought to provide syntactic analyses of grammatical utterances without recourse to considerations of meaning. In the context of this tradition, therefore, the tenor of Chomsky's research was unremarkable. Nevertheless, although Chomsky's focus on syntax was conventional, the manner in which he came to formulate the task of syntactic analysis in the mid-1950s was certainly provocative. As is well known, the basic development that Chomsky advocated was a general shift away from (overly restrictive) discovery procedures of the type favoured by Harris, towards evaluation procedures, such as the simplicity criteria discussed in section 4.3, which were designed to facilitate the task of selecting one of many competing grammars rather than to permit the creation of a grammar from scratch given a specific corpus. This basic development is well known and has been discussed extensively.[5] However, Chomsky's switch from discovery to evaluation procedures has never really been adequately considered in the light of his changing response to the kind of logical empiricism advocated by Goodman (in particular). Consequently, these aspects of Chomsky's work will be discussed here.

As mentioned in section 4.4, Chomsky's first published paper, 'SSA', appeared to suggest that he was contentedly working within a post-Bloomfieldian paradigm, since the point of that paper was to explore the possibility of utilising Goodman's calculus of individuals as a mechanical discovery procedure that could automate grammatical analysis. However, by the mid-1950s Chomsky's understanding of the general purpose and function of linguistic theory had clearly begun to change with the result that, between the appearance of 'SSA' in 1953 and the completion of the first draft of *LSLT* some time in early 1955, the emphasis of his research had shifted away from taxonomic discovery procedures towards the type of theory that would later be referred to as TGG. Chomsky's own account of this change in direction is well known but is still worth quoting in this context.

> By 1953 I came to the same conclusion [i.e., as Halle]: if the discovery procedures did not work, it was not because I had failed to formulate them correctly but because the entire approach was wrong. In retrospect I cannot understand why it took me so long to reach this conclusion – I remember exactly the moment when I finally felt convinced. On board ship in the mid-Atlantic, aided by a bout of seasickness, on a rickety tub that was listing noticeably – it had been sunk by the Germans and was now making its first voyage after having been salvaged. It suddenly seemed that there was a good reason – the obvious reason – why several years of intense effort devoted to improving discovery procedures had come to nought, while the work I had been doing during the same period on generative grammar and explanatory theory, in almost complete isolation, seemed to be consistently yielding interesting results. (Chomsky 1979a: 131)

Whatever the truth of this story (and whatever 'the obvious reason' might actually have been), the underlying causes of this general shift in perspective were many and various, though, certainly, the fact that 'several years of intense effort' had been (seemingly) wasted on discovery procedures could have provided the main motivation for the change. In addition, though, there is no doubt that the prioritising of evaluation over discovery procedures was partly prompted by Chomsky's evolving appreciation of the work of Goodman and Quine. In particular, during the early 1950s the type of hard-line Carnapian logical empiricism espoused by Goodman, and (seemingly) championed so assertively by Chomsky in 'SSA', ceased to impress him, and his increasing disillusion was apparently bolstered by his sympathy for the trenchant questioning of reductionist logical empiricism offered by Quine in 'Two Dogmas of Empiricism'. Chomsky's 1975 recollection of the general progress of his thinking during the formative years 1947–1955 was quoted in the introduction, but it will be reproduced here for ease of reference.[6]

> At Harris's suggestion I had begun to study logic, philosophy, and foundations of mathematics more seriously as a graduate student at the University of Pennsylvania, and later at Harvard. I was particularly impressed by Nelson Goodman's work on constructional systems. In its general character, this work was in some ways similar to Harris's, and seemed to me to provide the appropriate intellectual background for the investigation of taxonomic procedures that I then regarded as central to linguistic theory. But Goodman's ongoing critique of induction seemed to point in a rather different direction, suggesting the inadequacy in principle of inductive approaches. Goodman's investigation of the simplicity of systems also suggested (to me at least) possibilities for nontaxonomic approaches to linguistic theory. Quine's critique of logical empiricism also gave some reason to believe that this line of enquiry might be a plausible one. Quine argued that the principles of scientific theory are confronted with experience as a systematic complex, with adjustments possible at various points, governed by such factors as general simplicity. (Chomsky 1975[1955]: 33)

If these remarks can be trusted, then this passage is of particular interest since it reveals a considerable amount about the underlying philosophical motivations that prompted the development of TGG. Crucially, it identifies some of the causes for the dramatic shift away from the sort of empirical discovery procedures that had characterised post-Bloomfieldian linguistics, and which had provided the focus for Chomsky's own early work. Specifically, it is perhaps surprising that, in the above account of the development, Chomsky's motivation seems to have been primarily philosophical in origin rather than purely linguistic. As was discussed in section 3.5, ever since Carnap had formulated constructional system theory in the *LCW*, the use of such systems had been strongly associated with Carnapian logical empiricism, which, as a theoretical approach to the problem of knowledge acquisition, was (as the name suggests) fundamentally empirical, with objects in a given system (i.e., the *'Gegenstanden'*) being ultimately derived, by means of definition, from sensory experience. However, the above passage suggests (ironically) that Goodman's attempts in the early 1950s to justify the type of inductive procedures required by logical empiricism, combined with Quine's probing scepticism about empiricism in general, caused Chomsky to question the validity of the sort of inductive assumptions inherent in the standard taxonomic discovery procedures proposed by the post-Bloomfieldians. Although Chomsky does not give specific details, it is likely that he had Goodman's *Fact, Fiction and Forecast* (1954) in mind. As mentioned briefly in section 3.6, in this work Goodman discussed the role of induction in philosophical research and, consequently, was obliged to consider some of the difficulties associated with inductive procedures. In particular, the emphasis in his discussion was upon the task of prediction, and it should be recalled that Chomsky's nascent theory of TGG was specifically designed to accomplish the task of predicting all grammatical sentences in a given natural language, hence the relevance of Goodman's discussion to Chomsky's work. For Goodman (following David Hume (1711–1776)), one of the main issues that must be addressed was 'the question of how predictions are related to past experience' (Goodman 1954: 60), and he observes that 'the problem of justifying induction has called forth as much fruitless discussion as has any half-way respectable problem of modern philosophy' (Goodman 1954: 61). From the outset, then, the tone of Goodman's summary is negative, and he continues

> Understandably, then, more critical thinkers have suspected that there might be something wrong with the problem we are trying to solve. Come to think of it, what precisely would constitute the justification we seek? If the problem is to explain how we know that certain predictions will turn out to be correct, the sufficient answer is that we don't know any such thing. If the problem is to *find* some way of distinguishing antecedently between true and false predictions, we are asking for prevision rather than for philosophical explanation. (Goodman 1954: 62)

The clear implication of this overview is that inductive procedures are beset with real difficulties and, to provide a contrast, Goodman then considers 'non-inductive inferences' (i.e., deductive processes) and, in this case, the situation is less complex.

> How do we justify a *de*duction? Plainly by showing that it conforms to the general rules of deductive inference. An argument that so conforms is justified or valid, even if its conclusion happens to be false. An argument that violates a rule is fallacious, even if its conclusion happens to be true. To justify a deductive conclusion therefore requires no knowledge of the fact it pertains to. (Goodman 1954: 63)

Although Goodman then goes on to discuss the relationship between induction and deduction, and although the main point of the essays in *Fact, Fiction and Forecast* is to attempt to resolve some of the difficulties associated with inductive procedures, it is certainly possible that Goodman's critique of induction is sufficiently powerful to induce scepticism concerning its validity as a research method in the empirical sciences. Consequently, the above extracts (and other similar passages) from Goodman's argument, which were intended simply to provide the motivation for the development of an epistemic system of projections, could certainly appear to constitute an alarming condemnation of empiricism as a practical philosophy.

So much for Goodman's 'ongoing critique of induction'. As for Quine, his growing scepticism concerning logical empiricism was well expressed in *LPV*. In 'Two Dogmas of Empiricism' (the text Chomsky explicitly cited as an influence in 1975), for instance, Quine considers the nature of the relation between statements in natural language and the experiences that are involved in the confirmation of said statements. In this context, he continues,

> The most naïve view of the relation is that it is one of direct report. This is *radical reductionism*. Every meaningful statement is held to be translatable into a statement (true or false) about immediate experience ... So stated, the doctrine [i.e., of radical reductionism] remains ambiguous as between sense data as sensory events and sense data as sensory qualities; and it remains vague as to the admissible ways of compounding. Moreover, the doctrine is unnecessary and intolerably restrictive in its term-by-term critique which it imposes ... (Quine 1953: 38)

Having outlined his basic concerns in this general fashion, Quine then launches a blistering attack on logical empiricism, as practised by Carnap in *LCW* (and Goodman in *SA*, and Chomsky in 'SSA'), and his basic criticism is that the whole approach was 'left in a sketchy state' (Quine 1953: 40) since Carnap never adequately indicated how statements such as 'Quality q is at point-instant (x, y, z, t)' could ever be translated into the parsimonious initial language that consisted solely of logical axioms, extralogical primitives, and sense data. As a result, the whole methodology was flawed. It is important to emphasise, though, that Quine's purpose in his paper was to propose a modification of empirical philosophy, not entirely to reject it ('As an empiricist I continue to think of the conceptual scheme of science as a tool, ultimately, for predicting future experience in the light of past experience' (Quine 1953: 44)), and, in this respect, his position is similar to Goodman's concerning induction: both men destabilise aspects of empiricism and then proposed ways of rendering them more secure. As indicated in this brief summary, the critique of induction and logical empiricism that was developed in the work of Goodman and Quine would certainly have interested Chomsky in the early 1950s, given his experiments with constructional systems, and, as he himself acknowledged in 1975, Goodman's and Quine's arguments were partly responsible for propelling him towards the (now) more characteristic rationalist stance that he began publicly to adopt in the early 1960s. One consequence of the (often neglected) influence of Goodman and Quine upon Chomsky's work is that Chomsky's later well-known criticism of behaviourism should be reassessed. Indeed, it seems most likely that the robust rejection of behaviourism, which became one of the defining characteristics of the general philosophy of mind that underpinned research into generative grammar in the 1960s, actually had its roots in Chomsky's changing response to logical empiricism of the Carnapian variety.[7] Gradually, therefore, during the years 1953–1955 the focus of Chomsky's research began to shift away from pure post-Bloomfieldian methodologies and, as a result, he felt obliged to reassess the fundamental aims and purpose of linguistic theory in general.[8] Specifically, and in accordance with his rejection of inductive procedures, Chomsky was keen to simplify the basic task that linguists had set for themselves. To this end, in *SS* he defined three different approaches to the task of syntactic analysis, which he described as follows:

1. Discovery Procedure: 'the theory must provide a practical and mechanical method for actually constructing the grammar, given a corpus of utterances' (Chomsky 1957b: 50)
2. Decision Procedure: 'the theory must provide a practical and mechanical method for determining whether or not a grammar proposed for a given corpus is, in fact, the best grammar' (Chomsky 1957b: 50–51)
3. Evaluation Procedure: 'given a corpus and given two grammars G_1 and G_2, the theory must tell us which is the better grammar of the language from which the corpus is drawn' (Chomsky 1957b: 51)

and, having provided these definitions, Chomsky went on to state that

> The point of view adopted here is that it is unreasonable to demand of linguistic theory that it provide anything more than a practical evaluation procedure for grammars. That is, we adopt the weakest of the three positions described above. As I interpret most of the careful proposals for the development of linguistic theory, they attempt to state methods of analysis that an investigator might actually use, if he had the time, to construct a grammar of a language directly from the raw data. I think that it is very questionable that this goal is attainable in any interesting way, and I suspect that any attempt to meet it will lead to a maze of more and more elaborate and more complex analysis procedures that will fail to provide answers for many important questions about linguistic structure. (Chomsky 1957b: 52–53)

The thrust of Chomsky's argument, then, was that while the mechanical production of a grammar by means of discovery procedures may be a desirable accomplishment, it may simply be impossible to achieve, whereas a less ambitious approach could actually provide 'answers'. As Chomsky indicates, the fundamental difference between the three positions can be simply stated as the privileging of evaluation procedures (i.e., the selection of one grammar from amongst many, given a particular corpus) over either discovery or decision procedures (i.e., either the automatic inferring of a grammar from a given corpus, or the automatic assessment of the validity of a grammar), and the advice is to focus upon the relativistic exploration of the validity of competing grammars, rather than upon the notion of absolute correctness. As noted in section 4.3, Goodman's research into simplicity measures for constructional system theory partly motivated this reassessment of the linguist's task by considering the relative simplicity of the extralogical components in various competing systems. In addition, it should also be obvious that the task Chomsky came to advocate was the least empirical of the three tasks defined; a change that can be viewed as a manifestation of his response to Goodman's and Quine's critiques of induction and logical empiricism respectively.

Whatever the precise nature of the influences that prompted his revisions, there is no doubt that Chomsky actively set about redefining the goal of linguistics (and especially syntactic theory) in *LSLT*, a work in which the rejection of inductive discovery procedures is clearly stated. The avoidance of a purely nominalistic constructional methodology is signalled early in the book when Chomsky explains that, although such an approach is 'more natural' than the analytic framework adopted in *LSLT*, it will not be further developed because it necessitates the use of 'somewhat more elaborate constructions' (Chomsky 1975[1955]: 110); a remark that recalls Quine's complaint concerning the 'unnecessarily and intolerably restrictive' (Quine 1953: 38) methods required by the more extreme forms of logical empiricism. Nevertheless, despite this unambiguous change of direction, it is equally apparent that *LSLT* is securely rooted in constructional system theory. Indeed, it is a curious aspect of the development of TGG that, although the basic philosophy of inductive logical empiricism was spurned during the years 1953–1955, the technical devices associated with constructional system theory continued to be utilised extensively. Somehow, the rejection of the philosophy underpinning the theory did not invalidate the tools it provided, and, as will be shown in section 5.4, Chomsky continued to use and develop the core formal procedures, adapting them to the task of linguistic analysis.

5.4 Constructional levels

It was suggested in the preceding section that Chomsky's changing understanding of the implications of Goodman's strict logical empiricism, and his appreciation of Quine's critique of the same, caused him to reconsider the empirical aspects of syntactic analysis. Accordingly, he came to reject the standard taxonomic methodologies, favouring instead evaluation procedures that enabled a linguist automatically to choose between competing grammars. This rejection of Goodman-style empiricist concerns, and the corresponding disenchantment with the type of approach to syntactic analysis outlined in 'SSA', could have caused Chomsky to eradicate all vestiges of his early (and brief) constructive nominalist phase from his later work. In the event, this did not occur. For instance, in section 4.3 it was shown that considerations of grammatical simplicity continued to feature prominently in his work during the years 1953–1957, although his ideas concerning the purpose and function of grammatical analysis changed throughout this period. As another example, in this section the basic definition of a linguistic level as presented in *LSLT* is considered, and it will be shown that the influence of constructional system theory is still apparent even in his post-1954 work. If the following discussion demonstrates anything, it demonstrates Chomsky's remarkable ability to detach a useful procedure from its philosophical context and employ it with few subsequent qualms.

Throughout *LSLT* it is emphasised that there are three main tasks that confront the 'descriptive linguist' (Chomsky 1975[1955]: 77). These three tasks can be summarised as (i) the task of creating a general theory of linguistic structure, (ii) the task of constructing grammars for particular languages, and (iii) the task of justifying and validating experimental results, and they provide the main motivation for the type of theoretical approach to linguistic analysis adopted in the book. It is crucial to recognise (as Chomsky repeatedly asserts throughout the text) that, although the above tasks are distinct, they are not entirely independent, and therefore impinge upon one other to a considerable extent. For instance, the general theory of linguistic structure adopted for analysis will largely determine the nature of the resultant grammar that is ultimately constructed; and vice versa. With this interconnection in mind, Chomsky describes the fundamental problem of general linguistic theory as follows:

> A language is an enormously complex system. Linguistic theory attempts to reduce the immense complexity to manageable proportions by the construction of a system of *linguistic levels*, each of which makes a certain descriptive apparatus available for the characterisation of linguistic structure. (Chomsky 1975[1955]: 63)

In other words, the essential task is to create an hierarchical system, composed of various interrelated linguistic levels, that permits the analysis of natural language into basic units of some kind. The assumption is that simple regularities underlie the apparent surface complexity of all natural languages and, clearly, this type of method for analysing linguistic structure is a form of reductionism. Indeed, Chomsky freely acknowledges that the particular methodology developed in *LSLT* is characterised by 'a *strong kind* of reductionism'(Chomsky 1975[1955]: 85, italics added). However, as the above passage suggests, the sort of system required in order to reduce the full complexity of natural language to single components must be fundamentally hierarchical. This fact stresses the difference between the project proposed in *LSLT* and that outlined in 'SSA' (and discussed in section 4.4): while the earlier work was concerned exclusively with one level of linguistic analysis, the morphemic level, the latter is concerned with the attempt to develop a comprehensive analytic framework for the whole of language, hence the need for *multiple* linguistic levels. While acknowledging that the exact number of levels required in an exhaustively hierarchical linguistic theory is a contentious issue, Chomsky maintains that such a theory needs a minimum of six levels. These are abbreviated as **Pn** (the phonemic level), **M** (the morphemic level), **W** (the word level), **C** (the syntactic category level), **P** (the phrase-structure level), and **T** (the transformational level). In an abstract presentation, the schematic representation of each of the above is the same, since any linguistic level, **L**, can be defined as an independent system which contains the following components:

$$\mathbf{L} = [L, \frown, R_1, \ldots, R_m, \mu, \Phi, \phi_1, \ldots, \phi_n] \tag{5.7}$$

where

- L is a set of primes (i.e., level-specific primitive elements).
- $\frown$ is the concatenation relation.
- $R_1, \ldots, R_m$ are classes and relations defined within **L**.
- μ is a set of **L**-markers (i.e., elements created at level **L**).
- Φ is a mapping which, in particular, maps μ into the set of grammatical utterances.
- $\phi_1, \ldots, \phi_n$ are relations that express the relationship between **L** and all the other n levels.

It is clear from the above definition that at the core of any linguistic level there is a set of primitive elements (the primes) and various sets of relations. Of these relations, though, only the concatenation relation is primitive, and therefore Chomsky later observes that 'we have provided only one way of constructing elements in **L'** (Chomsky 1975[1955]: 107). Since mathematical logic is assumed as the basis of any general theory of linguistic structure (just as it is usually assumed as the basis of *any* scientific theory (see Chomsky 1975[1955]: 87)), the various primes, and the primitive concatenation relation associated with a given linguistic level, $\mathbf{L}_n$, can be viewed as the extralogical basis of a constructional system. Therefore, the general theory of linguistic structure proposed in *LSLT* extensively utilises an hierarchy of independent (though interrelated) constructional systems. Objects created at a given level, $\mathbf{L}_n$, using the level-specific primes and relations can be associated with objects on other levels by means of the mapping function, Φ, but the various levels are essentially distinct since objects existing at a specific level are created at that level. To consider a specific example, the linguistic level **Pn** contains a finite and fixed set of primes, which are phonetic symbols ($p_1, \ldots, p_n$), and various relations including the basic concatenation relation '$\frown$'. Therefore, if p_1 and p_2 are two primes in **Pn**, then the object '$p_1 \frown p_2$' is constructed by concatenating the two primes to form a sequence of primes. In this fashion, larger objects, or L-markers, can be constructed at each level in accordance with the basic principles of constructional system theory. It is revealing, incidentally, to note the presence of 'classes' (i.e., sets) in the definition of a level. The inclusion of such abstract entities once again underlines the difference between the nominalistic methodology adopted in 'SSA' and the freer, less restrictive, linguistic theory presented in *LSLT*, which willingly embraces abstract concepts of certain kinds.

In passing, it is worth emphasising that the use of concatenation as the basic primitive relation for the linguistic levels reveals the direct influence of Quine. As mentioned in section 3.5, Quine had explored the role of concatenation in formal language theory in the 1940s, and had claimed that the whole of arithmetic could be founded upon this single relation. He had made his ideas available in chapter 7 of his text *Mathematical Logic* (especially the revised second edition, published in 1951), and this text provided Chomsky with an important source of information concerning the core techniques of formal logic (as did chapter 4 of Paul Rosenbloom's *Elements of Mathematical Logic*). However, Chomsky borrowed more than concatenation from Quine. For example, the definition of 'occurrence' given in *LSLT* is taken unaltered from Quine's book (compare Chomsky 1975[1955]: 109 and Quine 1951: 297), and these borrowings indicate the full extent to which Quine's presentation of symbolic logic was influencing the type of formal linguistic theory that Chomsky was in the process of developing. Once again, this fact should prompt a reconsideration of Chomsky's views concerning logic and natural language. In section 4.5 it was shown that, following Harris, he discouraged the identification of linguistics with logic, questioning Bar-Hillel's advocation of Carnap's observation that linguists and logicians differ in 'degree' rather than in 'kind'. However, as his adaptation of Quinean concatenation and occurrence indicate, he was happy to make use of techniques from logic that were deemed to facilitate the analysis of natural language in its own terms. Indeed, as should be clear by now, constructional system theory itself was securely rooted in *PM*-style logic, so Chomsky's use of techniques from this theory in *LSLT* indicates the way in which he was willing to adapt logic-based procedures and incorporate them into the system he was constructing in order to analyse natural language.

5.5   Transforming transformations

The preceding section indicated that the influence of Goodman and Quine was still very much present in Chomsky's work from the mid-1950s despite his apparent rejection of Goodmanesque logical empiricism. However, other aspects of TGG can also be considered in relation to some of the developments in the formal sciences discussed in chapter 3. One such notion is the use of so-called 'transformations'. As mentioned in section 5.4, the 'transformational' part of TGG was one of its most influential characteristics, and this alone necessitates a consideration of the various ways in which the term 'transformation' was used in Chomsky's work from the period 1955–1957. A considerable amount of attention has been devoted to this topic over the years, and the main emphasis has usually been upon establishing the priority either of Harris' or Chomsky's use of the term.[9] While such investigations are undeniably entertaining, a more stimulating assessment can be provided if other sources of influence are considered. Therefore, while Harris' use of the term will be mentioned below, the issue of priority will not really be addressed. Rather, the intention is to examine the way in which Carnap's 'transformation rules' were transformed into Chomsky's 'transformations' during the 1950s. Carnap's use of formation and transformation rules was discussed at length in section 3.7, and it should be recalled that, in Carnap's system, the former are involved in creating sentences while the latter are essentially rules of logical inference that enable one sentence to be inferred from another. However, as will be shown below, the term came to be used in linguistics literature in a bewildering range of different ways.

Chomsky first uses the term 'transformation' in *MMH*, and, in particular, he makes extensive use of 'transformation statements' (Chomsky 1979b[1951]: 6), which constitute a key component of the type of grammar constructed in his thesis. Indeed, one component of the grammar presented there is described as 'a series of morphological and morphophonemic statements transforming any grammatical sequence of morphemes into a sequence of phonemes' (Chomsky 1979b[1951]: 4). So important are these statements to the grammatical formalism that Chomsky develops that he later defines a grammar entirely in terms of such statements: 'the grammar, then, will be a set of transformation statements each of which transforms a given representation of a sentence into a more specific one' (Chomsky 1979b[1951]: 6). Admittedly, as a definition of a grammar, this statement is rather vague, and, in recognition of this fact, Chomsky immediately starts to introduce the formal notation that he uses throughout the thesis. The basic transformation statements take the form '$\alpha \rightarrow \beta$', where α and β 'contain no notational elements but are simply sequences of the elements set up to represent parts of sentences (phonemes, morphemes etc.)' (Chomsky 1979b[1951]: 6). In addition, conditions can be imposed upon these transformations in order to restrict their scope. For instance, if $\alpha = \alpha_1 \beta_1 \gamma$ and $\beta = \alpha_1 \beta_1' \gamma$, then the corresponding transformation rule would be

$$\alpha_1 \beta_1 \gamma \rightarrow \alpha_1 \beta_1' \gamma \tag{5.8}$$

and this conversion could be written in the form

$$\beta_1 \rightarrow \beta_1', \text{ in environment } \alpha_1 - \gamma \tag{5.9}$$

where the context that determines the modification of β_1 is indicated in (5.9) as a general condition. In this way, key relationships between sequences of elements can be precisely stated in a concise fashion. It is of interest that some of the symbols Chomsky used in his transformation statements, particularly his use of the symbol '$\rightarrow$', recall some of the notations used in standard expositions of Hilbert's proof theory. For instance, although Hilbert himself usually employed the symbol '$\supset$' for implication, the symbol '$\rightarrow$' was commonly used for this in the sort of textbooks discussed in section 2.8, and, as a result, there is an apparent association, both in terms of symbolism and basic concept, between Chomskyan transformation statements and Hilbert's proof-schema given as (2.10) above. Essentially, in both cases, a string of symbols is obtained from another string of symbols by means of a formal mapping procedure. Consequently, in the following discussion the Chomskyan transformations will sometimes be referred to as rules of (quasi-)inference.

Harris' public use of the term 'transformation' apparently dates from 1952 when, in his paper 'Discourse Analysis', he included a section that considered the topic of 'grammatical transformations'. In this part of his discussion, Harris introduces two types of transformation, those that operate upon classes of morphemes and those that operate upon single morphemes, and both types are presented as ways of incorporating information from outside the text into the task of analysing a discourse. Harris' intention was basically to define equivalence classes in order 'to discover patterned (i.e., similar or partly similar) combinations of these classes in successive intervals of the text' (Harris 1952: 18–19). Consequently, the notation Harris uses is different from that which Chomsky had employed since, rather than employing a symbol that denotes some kind of (quasi-)inference, Harris simply uses the equality operator to enable him to state equivalences. For instance, in Harris' formalism, the equivalence of active–passive pairs enables sentences such as 'Casals plays the cello' to be considered equal to sentences such as 'The cello is played by Casals', and, in formal notation, Harris defines this equivalence as follows:

$$N_1 V N_2 = N_2 \text{ is } V - \text{en by } N_1 \qquad (5.10)$$

Equivalences such as (5.10) define grammatical transformations of various kinds, which Harris then uses to accomplish the task of discourse analysis.

So far, then, three different types of transformation have been considered (i.e., Carnap's logical inferences, Chomsky's context-dependent (quasi-)inferential statements, and Harris' equivalences) and the complex relationship between these different types was recognised during the 1950s by other linguists. As ever, Bar-Hillel's interdisciplinary background enabled him to perceive some of the connections that other linguists, less familiar with recent developments in logical analysis, may have missed. For instance, in his 1954 paper (discussed at length in section 4.5), Bar-Hillel explicitly considers Carnap's formation and transformation rules and regrets the fact that, while the former have been studied by linguists with reference to natural language, the latter have been almost entirely neglected. He refers to Harris' work in particular and notes that, although Harris uses the term 'transformation', the equivalence statements that he employs are actually formation rules, in the Carnapian sense:

> A recent attempt by Harris to reduce the transformational part of syntax to its formational part is based on a series of equivocations in the terms *language*, *equivalent*, *commutable* and their cognates, and so is without foundation. (Bar-Hillel 1954: 237)

The precise nature of the supposed 'equivocations' that Bar-Hillel identified in Harris' work is not of primary concern here, nor indeed is it discussed in Bar-Hillel's paper. What is of greater interest is Bar-Hillel's general identification of the type of distributional equivalence statements that Harris employed with Carnapian *formation* rules. For Bar-Hillel, at least, Harris' transformations were not the same as Carnapian transformations, since, as mentioned above, the latter are essentially rules of logical inference, while Harris' statements cannot obviously be classified as rules of this kind. Since it is known that Harris was familiar with Carnap's *LSL*, and since (presumably) he understood the structure of the logical system presented in that text, it is either to be assumed that Harris actually believed that his grammatical transformations defined rules of inference (which is unlikely), or else that he was consciously adapting a term taken from logical syntax and redefining it within the context of linguistic analysis. The latter alternative seems to be the most reasonable option, partly because (as indicated in section 3.7) Harris was adamant that logicians and linguists studied different things, and partly because (as stated above) Harris' transformations are not presented as if they were rules of inference. Also, revealingly, Harris never cites Carnap as a direct source for his use of the term 'transformation'. Indeed, he generally implied that his own use of the concept was developed to facilitate the analysis of utterances in natural language. For instance, writing in 1957, he observed that 'the study of transformations arose out of the attempt to construct a method for analysing language samples longer than a sentence' (Harris 1957: 283.n1), implying that a concern with discourse structure analysis provided the main inspiration. Obviously, this does not exclude the possibility that he knowingly adapted terminology that he had first encountered in the logical syntax literature, but his silence concerning this matter is curious nonetheless.

Bar-Hillel's interpretation of Carnap's transformation rules was reinforced in Chomsky's 1955 response (also discussed at length in section 4.5), providing further evidence to support the idea that, as far as linguists familiar with recent developments in logic were concerned, Carnapian transformations did indeed constitute rules of logical inference. For instance, while summarising Bar-Hillel's argument, Chomsky himself considers the nature of Carnapian formation and transformation rules. He observes that, for Carnap, the notion of formal consequence is given as a primitive in the system he constructs and, while indicating that such an assumption would not contribute to the task of analysing natural language, he comments that 'the transformation rules of logic are rules of valid inference; hence in this discussion the terms "inference" and "transformation" will be used interchangeably' (Chomsky 1955a: 37.n4). The phrase 'transformation rules of logic' is revealing, since the implication is that Chomsky was already thinking of linguistic transformations as being different kinds of formal devices from those encountered in logical syntax, and it should be remembered that, as mentioned above, the 'transformation statements' used in *MMH* were certainly not strictly rules of valid inference. A slight confusion occurs, though, when Chomsky goes on to consider Harris' grammatical transformations. Since he has declared that the word 'transformation' will be used interchangeably with the word 'inference', does it follow that he understands Harris' equivalence statements to be rules of inference, or is it the case that the adjective 'grammatical' is intended to indicate that linguistic, and not logical, transformations are being discussed here? Ambiguities such as these are prevalent in the various papers from this period that discuss transformations. What is clear, however, is that, by the mid-1950s, the active–passive relation had come to be the focus of attention when grammatical transformations were being discussed, and certainly this relation would continue to be associated with transformations in the TGG framework outlined in *LSLT* and *SS*.

So far, the topic of transformations has been discussed with reference to the work of Harris, Bar-Hillel, and Chomsky. However, it is crucial to recognise that the notion of linguistic transformations had begun to spread throughout the linguistics community by the mid-1950s, and this dissemination of ideas seems to have been partly inspired by Bar-Hillel's 1954 paper, which had advocated the exploration of Carnapian transformation rules within the context of natural language analysis. Not surprisingly, this suggestion appears to have resonated with mathematically minded linguists in particular. For instance, in his 1955 paper (already discussed in section 3.2 in a different context), Harwood explicitly responded to Bar-Hillel's plea for Carnapian transformations to be used in linguistic research, and, at the start of this paper, he unambiguously outlined his intentions as follows:

> Given a morpheme list for a language, the aim of a syntactic system is to tell us how to put together the sequences of morphemes which are used as sentences in the language. Such directions we shall call the FORMATION RULES. Additionally, works on syntax usually give a certain amount of information about the equivalences between some sequences and others, e.g. that *John discovered the path = The path was discovered by John*. We shall call such statements TRANSFORMATION RULES. Only a small part of the transformation rules is covered in syntax; some others are discussed in mathematical logic, e.g. Russell's theory of descriptions, procedures of generalisation and abstraction. So far in mathematical logic, most attention has been directed to developing formation and transformation rules of artificial languages, and no complete treatment has yet been made of the transformation rules of natural language. (Harwood 1955: 409)

The passage raises a number of issues that have already been discussed, and it indicates how these issues were considered to be deeply interconnected at the time. For instance, in the above passage we encounter the (by now familiar) belief that techniques from logic can be usefully employed when natural language is analysed, as well as the basic Carnapian distinction between formation and transformation rules. However, for Harwood, Harris' equivalences are indeed considered to be transformations of the Carnapian type, contrary to Bar-Hillel's assertion discussed above. Indeed, the basic difference between the two kinds of rules, as far as Harwood is concerned, is that formation rules are used to construct sentences, while transformation rules are used to modify the form of those sentences. There are clear parallels between this view of syntactic analysis and the mature theory of TGG, with its deep structure and surface structure levels, that Chomsky was then in the process of constructing. Once again, therefore, this serves to emphasise the extent to which particular concepts and techniques that eventually came to be associated with TGG were already spreading throughout the linguistics community, albeit in an imprecisely articulated form, by the mid-1950s.

Given the above discussion, it is necessary to consider the way in which Chomsky began to use the term 'transformation' between the years 1955–1957, and it is worth noting that he used it conspicuously, since (as indicated earlier) chapter 7 of *LSLT*, which he submitted as his Ph.D. thesis in 1955, was called 'Transformational Analysis'. As is well known, the transformational level of syntactic analysis presented in *LSLT* was motivated by perceived limitations in phrase structure analysis. For instance, Chomsky explicitly discusses particular constructions that the phrase structure component struggles to deal with, and these include (for example) yes-or-no questions and active–passive pairs.[10] The central idea behind the transformational component, as developed in *LSLT*, was that the transformational rules would operate upon the lowest-level strings of symbols output by the phrase structure component (i.e., the set $\bar{P}$ which consists of morphological heads and syntactically functioning affixes). In the sections on phrase structure analysis (i.e, chapter 7), Chomsky has already introduced ρ_1-derivations and **P**-markers; the former constitute the set of grammatical strings that consist of terminal symbols, and the latter encode a phrase structure analysis of the grammatical strings. Consequently, at the start of chapter 9, Chomsky summarises the fundamentals of transformational analysis as follows:

> We are thus led to develop a new level of syntactic analysis, the level **T** of transformations, and to assign **T**-markers to strings of words as markers of their 'transformational history'. That is, the **T**-markers of a string of words will tell us how this string is derived from a certain *kernel* of sentences which have ρ_1-derivations and **P**-markers. In terms of previous levels we can represent each sentence as a string of phonemes, words, syntactic categories, and, in various ways, as strings of phrases. Now we will be able to represent a sentence as a sequence of operations by which this sentence is derived from the kernel

of basic sentences, each such sequence of operations corresponding to a T-marker. (Chomsky 1975[1955]: 306)

This passage emphasises the fact that, as already indicated above, the transformations used in TGG operate upon existing strings of symbols (i.e., kernel sentences) and modify their structure in precisely specified ways. It is the need to restrict the applicability of the various transformations that leads Chomsky to specify three basic conditions - namely, **C1**, **C2**, and **C3** – which apply to the set of grammatical transformations. These conditions can be defined as follows (compare Chomsky 1975[1955]: 311):

> **C1** A grammatical transformation T is defined on ordered pairs (Z, K) where (a) Z and $T(Z, K)$ are strings in $\bar{P}$, (b) K is a set of strings in $\mathbf{P}$, and Z is a member of K.
> Thus T operates on a string Z of P, with the analysis given by K, and produces a new string of P which is denoted '$(T(Z, K))$'.
> **C2** $T(Z, K)$ is unique; that is, T is a single-valued mapping.
> **C3** The domain of each T is limited to strings of a certain structure. This limitation can be effected by associating with each T a finite *restricting class* Q of sequences of strings.

The purpose of each of these conditions is broadly as follows: **C1** specifies the elements that can be contained in the domain and range of a given transformation; **C2** ensures that only a single-valued mapping from a given ordered pair (i.e., (Z, K)) in the domain to a unique string in the range (i.e., in the set $\bar{P}$) is allowed; and **C3** ensures that each transformation applies only to a particular subsection of the potential domain. In summary, then, a given grammatical transformation, T, operates upon a string, Z, which has constituent interpretation K (which may or may not be a **P**-marker), and it converts it into a string, Z', which has interpretation K'. The transformation T is restricted so that it only operates upon a subset of the possible sets of pairs (Z, K), and this subset is determined by the restricting class Q.

Turning from abstract theory to the actual mire of English, in chapter 10 of *LSLT* Chomsky attempts to demonstrate that transformations can facilitate the analysis of English grammar. In particular, he identifies certain 'elementary transformations' (Chomsky 1975[1955]: 404) which involve specific modifications to kernel strings. For instance, the deformation transformation, δ, either deletes or adds a constant string to certain terms in a given string. Similarly, the permutation transformation, π, simply alters the order of the terms in a given string. In order to clarify how these elementary transformations operate, consider the case of π (and compare the discussion in Chomsky 1975[1955]:

404–405). Given a string $Y_1 - \ldots - Y_n$, the transformation π can be represented as

$$\pi^*(Y_1, \ldots, Y_n) = Y_{a_1} \frown \ldots \frown Y_{a_n} \qquad (5.11)$$

where $(a_1, \ldots, a_n)$ is a permutation of the integers $(1, \ldots, n)$. In addition, for each i, the following equivalence holds

$$(Y_1, \ldots, Y_i; Y_i, \ldots, Y_n) = Y_{a_i} \qquad (5.12)$$

Consequently, π is completely characterised by the sequence of integers $B = (a_1, \ldots, a_n)$. To give a concrete example, if $Y_1 - Y_2 - Y_3$ indicates the morpheme sequence '*he - can - come*', then the permutation transformation $\pi^*(Y_1, Y_2, Y_3) = Y_2 \frown Y_1 \frown Y_3$ enables the string '*can - he - come*' to be obtained. As this example indicates, the transformations in TGG essentially map **P**-markers into **P**-markers in a principled manner, and, as is well known, in his subsequent discussion Chomsky develops specific transformations that facilitate the analysis of a wide range of basic structures in English (e.g., yes-or-no questions, *wh*-questions, passives and so on).

Although transformations have been discussed primarily in an abstract fashion above, and a single example of a permutation transformation has been considered, it should be noted that the passive transformation receives considerable attention both in *LSLT* and *SS*, where it is discussed in relation to the phrase structure kernel.[11] While the basic difference between Chomsky's transformation rules and Harris' equivalence statements was discussed above, it is worth mentioning that during the years 1955–1957 Chomsky was keen to stress the difference between his approach and that of Harris; and it is particularly important to emphasise this since Harris had also used his transformations to effect an analysis of active–passive sentence pairs. As an example of Chomsky's desire to indicate the difference between his approach and that adopted by Harris, in *SS* he explicitly observes that Harris' use of transformation rules constituted 'a somewhat different approach to transformational analysis' (Chomsky 1957b: 44), though he refrains from exhaustively enumerating the differences between the two theories.

While assessing the deployment of transformations in TGG, and given the discussion of simplicity criteria in section 4.3, it is necessary to emphasise that, in *LSLT*, Chomsky repeatedly stresses the fact that a grammar with a transformational component is inherently simpler than a grammar that lacks such a component. In other words, as far as Chomsky is concerned, considerations of simplicity partly motivate the use of transformational rules. For instance, at the start of his formal development of transformational analysis, Chomsky states:

> I will try to show that a theory of transformations can provide a unified and quite natural approach to all the problems mentioned in [earlier sections], and that it can result in syntactic description which is considerably more economical and revealing. (Chomsky 1975[1955]: 307)

As ever, the key word here is 'economical': in the event, Chomsky is keen to demonstrate that the use of transformations greatly simplifies the proposed grammar since it enables all types of recursion to be eliminated from the phrase structure component. This important topic is discussed in greater detail in section 5.6.

As the foregoing discussion indicates, the confusion concerning the nature and purpose of grammatical transformations was widespread, and the relationship between the transformations employed by Harris, Chomsky, Harwood, and others, and those utilised by Carnap and his fellow logicians provided the main focus for discussions of such topics throughout the 1950s. By the early 1960s the situation seems to have become slightly clearer, mainly because Chomsky's detailed grammatical formalisms provided secure definitions of the terms as used in the mature theory of TGG. For instance, writing in 1963, Bar-Hillel indicated that, while he was personally convinced of the importance of TGG-style transformation rules, he felt obliged to re-emphasise the fact that they were not 'transformation' rules in the Carnapian sense, but rather 'formation' rules (again in the Carnapian sense). Indeed, as far as Bar-Hillel was concerned, they were a new kind of formation rule which permitted the analysis and description of 'many more linguistic facts than I had originally thought' (Bar-Hillel 1963: 542). However, as a result of the terminological confusion, Bar-Hillel felt obliged to offer the following words of caution:

> those formation rules that can handle these facts are of a type which has only recently been analysed and understood ... It is interesting that this novel type of formation rules has been called by Harris and Chomsky (and is now being called by everyone else) 'rules of transformation', and the reader should beware of the confusion. (Bar-Hillel 1963: 543)

Confusion is perhaps an understatement. Throughout the period 1951–1957 the word 'transformation' is used in a wide variety of ways, and it is not always a simple task to determine the precise connotations that the term was intended to imply. Somehow, from out of this general haze, TGG emerged in the late 1950s as a coherent, identifiable theory which used well-defined rules that were called 'transformations'. As the years passed, the relationship between these rules and those proposed by Carnap became a less pressing issue, and the original terminological complexities were forgotten. The purpose of the above discussion, however, has been partly to revive something of the original chaos. To summarise therefore, it seems likely that the transformations developed by Harris and Chomsky were related to the transformation rules presented in (the English translation of) Carnap's *LSL*. However, since Harris' grammatical equivalences and Chomsky's transformations are not obviously rules of valid inference, they must be viewed as formation rules from a Carnapian perspective (the perspective consistently adopted by Bar-Hillel). However, as Harwood's work shows, during the 1950s transformation rules came generally to refer to rules that operated upon complete sentences that had been generated by other rules, with the transformations causing modifications to the order of the elements in the existing sentences. Obviously, it was this kind of transformation that came to characterise Chomsky's work in the years 1955–1957 (and beyond).

5.6 Recursive rules

As shown in the previous section, the origins of the technical devices that came to be referred to as 'transformations', and which played such a crucial role in the development of TGG, can be traced back to advances in logical syntax that were largely due to Carnap, who, in turn, had been profoundly influenced by (Hilbertian) Formalism. Appropriately, the same is also true of the 'generative' aspects of TGG. It was mentioned in section 3.3 that recursive functions became central to Hilbert's proof theory when it was recognised that they were essential elements in finitistic proofs, and that research into the nature of recursion resulted in the general theory of recursive functions, with associated developments such as the theory of recursively enumerable sets. Similarly, in the same section, it was shown that Kleene's discussion of recursive definitions was adapted by Bar-Hillel and considered in the context of grammatical analysis in the early 1950s. The main consequence of this work was that recursive definitions came to be explored within the broad framework of syntactic theory, and, eventually, they came to provide a core component of the TGG formalism. The course of this gradual development must now be considered.

Not surprisingly, recursion is a crucial factor in TGG for the same reason it is a crucial factor in finitistic proofs; namely, it provides a way of analysing the (potentially) infinite in terms of the finite. Specifically, during the 1950s syntacticians began to re-emphasise the fact that, although the grammar of a given natural language must itself necessarily be finite, it must also be able to produce a potentially infinite number of sentences, and this observation prompted the basic conceptual shift away from post-Bloomfieldian corpora-based analytical discovery procedures that iteratively decomposed given linguistic complexes into their constituent parts, towards a synthetic or 'generative' grammar that iteratively produced all the grammatical sentences of a given language using a given lexicon, a finite set of initial assumptions, and certain formal devices. Consequently, the problem for syntactic theory became one of constructing a potentially infinite number of sentences using finite procedures and, clearly, the theory of recursive functions offered a simple mechanism for achieving this. It is important to realise, however, that the post-Bloomfieldian tradition prepared the way for such a development by emphasising the predictive nature of the grammars obtained from analytical procedures. In other words, discovery procedures were often only considered valid if the resultant grammar could be successfully transferred to new corpora, and Hockett, in particular, emphasised this requirement.[12] Once again, therefore, from this perspective, TGG can be viewed as the logical outcome of one particular branch of the post-Bloomfieldian research programme. Accordingly, in 'TMDL' Chomsky emphasised the desirability of predictive formal grammars, and stated plainly that a TGG-style approach to syntactic analysis requires some kind of recursive component in order to construct the full range of possible grammatical sentences: 'If a grammar has no recursive steps ... it will be prohibitively complex ... If it does have recursive devices, it will produce infinitely many sentences' (Chomsky 1956: 116). In particular, Post's theory of recursively enumerable sets, described in section 3.3, provided a useful framework that could be adapted for the purposes of theoretical syntax. As mentioned previously, the intuition behind Post's theory was that all the elements belonging to a recursively enumerable set are in the range of a general recursive function, and, in a 1959 paper, Chomsky explained why such sets were important to the basic TGG framework.

> Since any language in which we are likely to be interested is an infinite set, we can investigate the structure of **L** only through the study of the finite devices (grammars) which are capable of enumerating its sentences. A grammar of **L** can be regarded as a function whose range is exactly **L**. Such devices have been called 'sentence-generating grammars'. (Chomsky 1959a: 137)

This passage indicates that, in mature TGG, the set of grammatical sentences, **L**, is considered to be an infinite set of sentences, the elements of which can be generated by the function, g, where g constitutes the grammar of the language **L**. It is worth noting that (as indicated in section 3.3) even the terminology used here reveals the connection between the theories: Post frequently used the verb 'generate' in order to describe how a recursively enumerable set is obtained from its associated general recursive function, and Chomsky explicitly acknowledges this terminological source, suggesting that he adapted these techniques directly from Post's work. In a footnote following his use of the phrase 'sentence-generating grammars', Chomsky adds:

> Following a familiar technical use of the term 'generate' cf. Post (1944). The locution has, however, been misleading, since it has erroneously been interpreted as indicating that such sentence-generating grammars consider language from the point of view of the speaker rather than the hearer. Actually such grammars take a completely neutral point of view. Compare Chomsky ([1957b], p.48). We can consider a grammar of **L** to be a function mapping the integers onto **L**, order of enumeration being immaterial (and easily specifiable, in many ways) to this purely syntactic study ... (Chomsky 1959a: 137.n1)

This passage indicates that Post's work concerning recursively enumerable sets was 'familiar' to Chomsky, and that the latter knowingly adapted the terminology that the former had deployed. This fact should be borne in mind throughout the following discussion since it is crucial to recognise that Chomsky was familiar with Post's own research and did not simply obtain his ideas concerning recursively enumerable sets from later expositions of the theory.

The above discussion indicates that TGG, as it was presented in the 1950s, required 'recursive devices' (Chomsky 1956: 116) in order to generate an infinite number of sentences from a finite grammar, and, although Post provided some kind of impetus for this assumption, Chomsky's ideas concerning these topics were also directly influenced by the work of Bar-Hillel. For instance, as noted previously, Chomsky had remarked in 'LSS' that

> At one point, Bar-Hillel suggests that recursive definitions may be useful in linguistic theory; whether this turns out to be the case or not, I agree in this instance with the spirit of his remarks. (Chomsky 1955a: 45)

It is no surprise, then, that recursive techniques were used extensively in TGG, and the recursive aspects of the theory are meticulously presented in *LSLT*. In order to clarify the following discussion, two different types of recursion in TGG will be considered. The first type involves the successive application of the sequentially ordered rules of the grammar, while the second type involves the inclusion of rules within the grammar which are themselves recursive by definition. Both types will now be assessed in turn.

In chapter 7 of *LSLT* Chomsky elaborates his basic theory of the phrase structure component of the grammar; in particular, he proposes that this component can be specified as a sequence of conversions of the familiar form '$X \rightarrow Y$', and he refers to this type of formulation as 'a linear grammar' (Chomsky

Recursive rules 171

1975[1955]: 194). However, Chomsky is quick to note that the finite nature of a linear grammar requires the sequence of rules to be applied iteratively.

> The linear grammar is a sequence of conversion statements $S_1, \ldots, S_n$, where each S_i is of the form $X_i \rightarrow Y_i$. We can produce derivations from this linear grammar by applying the conversions S_i (interpreted as the instruction 'rewrite X_i as Y_i') in sequence. Among the S_i we distinguish between obligatory conversions that must be applied in the production of every derivation, and permissible conversions that may or may not be applied. There are only a finite number of ways to run through the linear grammar, applying all obligatory and some permissible conversions; hence only a finite number of derivations can be produced by the linear grammar $S_i, \ldots, S_n$. This was not a difficulty on earlier levels [e.g., the phonemic level, the syntactic categories level, etc.] but we know that infinitely many sentences must be generated by some mechanism in the grammar. We can permit this infinite generation on the level **P** by allowing the possibility of running through the linear grammar $S_1, \ldots, S_n$ an indefinite number of times in the production of derivations. If the derivation formed by running through the sequence of conversions does not terminate with a string in P [the set of strings composed of morphological heads and syntactically functioning affixes], then we run through the sequence again. Thus we can understand the linear grammar to be the sequence of conversions $S_1, \ldots, S_n, S_1, \ldots, S_n, S_1, \ldots, S_n, \ldots$. We then say that a derivation D is *recursively produced* by the linear grammar $S_1, \ldots, S_n$. We define a *proper linear grammar* as a linear grammar which is so constructed that it is impossible to run through it over and over again vacuously. (Chomsky 1975[1955]: 194–195)

This passage indicates that the iterative application of the conversion statements in the linear grammar was viewed (by Chomsky) as a recursive procedure, and this type of recursion was explicitly introduced in order to enable an infinite number of sentences to be produced by the grammar. In the light of the discussion of simplicity criteria in section 4.3, it is worth considering the recursive application of conversion statements from a grammar-internal perspective. Specifically, it is important to note that, for Chomsky, the issue of recursive rule application was closely connected to the issue of determining the simplicity of the resultant grammar, and the following passage is crucial:

> The recursive extension which permits infinite production of derivation might pose a problem for the determination of simplicity. Thus we may ask whether a grammar is simpler if it is necessary to run through it fewer times to set up derivations. There are several possible ways to place conditions on grammars that will eliminate a conflict between this consideration and the criterion of simplicity already established. (Chomsky 1975[1955]: 200–2001)

172 *Transforming generative grammar: 1955–1957*

This passage is of interest because it indicates that, while constructing TGG, Chomsky was forced to struggle with various technical problems that resulted from his attempts to adapt both simplicity criteria and recursion for his current purposes. However, Chomsky does not develop in detail the particular 'considerations' that could eliminate the apparent conflict, for, in chapter 10 of *LSLT*, he proposes that all recursive procedures should be removed entirely from the phrase structure part of the grammar, a proposal that is considered in detail below.

As indicated previously, if the repeated application of conversions constitutes one type of recursive procedure introduced in *LSLT*, another type manifests itself in certain rules contained within the phrase structure part of the grammar. Initially (as mentioned above), this kind of recursion was introduced in the form of rewrite rules such as '$X \rightarrow YX$', where the category to the left of the arrow, 'X', also appears on the right-hand side of the rule, 'YX'. Chomsky's initial presentation of the topic at the start of chapter 7 of *LSLT* clarifies the manner in which these rules were used in TGG:

> When we turn to the level of phrase structure, we find that certain rules may have a recursive character. Thus *Noun Phrase* (NP) might be analyzed in such a way that one of its components may be a NP as in such sentences as 'the man who made the discovery is my brother', which might be derived by means of a set of such conversions as
>
> (i) NP $\rightarrow$ NP$_1$ ⌢ who ⌢ VP
> VP $\rightarrow$ V ⌢ NP[3]
>
> Conversions of this sort will permit the generation of infinitely many sentences by that part of the grammar that deals with phrase structure ... (Chomsky 1975[1955]: 171–172)

As should be obvious, the formalism that Chomsky gives here is (to use Bar-Hillel's term) 'recursive in disguise' (Bar-Hillel 1953: 163) since he does not provide the definitions of NP that are required in order to terminate the recursion, yet these are provided in the main discussion of the topic that follows later in the chapter. The basic point is clear, though, nonetheless: the phrase structure component of the type of grammar developed in *LSLT* contains recursive rules. In the above example, the rule indicates that NPs can be rewritten as larger structures (containing relative clauses) which in turn contain NPs, and so on *ad infinitum*, at least in theory if not in practice. The rest of chapter 7 constitutes an exploration of the abstract theory underlying level **P** (i.e., the phrase structure level of the grammar), and when Chomsky actually begins to develop this component for English in chapter 8, he introduces a number of recursive rewrite rules. Sometimes these take the form of potentially infinite expansions. For example, when discussing the structure of verb phrases, Chomsky proposes the rules

Sentence → $NP\ VP$
$VP \to VP_A \frown VP_1$
$VP_1 \to\ <VP_B>\ VP_2$
$VP_A \to VP_{A1} < VP_{A2} >$
$VP_{A1} \to \{C, ed\} < M >$
$VP_{A2} \to\ < have \frown en >< be \frown ing >$
$VP_B \to Z_1 < Z_2 < \ldots < Z_n >>>$, where each Z_i is one of the forms
$V_c \frown to, V_y \frown ing$
(Chomsky 1975[1955]: 249–250)

where VP_A and VP_B both enable certain kinds of auxiliary verb constructions to be generated, with the difference that VP_B is defined so as to permit an unlimited number of Z_is. In order to illustrate how this particular group of rules works, the sentence 'John wants to read the book' can be obtained from the given conversions as follows:

Sentence
$NP \frown VP$
$NP \frown VP_A \frown VP_1$
$NP \frown VP_A \frown VP_B \frown VP_2$
$NP \frown C \frown VP_B \frown VP_2$
$NP \frown C \frown want \frown to \frown VP_2$
$John \frown C \frown want \frown to \frown read \frown the \frown book$
(Chomsky 1975[1955]: 250)

As these examples indicate, the recursive rules were initially introduced into the phrase structure component of TGG; that is, they appeared in the part of the grammar that was responsible for generating the kernel of basic sentences, enabling infinite structures to be generated. However, as Chomsky begins to elaborate his theory of transformations in chapters 9 and 10 of *LSLT*, he is compelled to reduce the recursive elements in the phrase structure component. More specifically, as the theory develops, the recursive rules are moved out of the phrase structure component entirely, and are placed in the transformational component of the grammar instead. In addition, Chomsky suggests that the first type of recursion discussed above, which permits the conversion statements to be applied recursively in sequence, should also be removed. Ultimately, these developments led Chomsky to make the following claim towards the end of chapter 10:

In the course of this analysis we have found that much of the recursive part of the grammar of phrase structure ... has been cut away. It seems reasonable to place the formal requirement that no recursions appear in the kernel grammar. Specifically we rule out such statements as $[VP_B \rightarrow Z_1 < Z_2 < \ldots < Z_n >>>]$, and we drop the constructions ... that permit running through the grammar indefinitely many times. As far as I can determine, this formal requirement on **P** does not exclude anything that we would like to retain in **P**; nor does it impose any artificial or clumsy limitation on the actual statement of the grammar corresponding to **P**, now that the transformational analysis presents an alternative way of generating sentences ... Now that the higher level of transformational analysis has been established, it is no longer necessary to require that generation by the grammar of phrase structure is infinite. As the level **T** has been formulated, the process of transformational derivation is recursive, since the product of a **T**-marker can itself appear in the **P**-basis of a **T**-marker. (Chomsky 1975[1955]: 516–518)

The requirement that the phrase structure component should not contain recursive elements ensures that the recursive parts of the grammar must all be implemented in the transformational component; a development which, at the time, no doubt emphasised the potential importance of Chomskyan transformations. Nevertheless, as the above extract indicates, whether they are situated in the phrase structure kernel or in the transformational component, TGG requires recursive rules since such rules enable a grammar, g, to generate all the sentences of the recursively enumerable language **L**, and, as suggested above, such rules clearly have their roots in recursive function theory.

5.7 Formal syntax

The preceding sections of this chapter have considered various aspects of TGG that can be associated with specific techniques used in the formal sciences. In this final section the general correspondences between TGG and Formalism will be discussed. Section 3.7 attempted to indicate how key concepts of the (caricatured) Formalist creed were disseminated amongst mathematically inclined linguists during the first decades of the twentieth century, and there is no doubt that many of the characteristic features of TGG were derived from the type of sources mentioned in section 2.8, since specific references to named texts (such as Quine's *Mathematical Logic* and Rosenbloom's *Elements of Mathematical Logic*) are frequent in Chomsky's publications from the years 1953–1957. To some extent the discussion in sections 5.4–5.6 has anticipated the following analysis, since it has already been established that specific methods strongly associated with proof theory, such as the use of recursive rules, were incorporated into TGG at a comparatively early stage. However, the full influence of Formalism upon the theory has yet to be illustrated.

As discussed at length in section 3.7, the need to formalise linguistic theory became a pressing concern for particular groups of researchers in the late 1940s, and this task had been partially accomplished by certain post-Bloomfieldians (especially Bloch, Wells, Chao, Hockett, and Harris) by the mid-1950s. As indicated previously, Harris was aware of contemporaneous developments in logic and metamathematics and therefore it is no surprise that he encouraged the young Chomsky to attend lectures on mathematics and philosophy. Once again, therefore, although the following passage from Chomsky's 1975 recollections was quoted in the introduction, it merits being reproduced here since it provides a fascinating insight into the eclectic intellectual climate at MIT in the early 1950s.[13]

> Perhaps a word might be usefully added on the general intellectual climate in Cambridge at the time when it [i.e., *LSLT*] was written. Interdisciplinary approaches to language communication and human behavior were much in vogue ... Roman Jakobson's work was well known and influential. Oxford ordinary language analysis and Wittgenstein's later work were attracting great interest. The problem of reconciling these approaches (if possible) with Quine's provocative ideas on language and knowledge troubled many students. Mathematical logic, in particular recursive function theory and metamathematics, were becoming more generally accessible, and developments in these areas seemed to provide tools for a more precise study of natural language as well. All of this I personally found most stimulating. (Chomsky 1975[1955]: 39)

The explicit references here to 'mathematical logic', 'recursive function theory' and 'metamathematics' clearly indicate that, as shown in chapter 3, during this period linguistics and mathematics were sufficiently closely connected to enable developments in logic and metamathematics to become a potent source of inspiration for young linguists, although, as indicated in section 4.5 and elsewhere, the precise nature of the relationship between logic and natural language was a topic that was frequently debated. However, even if, like all recollections, the above comments are not to be trusted entirely, there is plenty of contemporaneous evidence which suggests that Chomsky inherited from his immediate post-Bloomfieldian predecessors the belief that techniques adapted from metamathematics could provide useful tools for syntactic theory. As mentioned previously, with particular reference to Chomsky's own work, it is important to emphasise the fact that the very title of his weighty *LSLT* manuscript (i.e., '*The Logical Structure of Linguistic Theory*') appeared explicitly to associate his research with Carnap's research into logical syntax (i.e., in English translation, Carnap's *The Logical Structure of Language*), the main difference being that, while Carnap had signalled his concern with the logical structure of language, Chomsky was keen to stress his interest in the logical structure of linguistic theories devised to analyse natural language. It is crucial to note the difference in emphasis here: Chomsky's title implies that, while it may not be possible to demonstrate that the structure of natural language can be reduced to logic, it is certainly possible to ensure that the structure of a linguistic theory is elaborated in a logical manner. Clearly, though, despite this difference in emphasis, Chomsky seems to have been happy to associate himself (to some extent) explicitly with the logico-philosophical Formalist tradition (as manifest in Carnap at least), even if the association is intended primarily to illustrate the distinctive character of his own approach; and, as the previous sections have shown, such an association was a natural extension of the more formal approach to the methodology of linguistics advocated by certain subsets of the post-Bloomfieldians.

Given that developments in metamathematics were accessible to linguists in the 1950s, and given that certain post-Bloomfieldians had sought to develop a more systematic approach to linguistics by adopting a more (meta)mathematical methodology, it is no surprise that, when TGG began to coalesce in the mid-1950s, considerable emphasis was placed upon its status as a *formal theory*. Indeed, Chomsky addresses this very issue in chapter 2 of *LSLT*, and the Formalist nature of the project he is in the process of outlining is clear.

> In the strict sense of the word, an argument, a characterization, a theory, etc. is 'formal' if it deals with form as opposed to meaning, that is, if it deals solely with the shape and arrangement of symbols. In this sense, any distributional theory or argument is formal. But the word 'formal' has misleading connotations, implying 'rigorous', 'clear', etc. Suppose that we use the word 'formalized' when we have the latter sense in mind. A formalized theory, then, is one that is formulated in accordance with clear canons of rigor and precision: definitions are given explicitly in such a way that defined terms are always eliminable, and the axioms and methods of proof are precisely stated. We can thus have a formalized theory purporting to be about form or about meaning. A formalized theory is, of course, not necessarily an acceptable or enlightening theory. And the fact that a certain subject matter is stated to constitute the intended interpretation of a presented formalized theory does not confer any desirable properties upon this subject matter, or upon the theory. It is possible to construct a formalized theory with no interesting interpretation, or with intuition, ghosts, etc., in its intended

interpretation. What concerns us here is the possibility of a formalized theory of linguistic form, and the problems involved in constructing such a theory. (Chomsky 1975[1955]: 83)

This passage (or at least sections of it) could have been taken from any of the textbooks discussed in section 2.8, and clearly the basic approach to syntactic theory proposed here is entirely in keeping with Bloomfield's recommended axiomatic-deductive approach to theoretical linguistics. Indeed, the foregoing sections of this book should already have illuminated the way in which the above passage is richly embedded in a specific cultural tradition – namely, the drive towards greater 'rigour' that was revived by Cauchy in the nineteenth century in order to secure the foundations of the calculus, but which spread to many other scientific disciplines during the twentieth century, largely due to the influence of Logicism and Formalism. Before continuing, though, it is necessary to emphasise Chomsky's attitude towards the task of formalising a linguistic theory.

As the above passage indicates, for Chomsky, formalisation for the sake of formalisation is not the point: any theory can be converted into a 'formalized' theory, but this does not guarantee that the theory is 'enlightening'. Consequently, the motivation for propounding a formal linguistic theory is not to spare the linguist the arduous task of analysing complicated and confusing data; rather, the process of formalisation is desirable primarily because it enables specific conjectures concerning particular data to be stated more precisely. Indeed, for Chomsky, formalisation was never a soulless activity that could be accomplished only when a theory was already complete; rather, it was a fundamental aspect of the process of theory development. Indeed, as he observes elsewhere in *LSLT*, 'formalization can play a very productive role in the process of discovery itself' (Chomsky 1975[1955]: 59).

In the passage concerning formalisation quoted at length above, Chomsky refers only in very general terms to the use of 'axioms and methods of proof'. However, the axiomatic nature of TGG is clear from the various presentations of the basic theory that appeared in the mid-1950s. Once again, though, it is necessary to make a basic distinction between the way in which Chomsky presented his expositions of the basic theory, and the way in which language was analysed within that theory. For example, the main chapters of *LSLT* conspicuously reveal the axiomatic-deductive nature of Chomsky's exposition. To take one example virtually at random, when Chomsky introduces the 'relation of representation', ρ, which he uses to specify relations such as '$\rho(NP, the \frown man)$', indicating that '*the $\frown$ man*' is an NP, he provides specific axioms and definitions, and then proceeds to deduce theorems from these. For instance, the axioms and definitions take forms such as[14]

> **Axiom 1**: ρ is irreflexive, asymmetrical, transitive and nonconnected.
> **Definition 2**: P is the set of strings X such that for Y, $\rho(X, Y)$.

and the theorems are constructed using these axioms and definitions in the standard axiomatic-deductive fashion. As is obvious even from these two examples, unlike Bloomfield and Bloch (discussed in section 3.2), Chomsky was not content solely with natural language descriptions of his various technical entities and procedures; consequently, he introduces a rich symbolic metalanguage that enables the various axioms and definitions to be presented as precisely as possible.

While the presentation of TGG as a linguistic theory evinces a predilection for the axiomatic-deductive method, it is important to emphasise the fact that the basic sentence construction mechanism, as viewed from the perspective of TGG, can also be classified as an axiomatic-deductive procedure. To consider just one presentation, the rudiments of the theory were discussed explicitly in 'TMDL', and, in this presentation, Chomsky seems to promote a distinctly axiomatic-deductive interpretation of his theory since he describes the core components of the phrase structure component as follows:

> A phrase-structure grammar is defined by a finite vocabulary (alphabet) V_p, a finite set Σ of initial strings in V_p, and a finite set F of rules of the form: $X \rightarrow Y$, where X and Y are strings in V_p. (Chomsky 1956: 117)

This passage recalls Hilbert's specifications for metamathematical formal systems within the proof theory tradition, and, accordingly, it implies that the phrase structure grammar component can be viewed as a particular kind of formal system. This interpretation is implied by the description of the grammar as consisting of a finite alphabet of primitive elements, V_p, which are combined using rules of the form, $X \rightarrow Y$, in order to create well-formed formulae (i.e., grammatical sentences). For example, a simple phrase structure grammar of this type could take the form (compare Chomsky 1957b: 26):

(i) Sentence → NP + VP
(ii) NP → T + N
(iii) VP → Verb + NP
(iv) T → the
(v) N → man, ball, etc.
(vi) Verb → hit, run, etc.

and, in this example, every well-formed formula (i.e., grammatical sentence) is ultimately derived by means of rules (i.e., conversions) from the initial 'Sentence' symbol. This suggests that Chomsky initially considered the task of generating grammatical sentences to be comparable to an exercise in finitistic proof theory, and the use of terminology such as 'well-formed formulae', which was directly borrowed from the metamathematics literature and used in early TGG papers, underlines the extent of the correspondence. Just in case there could be any doubt concerning the analogy between sentence generation and proof construction, Chomsky himself explicitly acknowledged this connection on several occasions in the mid-1950s. For instance, when discussing the way in which sentences are derived in a formal TGG-style grammatical framework, he stated in *LSLT* that the process of derivation is 'roughly analogous to a proof' (Chomsky 1975[1955]: 67), and this seemingly innocent analogy between the derivation of a grammatical syntactic structure and the construction of proof in a metamathematical framework became one of the more characteristic features of TGG-style syntactic theory.

As indicated above, in the main expositions written during the years 1955–1957, TGG-style grammars were presented as if they were formal systems, and the process of sentence generation was deemed to be similar to the task of proof-theoretical deduction. These assumptions had profound consequences for the type of syntactic theory that TGG advocated. For instance, as indicated earlier, the role of meaning in Hilbertian proof theory was necessarily reduced to a minimum (indeed, it was entirely negated by the extremists) since the construction of a valid proof was considered to be a meaning-less task accomplished by a sequence of purely syntactic manipulations. The advantage of this approach was that it provided a general axiomatic-deductive framework that enabled valid derivations to be obtained within any formal system irrespective of the specific domain of application. In other words, the abstract generality of the theory appeared to eliminate relativism. Therefore, given the explicit analogy between TGG-style syntactic analysis and proof theory, it is not surprising that, within the broad TGG framework (as in the Bloomfield–Harris tradition) the role of semantics was minimised, while abstract syntactic structure was considered to be of fundamental importance. For instance, in the preface to *LSLT* (which was added to *LSLT* after *SS* had been written), Chomsky specifically discussed the distinction between syntax and semantics.

> Linguistic theory has two major subdivisions, syntax and semantics. Syntax is the study of linguistic form ... Semantics, on the other hand, is concerned with meaning and reference of linguistic expressions ... Syntax and semantics

are distinct fields of investigation. How much each draws from the other is not known, or at least has never been clearly stated. The subject of investigation in the following pages will be syntactic structure, and we shall study it as an independent aspect of linguistic theory ... In part, our desire to place no reliance on meaning in systematic development is motivated by a feeling that the theory of meaning fails to meet certain minimum requirements of objectivity and operational verifiability. (Chomsky 1975[1955]: 57)

None of the above is startling given the aforementioned Formalist slant of TGG, and, as indicated on numerous occasions already, this preoccupation with 'form' rather than 'meaning' had been a characteristic feature of certain kinds of linguistic research since Bloomfield (at least). Therefore it is no surprise that a comparable tendency manifests itself in the type of syntactic theory outlined in *LSLT* and *SS*, where grammatical sentences are exhaustively defined in terms of their formal structure without reference to semantics. Consequently, it is possible to view the explicit association between TGG and proof theory as yet another manifestation of the Formalist tendency of syntactic theory during the first half of the twentieth century, which resulted in the separation of syntax from semantics.

In the light of the above, it is worth considering the arguments Chomsky used at the time in order to justify the purely syntactic definition of grammaticality that his research espoused. Standardly, his basic assumption appears to have been that grammaticality, which is repeatedly associated with the notion of 'well-formedness', can be completely determined without any reference to meaning:

the notion 'grammatical' cannot be identified with 'meaningful' or 'significant' in any semantic sense. Sentences (1) and (2) are equally nonsensical, but any speaker of English will recognise that only the former is grammatical.

(1) Colorless green ideas sleep furiously.
(2) Furiously sleep ideas green colorless.

Such examples suggest that any search for a semantically based definition of 'grammaticalness' will be futile. (Chomsky 1957b: 15)

This argument essentially restates that already presented in 'TMDL', and, once again, the influence of the logico-philosophical Formalist tradition is clear. For instance, Chomsky's celebrated examples and general argument in the above passage seem consciously to echo those introduced by Carnap in his *LSL*. As mentioned in section 3.7, Carnap constructed the sentence 'Pirots karulize elatically' in order to demonstrate that well-formedness could be analysed in purely syntactic terms without reference to semantic considerations, and, obviously

Chomsky is employing a similar strategy in order to make the same basic point. Indeed, it is worth noting that Carnap's example is actually more extreme than Chomsky's since the use of neologisms complicates the situation even more from a semantic perspective, but there is no doubt that the main thrust of both arguments is essentially the same.

It is clear that the type of argument summarised above is understood to apply to syntactic research at a very general level; that is, the main recommendation is that any sensible and self-respecting syntactic theory will distance itself entirely (if possible) from considerations of meaning. However, while it is sufficiently important to consider this kind of general recommendation, it is equally revealing to explore the way in which Chomsky handles the problem of meaning in his detailed developments of TGG. To give just one example of this, in *LSLT*, when he is in the process of motivating the use of transformations in addition to the conversions in the phrase structure component of the grammar, Chomsky states:

> We do not want a transformation to depend on the 'content' of the particular strings into which Z [i.e., a string produced by the kernel] is decomposed for the purposes of transformation, but only on the number and order of these substrings. Only such transformations will reflect general structural relations between classes and strings. Once we have settled on some fixed way of characterizing grammatical transformations in terms of certain structural properties, it will be possible to take the complexity of this fixed form of characterization into account as a feature in the evaluation of given grammars. (Chomsky 1975[1955]: 315)

The emphasis of this passage should already be familiar given the previous discussion: Chomsky wishes to ensure that the transformations do not need to take semantic information into account, and that they should consider only the 'number and order' of substrings, since only a system of this kind will enable the transformations to reflect 'general structural relations'. The implication of this (and similar passages scattered throughout *LSLT* and *SS*) is clear: Chomsky assumed that syntactic form could be exhaustively analysed independently of meaning and, in assuming this, the type of theory he proposed in the mid-1950s reveals something of its Formalist inspiration. At the very least, it demonstrates how far syntactic theory had come since Hjelmslev distinguished between meaning-less metamathematics and meaning-full natural language analysis in the 1940s. Indeed, Chomsky's position is more extreme even than that of second-generation Formalists, such as Carnap in the 1930s, since, as indicated above, Carnap maintained that, due to their complexity, natural languages could not be analysed adequately using techniques that were devised to analyse formal languages, while, by the mid-1950s Chomsky had begun to challenge such views by adapting various techniques from mathematics, logic, and metamathematics, and deploying them for the purposes of natural language analysis. In order to accomplish this, it was necessary to assume that natural languages and formal languages were amenable to similar analytical techniques. Given the apparent diversity and idiosyncrasy of human language, this assumption necessitates the development of an abstract syntactic theory that seeks to identify underlying regularities lurking beneath apparent surface irregularities, and a research programme of this type has largely determined the course of generative grammar from the 1950s to the present day.

6 *Conclusion*

As indicated in the introduction, and as demonstrated in the subsequent chapters, this book manifestly constitutes an exercise in historiography, and the general purpose has been to reveal the nature and extent of the influence of the formal sciences upon the development of linguistic theory in the twentieth century, with the main emphasis falling upon the advent of TGG. At this stage, therefore, it is probably worth summarising the main issues considered, in order to review the central conclusions of the various intertwined investigations presented in the foregoing chapters.

One of the main tasks attempted in several sections of this book has been the re-evaluation of certain aspects of Bloomfield's work in the light of his interest in the foundations crisis and (specifically) in Formalism, aspects which appear to anticipate some of the preoccupations that obsessed mathematically minded linguists in the 1950s. In particular, it was suggested that Bloomfield's well-known mistrust of semantic considerations in the study of natural languages may have been influenced by his knowledge of Hilbertian proof-theoretical techniques which (at least in their popularised form) recommend the avoidance of semantic considerations in (meta)mathematical proofs in favour of non-contentual syntactic manipulations. In general, recent research has neglected Bloomfield's knowledge of the foundational debates of the 1920s and 1930s, as well as his professional interest in the relationship between linguistics and mathematics. However, if indeed it was the case that part of Bloomfield's own research into natural language was influenced by Formalism in the manner proposed in chapter 3, then full recognition of this fact may help to explain why the distributional procedures that grew out of his research, and which were developed by the post-Bloomfieldians, were considered to share similar characteristics with various methods employed in the formal sciences in the 1940s and 1950s. The conclusion offered in this book is that the formal sciences and post-Bloomfieldian linguistics appeared to approach their different tasks in a similar fashion partly because the methodologies used in both disciplines were directly influenced by Formalism during the first half of the twentieth century.

In addition (and more specifically), Bloomfield was an early proponent (possibly the earliest?) of the use of the axiomatic-deductive method in linguistics, an approach that was revived first by Bloch in the 1940s, and then by Bar-Hillel, Harwood, and others in the 1950s, and which gradually became the dominant method of syntactic analysis after the appearance of *SS*. Consequently, the analogy between syntactic theory and proof theory, that was explicitly articulated by Chomsky in *LSLT*, has its linguistic roots in Bloomfield's 1926 set of postulates for the study of language, and, more generally, in his fascination with contemporary mathematics.

If one of the accomplishments of the preceding chapters has been the rehabilitation of the mathematical aspects of Bloomfield's linguistic research, in a similar manner the work of Bar-Hillel may also have been revived. As mentioned previously, Chomsky has stated that he considers Bar-Hillel to have been a 'constructive participant' (quoted in Kasher 1991: 6) in the development of TGG, and it is hoped that the various explorations of different aspects of Bar-Hillel's work that have been presented here have largely validated this epithet. In particular, it has been shown that Bar-Hillel responded directly to some of Bloomfield's ideas concerning the relationship between mathematics and natural language, and that he was instrumental in exploring the relationship between logic and linguistic theory. His extension of Ajdukiewicz's work, which alerted the linguistics community to the existence of the Lvov-Warsaw school of logicians, and which eventually resulted in the advent of Categorial Grammar, should be recognised as an impressive early attempt to incorporate techniques from logic into systems of syntactic analysis. To some extent, therefore, Bar-Hillel was one of the main researchers who made the fusion of linguistics and logic appear a real possibility in the early 1950s. Further, with his appropriation of recursive definitions for the purposes of syntactic analysis, and with his claim that natural and artificial languages are essentially identical types of linguistic systems, Bar-Hillel influenced and provoked Chomsky, compelling him to formulate his own ideas more precisely. Sometimes he agreed with Bar-Hillel (e.g., concerning the use of recursive definitions in syntactic theory), sometimes he disagreed with him (e.g., concerning the use of techniques from logical semantics in natural language analysis), but, either way, he invariably felt obliged seriously to consider the implications of the various ideas that Bar-Hillel introduced. The closeness of their association and the particular details of their differences have not been fully considered in the past, with the result that Bar-Hillel has faded rather from the official histories of TGG. It is hoped that, to some extent, this book has revealed the centrality of his role.

If Bloomfield and Bar-Hillel have been dusted off a little in this book, then perhaps a third rehabilitation has also been achieved – or perhaps even a third *and* a fourth, depending on whether Goodman and Quine are sufficiently strong collocators to count as a single entity or not. However that may be, one of the aims of this research has been to explore the nature of the influence that the work of Goodman and Quine exerted upon the development of TGG, particularly since this topic has been so often neglected. As mentioned earlier, this neglect is rather curious, since Chomsky himself has invited a consideration of these issues. In the preface to *SS*, for instance, after dutifully thanking Harris for his assistance, he adds that 'in less obvious ways, perhaps, the course of this research has been influenced strongly by the work of Nelson Goodman and W. V. Quine' (Chomsky 1957b: 6). Therefore, to this end, certain sections of this book have simply explored this influence in greater detail than has been accomplished in the past, and, as a result, various aspects of TGG have been (re)assessed. For example, the use of simplicity criteria in Chomsky's earliest publications can be viewed as a direct adaptation of Goodman's research into the basal simplicity of constructional systems. Further, it has been demonstrated that 'SSA', Chomsky's first published paper, is clearly an attempt to fuse Harris-style discovery procedures with the particular constructional system that Goodman had developed in *SA*. These early (i.e., pre-*c*. 1954) projects suggest that, at this stage, Chomsky was still viewing linguistics as an empirical science that required the elaboration of automatic discovery procedures. However, at some point during the period 1953–1954 he appears to have rejected some of the philosophical implications associated with the type of constructive nominalism he had learnt from Goodman (and, to a lesser extent, Quine), and one of the many consequences of this rejection was the rejection (in turn) of the use of discovery procedures in linguistic theory in favour of evaluation procedures designed to choose between competing grammars (or were the rejections in the inverse order? or were they effectively simultaneous?). As indicated earlier, this profound shift in Chomsky's understanding of the purpose and function of linguistic methodology has never really been assessed before in the light of his changing attitudes towards constructive nominalism. Since Chomsky is universally categorised these days as a self-professed 'mentalist', it is sometimes difficult to accept that the pre-*c*. 1954 Chomsky seems to have been a logical empiricist of the Carnap–Goodman variety, but the evidence contained in his first publications and manuscripts certainly seems to point towards this conclusion. However, it should be emphasised that, even if Chomsky's rejection of logical empiricism was involved in his rejection of discovery procedures, the evaluation procedures (i.e., simplicity criteria) that he recommended as a preferable alternative also have their roots in the work of Goodman and Quine. Indeed, it is a strange fact that, while Chomsky apparently came to view constructive nominalism as having a deleterious effect upon linguistics, the same theory nevertheless provided technical procedures that were involved in his redefinition of the methodology of syntactic analysis. This conclusion is admittedly rather complex, but it is to be hoped that the complexity offered here is closer to the truth than the simplifications (or, worse, eerie silences) that have characterised historiographical studies of the genesis of TGG in the past.

In addition to the three broad topics summarised above, a number of smaller insights have been gained. For instance, with reference to non-TGG topics, some forgotten linguists have been resuscitated, most notably Harwood, whose early attempt to provide a formal axiomatic approach to syntactic theory seems, unfortunately, to have fallen out of the collective consciousness. With reference to TGG, though, the influence of White's critique upon Chomsky's rejection of methods from logical semantics has been explored in a preliminary fashion, and this association has not been fully recognised previously. Indeed, the treatment of this topic (i.e., the influence of Quine–White style analytic philosophy from the early 1950s upon TGG) is only sketchily accomplished in this book, and the White–Chomsky relationship in particular still awaits comprehensive consideration. In addition, there is the influence of Carnap's research into logical syntax upon the development of TGG, an association that has been generally acknowledged in the past, but never discussed in depth. Specifically, in this book, the difference between Carnapian and Chomskyan transformations has been investigated, and it is hoped that some of the terminological complexities have been elucidated. In general, though, perhaps the main achievement of this book has been to associate TGG with both Formalism and Logicism, two intellectual movements that profoundly influenced scientific methodology in the early twentieth century. Indeed, this general issue seems to have been the single destination towards which the various paths of enquiry have led. With its focus on syntax as opposed to semantics, with its use of a logic-based notational system, with its identification of the analogy between a proof and the generation of a grammatical sentence, and with its use of such procedures as recursive definitions and axiomatic deduction, TGG unambiguously reveals its associations with the formal sciences.

Having summarised the main topics that this book has addressed, it is necessary briefly to emphasise the main issues that have *not* been presented here. In particular, it should be recalled that, as stated in the introduction, this study of the development of TGG effectively ceases when the year 1957 has been reached (this being the year in which *SS* was published), and one reason for choosing this date as the terminus of the current study is to illustrate the void at the core of the various discussions of the history of TGG that take 1957 as their starting point. However, as a result of adopting 1957 as an upper-bound, there has been no attempt in the present study to discuss Chomsky's research into formal language theory, which constituted one of his main academic preoccupations between the years 1958–1965. In particular, the work he published jointly with both Miller and Marco Schützenberger (1920–1996) has not been assessed, although such a re-evaluation is obviously necessitated by the various topics addressed in the foregoing chapters. Similarly, with 1957 as the chosen cut-off point, there is no space here for discussing the emergence of the innateness hypothesis in exhaustive detail, the reason being that, although this hypothesis was eventually to become one of the most characteristic features of generative grammar, the initial expositions of this hypothesis were not presented until the late 1950s and early 1960s. Given the subsequent dominance of this hypothesis in the generative grammar tradition, this work clearly merits reconsideration (in particular, Chomsky's interactions with Eric Lenneberg (1921–1975) await discussion), but such a task is outside the scope of the present study. In addition to this nexus of interrelated topics, there are fascinating sociopolitical aspects of the development of TGG that demand further exploration. For example, in the late 1950s and early 1960s research into generative grammar was often funded by the US defence department. However, as the 1960s advanced, such funding sources ceased to be available for such work, although other kinds of research, such as automatic speech recognition and machine translation, saw no diminution in their financial support during these years. The reasons for this shift in perception from the institutions that initially financed TGG research have never been discussed, barely even mentioned; and, alas, they remain neglected in this book too, although the omission has (at least) been acknowledged. The questions are enticing, though. For instance, surely it can only be a coincidence that the defence department funding of generative grammar research should diminish in the late 1960s; that is, around the time that Chomsky started to promulgate political views that were severely critical of US foreign policy.

Having provided this overview of the genesis of TGG in the light of various developments in the formal sciences, it would be possible to terminate the discussion here, safe in the realm of conventional, retrospective historiography. However, since it is always necessary to resist the artificial sense of completeness that is inevitably associated with the conclusion of an investigation of this kind, the discussion will be extended a little longer. The motivation for continuing can be simply explained, and (perhaps predictably) it is prompted by contemporary preoccupations concerning the nature of generative grammar.

Possibly such considerations seem out of place in a study of this kind, but it should be remembered that, although TGG in its initial guise has long passed into the historical twilight, more modern variants of the theory are still very much in the full glare of daylight. Indeed, despite the many changes that have occurred since the late 1950s (i.e., the influential reconstruction(s) of the 1960s and 1970s that came to be referred to as the Extended Standard Theory (EST), the advent of the Principles and Parameters (P&P) model in the 1980s, and the subsequent inauguration of the controversial Minimalist Program (MP)), the essential elements of the syntactic theory broadly known as 'generative grammar' have remained remarkably constant. Consequently, certain aspects of the theory that were originally bold assumptions (some of which were ultimately derived from the formal sciences) have crystallised and have become incontrovertible components. As ever, though, consequences eventually follow from assumptions, and it is worth pausing to assess some of the implications that are inherent in the framework adopted by generative grammar.

One aspect of TGG that has been emphasised throughout the foregoing chapters is the conspicuously axiomatic-deductive (quasi-)proof-theoretical character of the theory. As demonstrated in sections 3.2 and 5.7, the axiomatic-deductive method fascinated certain linguists during the first half of the twentieth century, and it clearly provided the conceptual foundation for the type of computational syntactic theory that Chomsky outlined in *LSLT*. Indeed, to take this discussion back to where it (almost) began, it should be recalled that Lees had noted, in his 1957 review of *SS*, that Chomsky's theory utilised 'an overt axiom system' (Lees 1957: 378), suggesting that this was one of the characteristic features of the theory that made it 'rigorous' (Lees 1957: 378); and certainly the axiomatic-deductive framework (with all its attendant logico-philosophico-mathematical baggage) has remained a fundamental component of generative grammar ever since. In his 1995 presentation of the MP, for example, Chomsky sketched the basic structure of C_{HL}, the computational component of Universal Grammar (UG), and the proof-theoretical nature of this system is clear. For instance, recursion is still explicitly utilised (i.e., 'the operations of C_{HL} recursively construct *syntactic objects*' (Chomsky 1995: 226)), and derivations are 'generated' in a derivational (as opposed to a representational) fashion, starting with primitive elements (i.e., ultimately lexical and formal features) and resulting in phonological form and logical form pairings (i.e., (π, λ)) (Chomsky 1995: 219ff.). Although it is not possible exhaustively to consider all aspects of the various proof-theoretical features of contemporary generative grammar here, it is revealing to probe the implications of certain assumptions that have been retained; and, to this end, the formulation of recursion within contemporary versions of the theory will be discussed, primarily because the importance of recursion within the generative grammar framework has increased dramatically in recent years.

As indicated above, in *The Minimalist Program* (from henceforth *MP*) Chomsky states that the operations of C_{HL} 'recursively construct' syntactic objects, and he later defines such objects as follows (see Chomsky 1995: 243):

Definition 6.1: Syntactic Objects
1. lexical items
2. $K = \{\gamma\{\alpha, \beta\}\}$, where α, β are objects and γ is the label of K

Chomsky explicitly notes that clause 2 of definition 6.1 provides the 'recursive step' (Chomsky 1995: 243):

> Suppose a derivation has reached state $\Sigma = \{\alpha, \beta, \delta_i, ..., \delta_n\}$. Then application of an operation that forms K as in [definition 6.1, clause 2] converts Σ to $\Sigma' = \{K, \delta_i, ..., \delta_n\}$ including K but not α, β. (Chomsky 1995: 243)

This summary is rather brief, and it is useful to work through a specific example in order to appreciate the framework that is being proposed. For instance, if it is assumed that the only operation that creates K is Merge, then derivation creation can be viewed primarily as a process involving the repeated application of this operation, which terminates when the initial numeration is mapped to a single syntactic object. Schematically, if $\alpha_1, \alpha_2, \alpha_3$, and α_4 are the lexical items in a given numeration, then for a derivation that begins in state $\Sigma = \{\alpha_1, \alpha_2, \alpha_3, \alpha_4\}$, one possible series of subsequent steps can be explicitly represented as follows:

Derivation: Example 1
Given $\Sigma = \{\alpha_1, \alpha_2, \alpha_3, \alpha_4\}$:
Step 1: $K_1 = \text{Merge}(\alpha_1, \alpha_2)$ and $\Sigma' = \{K_1, \alpha_3, \alpha_4\}$
Step 2: $K_2 = \text{Merge}(K_1, \alpha_3)$ and $\Sigma' = \{K_2, \alpha_4\}$
Step 3: $K_3 = \text{Merge}(K_2, \alpha_4)$ and $\Sigma'' = \{K_3\}$

Chomsky stresses that, during the course of derivation generation, 'no new objects are added ... apart from rearrangements of lexical properties' (Chomsky 1995: 228), and therefore the whole process is determined by the operation Merge and the features associated with the lexical items. In essence, as Chomsky formulates it, the 'recursive step' constructs syntactic objects that possess hierarchical structure. More precisely, Merge causes two syntactic objects, α and β, to be combined in a principled manner in such a way that a label derived from either α or β can be determined and associated with the resulting hierarchically structured syntactic object. In later work, the need for labels was questioned (for example, see Collins 2002 and Chomsky 2000a), but even if a label-free system is proposed, the essential constructional procedure remains the same. It is of interest, though, that, rather than associating recursion explicitly with self-reference and other possible characteristic properties discussed at length in section 3.3, Chomsky associates it primarily with finite computations: a finite set of primitive elements (i.e., lexical items) and a finite set of operations (i.e., Merge) are used to generate a potentially infinite set of hierarchical structures (i.e., sentences). Therefore, the 'recursive' aspect of this process, as Chomsky presents it, appears primarily to involve an operation (i.e., Merge) that takes its own output (e.g., the Ks in example 1) as its own input. In 1995, then, a 'recursive' component, which enabled infinite structures to be created using finite means, was still posited within MP-style generative grammar, even though (inevitably) the exact details of its expression had altered since such a component was first incorporated into TGG in the 1950s.

Although, as indicated above, a 'recursive step' was included in the MP in 1995, in recent years Chomsky has suggested that, rather than merely constituting a useful constructional procedure that was initially derived from the formal sciences and incorporated into formal grammars, recursion may actually constitute a unique language-related aspect of human cognitive function. For instance, in a 2002 paper, 'The Faculty of Language: What Is It, Who Has It, and How Did It Evolve', which Chomsky co-authored with Marc Hauser and Tecumseh Fitch, the authors discuss the Faculty of Language in the Narrow sense (FLN) and they indicate that this term denotes 'the abstract linguistic computational system alone, independent of the other systems with which it interacts and interfaces' (Hauser, Chomsky, and Fitch 2002: 1571). Further, they state explicitly that 'a core property of FLN is recursion', before clarifying this succinct statement by explaining that 'FLN takes a finite set of elements and yields a potentially infinite arrangement of discrete expressions' (Hauser, Chomsky, and Fitch 2002: 1571). So far, none of this is especially unusual within the tradition of generative grammar. However, in addition to these familiar claims, Hauser, Chomsky and Fitch go on to hypothesise that FLN is 'uniquely human' and that it consists primarily of a recursive component and procedures for mapping syntactic objects to the interfaces (Hauser, Chomsky, and Fitch 2002: 1573). More specifically, the claim (referred to from henceforth as the 'FLN hypothesis') is expressed as follows:

> we suggest that FLN – the computational mechanism of recursion – is recently evolved and unique to our species . . . we propose in this hypothesis that FLN comprises only the core computational mechanisms of recursion as they appear in narrow syntax and the mappings to the interfaces. If FLN is indeed this restricted, this hypothesis has the intriguing effect of nullifying the argument from design, and thus rendering the status of FLN as an adaptation open to question. (Hauser, Chomsky, and Fitch 2002: 1573)

Clearly, then, within the context of contemporary generative grammar, recursion has begun to play a crucial role. In the 1950s recursive definitions were simply viewed as useful procedures derived from the formal sciences which (as Bar-Hillel had indicated in 1953) could be incorporated into grammars in order to facilitate linguistic analyses. However, if the above hypothesis proves to be correct, then, in the most recent versions of the theory, recursion will have to be viewed as a fundamental and unique species-specific property that is particularly associated with the faculty of language. Obviously, given the magnitude of this claim, it is essential to establish precisely what 'the computational mechanism of recursion' means. Unfortunately, though, the discussion of recursion presented by Hauser, Chomsky, and Fitch in their 2002 paper is simply too vague to enable the details of the FLN hypothesis to be clarified. For instance, no formal examples of particular recursive procedures are provided, though it can probably be safely assumed that recursive definitions such as definition 6.1 (discussed above) are intended. However, while the uncertainty is caused in part by a lack of detailed examples, it is also partly due to the fact that the term 'recursion', as it is currently used in the formal sciences, is fundamentally ambiguous. As mentioned briefly in section 3.3, from the late 1930s onwards recursive function theory has been associated both with λ-definability and with computability theory, and some of the problems caused by this association must now be addressed.

As discussed in section 3.3, Gödel was one of the leading researchers responsible for advancing recursive function theory, especially in his influential 1931 and 1934 publications. However, in 1936 two mathematicians provided alternative definitions of effective calculability. First, Alonzo Church published a paper which claimed that there was a close association between recursive function theory and λ-definability since general recursive functions could be shown to be λ-definable functions (and vice versa). Second, Alan Turing published his precocious paper 'On computable numbers, with an application to the *Entscheidungsproblem*', in which he introduced the notion of a computing machine (i.e., the mathematical entity now generally known as a Turing machine), thus initiating computability theory, an independent branch of mathematics that was characterised by its own procedures and techniques (e.g., Turing machines, Turning computable functions, the Turing Thesis, and the like) and which eventually provided the theoretical foundations for many advances in electronic computing in the 1950s. The relationship between recursive function theory and computability theory was recognised from the very beginning, since both theories attempted to define finite computable procedures, and Gödel himself was quick to realise that Turing's work effectively subsumed his own research into recursive function theory by providing a more general theoretical framework. Inevitably, as a result of the perceived associations between these three distinct theories, recursive function theory, λ-calculus, and computability theory became conflated in the late 1930s, and one undesirable consequence of this was that research undertaken within the framework of (say) computability theory (i.e., research which explicitly used Turing machines, Turing computable functions, and so on) was often formally expressed in terms of recursive function theory – and vice versa. This situation is clearly undesirable since (for example) while all primitive recursive functions can be re-expressed as Turing computable functions, it is certainly not the case that all Turing computable functions can be re-expressed as primitive recursive functions, and, therefore, if one speaks of the former while using terminology associated with the latter, misunderstandings inevitably abound. However, such unhelpful practices have become common in the literature concerning recursion and computability, and the mathematician Robert Soare has referred to this as the 'Recursion Convention' (Soare 1996: 28).

> The Recursion Convention has brought 'recursive' to have at least four different meanings... This leads to some ambiguity... Worse still, the Convention leads to *imprecise thinking* about the basic concepts of the subject; the term 'recursion' is often used when the term 'computability' is meant. (By the term 'recursive function' does the writer mean 'inductively defined function' or 'computable function'?) Furthermore, ambiguous and little recognized terms and imprecise thinking lead to *poor communication* both within the subject and to outsiders, which leads to isolation and a lack of progress within the subject, since progress in science depends upon the collaboration of many minds. (Soare 1996: 29)

This is a disquieting passage, and it certainly emphasises the current problematic state of the notion of recursion within the formal sciences.

In the light of the remarks quoted above, it is necessary to return to the work of Hauser, Chomsky, and Fitch. Obviously, given the FLN hypothesis, the first task is to attempt to determine which type of recursion is implicated. From their informal discussion of the subject, it appears to be the case that Hauser,

Chomsky, and Fitch are explicitly associating 'recursion' with the process of creating an infinite arrangement of discrete expressions from a finite set of elements (Hauser, Chomsky, and Fitch 2002: 1571, quoted above). This is reasonable, though it is essential to note that this is a far more general procedure than that associated with other interpretations of 'recursion'. For instance, if this elusive term is understood to mean 'definition by induction' (the interpretation that Bar-Hillel recognised in 1953 when he proposed that recursive definitions could be used in formal grammars), then in addition to the property of generating infinite structures from finite means, 'recursion' would also involve some kind of explicit self-reference. Since self-reference is not stressed in their paper, though, Hauser, Chomsky, and Fitch may be using the term 'recursion' to indicate something like 'effectively calculable' or 'specified by a finite algorithm', and if this were the case, then it would suggest that Chomsky's current use of the term is more closely related to the interpretation of 'recursion' that associates it with computability theory rather than with Gödelian recursive function theory. However, as mentioned previously, since the presentation offered in the Hauser, Chomsky, and Fitch paper is both brief and informal, it is simply not possible to determine with certainty which interpretation of 'recursion' is actually intended. Clearly, this is not the place in which to attempt to resolve some of these problems, and the preceding discussion is presented merely to indicate that it is impossible insightfully to assess the linguistic/biological role of the recursive components within contemporary generative grammar without first reflecting upon the tortive development of recursive function theory and its complex associations with λ-calculus and computability theory; and explorations such as that in section 3.3, which attempt to identify the way in which recursive definitions were incorporated into syntactic theories in the 1950s, simply seek to provide some kind of clarification.

If recursion is one topic that requires careful and dextrous consideration, then the notion of theory-internal simplicity is certainly another. As discussed (possibly *ad nauseam*) in sections 3.5 and 4.3, the characteristic concern with simplicity criteria in early TGG was directly motivated by Chomsky's interest in Goodman's research into the basal simplicity of constructional systems, and related concerns have haunted generative grammar ever since its inception. From the mid-1960s onwards, these concerns were often discussed in terms of explanatory, as opposed to descriptive, adequacy, and the opposing tensions caused by these guiding principles are well known: while descriptive adequacy requires the full complexity of those aspects of natural language that fall within the specified domain of enquiry to be captured by a formal linguistic theory, explanatory adequacy essentially demands that the theory developed should not become unnecessarily complex. Due to the fact that the introduction of explanatory adequacy as a theoretical prerequisite roughly coincided with the explicit adoption of the innateness hypothesis, the notion has conventionally been presented as a psychological/biological requirement in the generative grammar literature. In general, then, during the years *c*. 1965–1990 the main focus in mainstream generative grammar research was upon the task of improving the basic theory so that it could account more accurately for a larger number of linguistic phenomena, and the task of further developing the 'sketchy' ideas concerning simplicity criteria outlined in *LSLT* (Chomsky 1975[1955]: 116) was largely abandoned. Nevertheless, during this 25-year period of theory development, a basic sense of the importance of theory-internal simplicity was retained, and there were certainly times when the eradication of certain unnecessary theoretical complexities was openly acknowledged as a profound advance. For example, the development of X-bar theory in the early 1970s, which considerably simplified the orthodox theory of generative grammar by providing a unified analytical framework for phrasal projections, was widely recognised as a significant improvement. However, despite such cases, it is reasonable to claim that, in pre-*c*. 1990 generative grammar, considerations of 'economy' or 'theory-internal simplicity' never received the type of principled and sustained scrutiny that they began to receive when the MP emerged as an identifiable research programme in the early 1990s.

As is well known, the MP outlines an ambitious agenda, the main purpose of which is to determine the extent to which the human language faculty can be viewed as a 'perfect' solution to the problems posed by external constraints (i.e., the interfaces that connect the syntactic component with the phonological and semantic components). Put simply, one of the main goals of the MP is to reduce to a minimum the essential machinery required to represent the faculty of language, or, as Chomsky himself has expressed it recently,

> The minimalist program is the attempt to explore these questions [i.e., the questions 'what are the properties of language' and 'why are they that way']. Its task is to examine in detail every device (principle, idea, etc.) that is employed in characterizing languages to determine to what extent it can be eliminated in favor of a principled account in terms of general conditions of computational efficiency and the interface condition that the organ must satisfy for it to function at all. Put differently, the goal is to determine just what aspects of the structure and use of language are specific to the language faculty, hence lacking principled explanation at this level. (Chomsky 2004: 106)

Clearly, although it is important to stress that, in contrast to the use of simplicity criteria to select amongst competing grammars in TGG, in the MP the economy considerations determine the way in which operations such as Merge enable derivations to be generated by C_{HL}; nevertheless the basic concern with constructing a 'principled account' that is regulated by considerations of 'computational efficiency' can be directly associated with the exploration of the simplicity of grammars in the 1950s. Indeed, Chomsky himself has claimed that the MP effectively heralds a return to some of the concerns that originally motivated the creation of TGG. Writing in 1995, for example (and explicitly referring to chapter 4 of *LSLT*), Chomsky emphasised the distinction between 'an imprecise but not vacuous notion of simplicity that enters into rational enquiry generally' and 'a theory-internal measure of simplicity that selects among I-languages' (Chomsky 1995: 8), and he continues:

> The former notion of simplicity has nothing special to do with the study of language, but the theory-internal notion is a component of UG, part of the procedure for determining the relation between experience and I-language; its status is something like that of a physical constant. In early work, the internal notion took the form of an evaluation procedure to select among proposed grammars (in present terms, I-languages) consistent with the permitted format for rule systems. The P&P approach suggests a way to move beyond that limited though nontrivial goal to address the problem of explanatory adequacy. With no evaluation procedure, there is no internal notion of simplicity in the earlier sense ... Nevertheless, rather similar ideas have resurfaced, this time in the form of economy considerations that select among derivations, barring those that are not optimal in a theory-internal sense. The external notion of simplicity remains unchanged: operative as always, even if only imprecisely. (Chomsky 1995: 8-9)

In the terms of the MP, then, the concern with issues of theory-internal economy is formulated as a set of economy considerations that prevent non-optimal derivations converging, and (as indicated in the above quotation) Chomsky himself acknowledges that there is a noticeable similarity between this approach and the TGG focus upon simplicity criteria that selected between competing grammars. The implication is that the MP can be viewed (in part) as an attempt seriously to respond to certain questions concerning the theory-internal 'simplicity' of formal grammars that were asked in early work on TGG, but which have remained largely unanswered during the intervening decades. The fact that such concerns have 'resurfaced' is perhaps surprising, but it certainly indicates that research concerns that were responsible for prompting the emergence of TGG in the 1950s are closely related to the research concerns that prompted the advent of the MP, and such associations surely merit detailed consideration. Obviously, the task of determining the nature of theory-internal economy is non-trivial, and this is indicated by the various ways in which the topic is approached in standard collections of MP-focused papers such as Epstein and Hornstein 1999 and Epstein and Seely 2002. In these two collections alone, issues of economy and/or theory-internal simplicity are adduced in discussions of interpretable features and Case (Martin 1999), the copy theory of movement (Nunes 1999), multiple spell-out (Uriagereka 1999), 'elegant' syntax (Brody 2002), syntactic objects and labels (Collins 2002), and crash-proof derivations (Frampton and Gutmann 2002), to cite just a few instances. At various places, these discussions all utilise arguments involving some kind of notion of economy or theory-internal simplicity in order to justify the theoretical modifications or analyses that are presented; and this in turn suggests that such considerations are currently perceived to be central to the task of linguistic theory development within the MP tradition. Given the pervasive interest in such issues, it is necessary to emphasise that the centrality of such concerns has profound consequences for the methodology of syntactic research. For instance, it is an assumption to claim that considerations of simplicity (or 'economy', or 'elegance', or 'compactness', or any other related variant) are central to the task of linguistic analysis, whether they are expressed in terms of conversions in a given grammar itself or whether they are included as explicit conditions that delimit the types of permissible derivations generated by a particular grammar. Indeed, as Paul Feyerabend (1924–1994) argued in 1975, it is equally reasonable to assert that such issues are *never* necessary considerations for scientific research of any kind, and that the tendency to devote too much attention to these topics can be misleading (at best) and positively detrimental (at worst). In support of this provocative position, Feyerabend noted that the physicist Niels Bohr would 'dismiss the usual considerations of simplicity, elegance or even consistency with the remark that such qualities can only be properly judged *after* the event' (Feyerabend 2001[1975]: 14).[1] Feyerabend adds that 'science is never a completed process, therefore it is always "before" the event. Hence simplicity, elegance and consistency are *never* necessary conditions of (scientific) practice' (Feyerabend 2001[1975]: 15.n1). Statements such as these impinge directly upon syntactic theory as pursued within the MP tradition, suggesting that base-less assertions concerning the centrality of economy considerations in syntactic research (particularly unprincipled assertions which are used primarily in order to justify a proposed modification to the theory) are entirely insufficient. Consequently, it is not surprising that the role of 'simplicity' in contemporary generative grammar is necessarily a contentious issue. Once again, a detailed understanding of the origins of the initial concern with such issues, as they were expressed within the TGG framework, reveals the sources of these preoccupations, and so provides a foundation for a more insightful discussion of the role of economy considerations in contemporary versions of the theory; and such an understanding can only be achieved once the role of simplicity criteria in the work of Goodman (and Quine) in the 1940s and 1950s has been assessed.

If theory-internal considerations of simplicity and the use of recursive devices are all still central concerns within the MP, as they once were within TGG (although now manifest in very different ways), then it could also be claimed that the MP essentially (re)adopts a (constructive) nominalistic methodology for syntactic theory. This tendency manifests itself in the various developments that involve the elimination of abstract structures and/or processes that were formerly accepted within the theory in favour of a simpler lexicalist account, a development that is closely related to the topic of theory-internal simplicity. For instance, as mentioned above, one of the boldest developments that Chomsky proposed in *MP* was the rejection of X-bar theory in favour of bare phrase structure. As noted earlier, the X-bar framework, which had been a part of generative grammar since the 1970s, specified a unified framework for phrasal projections, thus providing a well-defined abstract hierarchical structure in advance of the actual construction process itself. However, in the bare phrase structure framework, all syntactic entities are defined in terms of the most primitive elements posited in the system – namely, the various features associated with the items in the lexicon, and formal features such as the EPP feature that are associated with the core functional categories. One consequence of this approach is that abstract structures such as VPs and N' projections are effectively eliminated from the construction process (though in practice they are often retained in expositions as a form of shorthand notation). Similarly, in his most recent work, Chomsky has suggested that the Spec-Head relation, which has played a central role in standard syntactic analyses since the 1970s, should be rejected since this relation cannot justifiably be unduly privileged, leading to the thesis that '[a]pparent Spec-H relations are in reality head-head relations involving minimal search' (Chomsky 2004: 113).

As mentioned above, in the MP, the process of syntactic object construction is viewed as a process in which 'no new objects are added . . . apart from rearrangements of lexical properties' (Chomsky 1995: 228), and therefore all syntactic objects constructed can be viewed as particular configurations of irreducible features. Clearly, this view of the process of grammatical construction is reminiscent of the approach to constructional system theory proposed by Goodman and Quine in the late 1940s; a framework in which they rejected abstract notions such as sets, defining instead a calculus of individuals (i.e., irreducible fundamental elements) that avoided the 'taint' of Platonism (Goodman and Quine 1947: 107). Consequently, the process of deriving a grammatical sentence in the MP framework is a feature-driven process that does not involve abstract X-bar theoretical structures. Although it is not possible here to examine this issue in detail, there are clearly parallels between the parsimonious analytical methodology advocated in the MP literature and that advocated by Goodman in his calculus of individuals, which Chomsky had considered in his earliest work. To some extent, the rejection of certain kinds of abstract entities, which is a characteristic feature of constructive nominalism and the MP alike, is related to the emphasis placed on simplicity criteria: if the task is to develop a maximally economical system, then there is a valid motivation for eliminating all non-essential components of the theory, and abstract structures are an obvious target, especially if they can be defined in terms of smaller, more fundamental units and processes.

As the above paragraphs imply, the relationship between TGG and the MP is a fascinating one that has yet to be explored in detail, and, obviously, the brief tour offered above is not intended to rectify this situation by providing deep insights into the nature of this relationship. Rather, the intention is simply to highlight some of the similarities, and to indicate that certain characteristics of 1950s-style TGG have remained constant throughout the evolution of generative grammar during the past fifty years, while others have reappeared with renewed prominence in the MP. These developments merit serious consideration, and a detailed exploration of the origins of TGG can enable us to view more clearly the various assumptions and analytical techniques associated with the MP; and if a reassessment of contemporary generative grammar is considered to be an important task, then it is necessary also to reconsider one of the words that has resonated throughout this book as it has resonated throughout the history of twentieth-century linguistics. The word (of course) is 'science'. Bloomfield, Sapir, Lees, Hockett, Chomsky,[2] and many more have all written about the scientific status (or the lack thereof) of linguistics, and the fundamental question that has been asked and reasked in so many different ways can be succinctly paraphrased as the cogent query: 'Is linguistics a science?' This question, of course, begs numerous other questions none of which can be discussed here. However, with specific reference to generative grammar, the whole issue of the scientific status of linguistics has been raised in a number of recent publications, and arguments both for and against have been constructed. To start with an example of a negative assessment, with reference to the validity of generative grammar, a disillusioned Paul Postal commented in 1995 that Chomsky[3]

> has good reason for being insecure because he cannot fail to have noticed that he has few substantial results in the sense that these are understood in more

serious fields such as logic, mathematics, computer science, or physics. And it is striking how elements of his position which were once considered to be profound contributions now have vanished or become enormously marginalized. Where are syntactic rule ordering, the principle of cyclic application, the A-over-A Principle etc? [today one could add 'Where are deep-structure, surface-structure, X-bar theory, etc?'] Many of the principles and accomplishments touted in recent years are almost embarrassing in their inadequacy and shoddiness ... The significant point, then, is that there is an extraordinary contrast between the paucity of genuine results in Chomskyan linguistics and the forests of paper which have been, and continue to be, devoted to the linguistic ideas involved. (quoted in Huck and Goldsmith 1995: 141–142)

In Postal's view, then, generative grammar does not deserve to be classified as a science (or at least as one of the 'serious' sciences) mainly because it has produced so few 'genuine results'. The various theoretical constructs that appeared to be 'profound contributions' at an earlier period have since faded or even vanished completely, suggesting that they were only ever of ephemeral value. However, the opposing viewpoint is well represented by Massimo Piattelli-Palmarini, who, in his introduction to Juan Uriagereka's *Rhyme and Reason* (Uriagereka 1998), claimed that generative grammar

> is well on the way to becoming a full-blown natural science, offering a serious promise of an advanced field of scientific inquiry whose idealizations, abstractions, and deductions will eventually match in depth and subtlety those of the most advanced domains of modern science. (Uriagereka 1998: xxv)

This pronouncement is unambiguous, and uttered only three years after Postal's contemptuous assessment. So which analysis is correct? Is generative grammar a science or not? The divergence between Postal and Piattelli-Palmarini's views is rather alarming to say the least. Surely it should not be possible for the opinions of informed, practising linguists to differ so greatly on this matter? Surely it should be possible for the linguistics community to agree as to whether generative grammar has indeed produced any genuine results or not? Surely it should at least be possible to determine whether, after over half a century of formalisms, debates, analyses, assertions, counter-assertions, misunderstandings, revelations, and revolutions, the researchers involved with the generative grammar enterprise (whether TGG or EST or P&P or the MP) have actually been responsible for some kind of scientific research or not? And if such possibilities are not, in fact, possible, then surely it is the case that something is rather deeply wrong with syntactic theory, or at least with the particular branch of it known as generative grammar? Unfortunately, there is not space here fully to explore all the implications raised by these queries. However, if the confusion and disagreement concerning the scientific status of generative grammar is indeed as profound as has been indicated above, then it is surely time to reconsider the various assumptions, intentions, and methods associated with this particular subset of linguistic theory; and, in order to reflect sensibly upon the scientific status (or otherwise) of contemporary generative grammar, it is perhaps necessary first to brood protractedly upon the scientific aspects of its past – a task that this book has attempted to accomplish.

Notes

Introduction

1 For short but insightful discussions of the standard classifications (and some of the attendant difficulties) see Suppe 2000 and Schaffer 1997.
2 For a notorious negative review of Chomsky's book see Aarsleff 1970. For a more dispassionate assessment, and for evidence of Chomsky's annoyance at the reception of *Cartesian Linguistics*, see the discussion in Koerner 1999, especially pp. 10–12, p. 178, and pp. 210–214.
3 Some of the mathematical aspects of Hockett's own work are discussed in section 5.2.
4 Chomsky's rejection of nominalism is discussed at length in section 5.3. For Lyons' discussion of Chomsky's critique of behaviourism, see 1970: 83ff., and for Chomsky's own words, see Chomsky 1959b.
5 For the details see Matthews 1993: 131–134.

The consequences of analysis

1 Throughout this chapter the term 'calculus' is used in the standard way to refer to the set of algorithmic procedures associated with differentiation and integration, while the term 'analysis' is used to denote various extensions of the calculus-based techniques, which include differential equations, the calculus of variations, and multivariate calculus.
2 'singulare ... calculi genus'.
3 For this particular example in full, see Newton 1967[1665]: 273.
4 'quantitates per singula temporis infinite parva intervalla augentur'.
5 For a detailed discussion of Newton's fluxional calculus, see Westfall 1980: 131–140.
6 For Leibniz's full response, see Leibniz 1863b[1695]: 332.
7 A useful collection of papers (in English translation) that contributed to the development of analysis during the eighteenth century can be found in Struik 1969, especially section 3. While often hostile towards each other, the researchers associated with the English and Continental traditions appear to have interacted more frequently than is sometimes suggested. For clear discussions of some of the complexities, see Boyer 1949 (chapter 6), Guicciardini 1989, and Fraser 1997.

8 See section 2.5 below for a brief summary of the development of logic in the nineteenth century.
9 The most authoritative overview of Cauchy's contribution to the nineteenth-century reformulation of analysis is Grabiner 1981. The development of Cauchy's ideas in relation to logic and set theory is considered in Grattan-Guinness 2000: 64–68.
10 Good surveys of various aspects of Weierstrass's work can be found in Dugac 1973 and Manning 1975. As an aside, it should be mentioned that the consensus amongst the mathematical community concerning the definitions of differentiation and integration was undermined when Abraham Robinson introduced Non-Standard Analysis in the 1960s. This theory provided a model-theoretic basis for Leibnizian infinitesimals, therefore reviving the very conceptual foundation for the calculus that Weierstrass had effectively eliminated. For further information about this fascinating development, see Robinson 1996 and Dauben 1995.
11 A good explanation of 'Dedekind cuts' can be found in Hrbacek and Jech 1984: 100–102.
12 An excellent introduction to Cantor's research into number theory can be found in Dauben 1979, especially chapter 2.
13 For more detailed accounts of Cantorian set theory, see Dauben 1979 (chapters 10 and 11), Jech 1991, and Grattan-Guinness 2000 (chapter 3). For a brief but insightful summary, see Hallett 1984: 1–11.
14 For more information about set theory in the twentieth century, see Johnson 1972.
15 For general overviews of the development of logic, see Kneale and Kneale 1962 and Grattan-Guinness 2000, chapter 4.
16 For more information about Frege's logical systems see Baker 1984 and Dummett 1991. As the twentieth century progressed Frege was gradually appropriated by analytical philosophers. For a recent attempt to reclaim him for logicians and mathematicians, see Grattan-Guinness 2000: 177–199.
17 By comparison with the work of other logicians concerned with foundational issues, Peano's work has been rather neglected. For a reasonably detailed overview, see Grattan-Guinness 2000, chapter 5.
18 For more information concerning Russell's intellectual development, see Clark 1975 (chapter 5), and Hylton 1990 (chapter 3).
19 In the years following the publication of Whitehead and Russell's ideas concerning the theory of logical types, a number of criticisms of the theory emerged. For a general overview of the theory itself and the controversy surrounding it, see Copi 1971.
20 For a more detailed discussion, see Grattan-Guinness 2000, especially chapter 7.
21 For more information about the terminology used in *PM*, see Grattan-Guinness 2000: 384–400.
22 For a succinct introduction to various non-classical logics, see Priest 2001.
23 For more biographical information about Hilbert, see Reid 1996, and, for more information about Formalism in general, see Kreisel 1958, Detlefsen 1993, and Hintikka 1995.

24 As mentioned in section 2.4, Hilbert seems to have known about Cantor's own doubts concerning set theory as early as 1896. For more information, see Grattan-Guinness 2000: 117–119.
25 For instance, see Hilbert 1932[1918], in which he considers the utility of such a language when constructing axiomatic-deductive arguments.
26 For timely words of caution see Ewald 1996: 1106–1107 and Mancosu 1998: 163–164.
27 By far the best source of information concerning all aspects of Brouwer's life and work is van Stigt 1990.
28 It is of interest, incidentally, that Brouwer's topological papers largely conform to classical assumptions about mathematics and do not overtly manifest his Intuitionist concerns. No doubt his reticence during these years was partly due to his desire to ingratiate himself with his peers.
29 'Brouwer, that is the revolution!'
30 For more information concerning Intuitionistic logic see Mancosu 1998 (part 4) and van Stigt 1990, especially chapter 5. For a discussion of the relationship between Intuitionism and proof theory, see Kino et al. 1970.
31 For more information concerning Intuitionist set theory see van Stigt 1990 (chapter 6) and Mancosu 1998: 1–27.

Mathematical linguistics

1 These particular examples can be found in Bloomfield 1926: 154.
2 For more information concerning the influence of Weiss upon Bloomfield's work, see Belyi 1967. Bloomfield cites Weiss' paper (Weiss 1925) explicitly in his own paper (Bloomfield 1926).
3 Certain aspects of Bloomfield's later work concerning this topic are discussed in section 3.7.
4 These particular examples can be found in Bloch 1948: 6–7.
5 Another important example, namely Bar-Hillel's development of Categorial Grammar, is discussed at length in section 3.4.
6 It should be noted that Chomsky discussed Harwood's paper explicitly in *Syntactic Structures* and compared Harwood's system with his own version of phrase structure grammar. For specifics, see Chomsky 1957b: 26n1. Some of the reasons why the axiomatic-deductive character of TGG impressed contemporary linguists are considered in various places in chapters 4 and 5.
7 Detailed discussions of the set of primitive recursive functions can be found in Kleene 1952 (chapter 9), Crossley and Dummett 1965, and Fitting 1981. For an approachable and insightful analysis of the various terminological problems that have enveloped recursive function theory since the late 1930s, see Soare 1996.
8 The well-known schemata discussed here were influentially presented in Kleene 1952: 219.
9 For more details, see Gödel 1986b[1934] and Kleene 1952: 270–276.
10 Various aspects of the work of Bar-Hillel are discussed in several sections of this chapter. This focus is necessary since his role in the development of TGG has often

been neglected. This neglect is unjustifiable, though, since, as Chomsky himself has acknowledged, Bar-Hillel was a 'constructive participant' (quoted in Kasher 1991: 6) in the development of TGG.

11 Bar-Hillel's work was also influenced by Carnap's 1952 paper 'Meaning Postulates', which is discussed at length in section 4.3.

12 The various ellipses in the following examples are Bar-Hillel's.

13 For more information about the Lvov-Warsaw school in general see Woléński 1989. A good collection of papers in English translation can be found in McCall 1967, and for an excellent collection of papers exploring the linguistic interests of the members of the school, see *Historiographia Linguistica* 25:1/2 1998. In the current study, the work of Tarski is considered separately in section 4.5.

14 For more information concerning Leśniewski's system, see Luschei 1962.

15 For more information concerning meaning-rules, see Ajdukiewicz 1978a[1934]: 57–66. His interest in pragmatics eventually culminated in Ajdukiewicz 1965.

16 The best source of information concerning Harris' 'procedures' is *MSL* itself. As an example, though, a typical distributional (morphophonemic) procedure was the one called 'Interchanging Phonemes among Alternates of One Morpheme'. The purpose and function of this procedure is summarised by Harris as follows: 'we group together into one morphophoneme the phonemes which replace each other in corresponding parts of the various members of a morpheme' (Harris 1951: 224). As a result, 'knife' and 'knive' are grouped together and associated with the single morphophonemic sequence //nayF//. For more information concerning distributional linguistics, see Matthews 1993, chapter 3.

17 The title of Carnap's text poses a few problems for translators. The actual title was *Der logische Aufbau der Welt: Versuch einer Konstitutionstheorie der Begriffe*, and the word '*Aufbau*' is commonly rendered into English in the philosophical literature as 'Structure'. This is done because Carnap also uses the noun '*Konstitution*' regularly, and it is usually deemed appropriate to reserve the term 'Construction' for this concept. However, '*Aufbau*' is more accurately converted into English if it is translated as 'Construction', and since these terminological difficulties are not a central concern here, this translation has been adopted. For further discussion of the complexities, see Richardson 1998: 6n3.

18 Like all paragraph-long accounts of the Vienna Circle, this summary is inevitably inadequate in many respects. Fortunately, there is a substantial body of literature concerning logical positivism in general and the work of the Vienna Circle in particular. For instance, Weinberg's classic book *An Examination of Logical Positivism* (1936) is still a revealing, contemporaneous introduction, as is Ayer's influential *Language, Truth and Logic* (1936). Two useful anthologies of core Vienna Circle papers are Ayer 1959 and Hanfling 1981. In recent years the standard interpretation of the whole movement has been destabilised by provocative revisionist accounts. Excellent examples of this current trend are Richardson 1998 and Friedman 1999.

19 The relationship between *LCW* and Russell's work has been reconsidered recently. For instance, see the assessment in Richardson 1998: 22–30.

20 For details, see Carnap 1967[1928]: 65ff.

21 Quine's own detailed account of his time in Vienna can be found in Quine 1985: 86ff. A useful recent assessment of Quine's work is Orenstein 2002, which includes some discussion of the complex relationship between Chomsky and Quine.
22 The complete text of Quine's 1934 lectures on Carnap can be found in Creath 1990: 47–103.
23 For specifics concerning Carnap's interpretation of the connection between his work and that of Goodman, see Carnap 1963: 19.
24 In brief, Goodman realised that 'joints' and 'segments' were more effective measures of simplicity. An n-place predicate joins each occupant of one of its n places with the occupants of the other places. Therefore, Goodman was able to define joints as follows: 'The number of joints ... is the number of places in any minimum set of pairs of places that ties all the places of the predicate together – i.e., that provides between every two places in the predicate a route consisting entirely of steps between places paired in the set' (Goodman 1949: 36). By contrast, the notion of a segment can be expressed in terms of place occupants that are identical, and the guiding intuition is that an n-place predicate is more complex if fewer of its places have the same occupant. As Goodman puts it: 'since all the places that have the same occupant as any given place belong to what I call a *segment*, clearly segments rather than places are to be counted in determining complexity' (Goodman 1949: 37).
25 An analytic truth is one that is true for logical reasons (e.g., $p \rightarrow (p \vee \neg p)$), while a synthetic truth depends upon extralogical considerations (e.g., 'Socrates is a man' is true or false depending upon the state of the universe of discourse).
26 For example, see Fries 1954. A broad discussion of these issues can be found in Matthews 1993: 118–122. The intensity of Bloomfield's distaste for semantics has been questioned from time to time. For some discussion of this position, see Murray 1994: 130–132.
27 The remaining fragments can be found in Bloomfield 1970b: 333–338.
28 This fact alone suggests some kind of familiarity with the work of Russell (perhaps his accessible *The Principles of Mathematics* (1903)?), since Russell had been the most assiduous paradox collector, and, as mentioned in section 2.5, the theory of logical types had been designed primarily to obviate the kind of set-theoretical self-reference that engendered the paradoxes.
29 A clear presentation of Grelling's paradox can be found in Grelling 1936.
30 This paper is mentioned briefly in Bloomfield (1970a[1937]: 333).
31 The redefinition of the notion of a set was one common response to the work of Cantor, Whitehead, and Russell during the first half of the twentieth century. For instance, as discussed in section 3.4, in the 1920s Leśniewski's 'mereology' was devised in order to avoid some of the problems of self-reference. For more information, see Luschei 1962.
32 The task of attempting to determine which researchers unambiguously belonged to the group now known as the post-Bloomfieldians has preoccupied a number of linguistic historiographers. For a consideration of the various complexities, see Hymes and Fought 1981[1975].

Systems of syntax: 1951–1995

1 For example, Chomsky 1988, Otero 1994b, Barsky 1997, and Smith 2004.
2 For instance, in the introduction to *The Minimalist Program* Chomsky writes:

> The shift in perspective provided by the P&P [i.e., Principles and Parameters] approach also gives a different cast to the question of how simplicity considerations enter into the theory of grammar. As discussed in the earliest work in generative grammar, these considerations have two distinct forms: an imprecise but not vacuous notion of simplicity that enters into rational enquiry generally must be clearly distinguished from a theory-internal measure of simplicity that selects among I-languages (see Chomsky 1975[1955], chapter 4). The former notion of simplicity has nothing special to do with the study of language, but the theory-internal notion is a component of UG [i.e., Universal Grammar], part of the procedure for determining the relation between experience and I-language; its status is something like that of a physical constant. In early work, the internal notion took the form of an evaluation procedure to select among proposed grammars (in present terms, I-languages) consistent with the permitted format for rule systems. The P&P approach suggests a way to move beyond that limited though nontrivial goal and to address the problem of explanatory adequacy. With no evaluation procedure, there is no internal notion of simplicity in the earlier sense. (Chomsky 1995: 8)

3 For this particular reference, see Chomsky 1979b[1951]: 67n5.
4 Since it is one of the core texts involved in the development of TGG, the publication history of *LSLT* deserves comment. The manuscript was complete by the spring of 1955 and revised for publication the following year. Having been rejected by the Technology Press at MIT, it circulated widely in a mimeographed version during the late 1950s, 1960s, and early 1970s. Chomsky finally agreed to have the book published, in a revised and truncated form, in 1975. For more detailed information concerning the complex genesis of this seminal text, see Chomsky's introduction to the 1975 edition of *LSLT*. However, as mentioned in the introduction, it is also worth reading Murray 1980 and Murray 1994 as an antidote, since Murray provides alternative reasons for the delay in publication.
5 The definition of grammatical levels in *LSLT*, which draws heavily upon constructional system theory, is considered in section 5.4.
6 Evaluation procedures are further discussed in section 5.3.
7 The advent of Generalised Phrase Structure Grammar in the late 1970s and early 1980s prompted a reassessment of these issues. For details, see Gazdar et al. 1985.
8 Chomsky had initially submitted this paper to the *Journal of Symbolic Logic* in October 1952.
9 In this context, constructional homonymity occurs whenever sentences sharing superficially identical forms are assigned to different syntactic classes. For instance, the two sentences

- The man stood by the woman (with the sense 'the man championed the woman')
- The man stood by the tree (with the sense 'the man stood beside the tree')

obviously differ significantly in their formal structure, despite apparent similarities.

10 Chomsky's shift from (apparent) empiricism to rationalism is considered separately in section 5.3.
11 Bar-Hillel's appreciation of Carnap was considered in section 3.7.
12 Carnap's formation and transformation rules are discussed in section 3.7, while the difference between Chomskyan and Carnapian 'transformations' is considered at length in section 5.5.
13 Bar-Hillel acknowledges that, in recent work, Harris had begun to introduce rules that he referred to as 'transformations', but he points out that this is merely an attempt to incorporate transformation rules into the formation part of syntax (Bar-Hillel 1954: 231–232).
14 For specifics, see Carnap 1942: x.
15 The paper 'The Concept of Truth in Formalized Languages' was presented to the Warsaw Scientific Society on 21 March 1931. It was published in Polish in 1933 and in German in 1936. An English translation appeared in Tarski 1956: 152–278.
16 The paper 'The Establishment of Scientific Semantics' appeared in Polish in 1936 and in German later the same year. An English translation appeared in Tarski 1956: 401–408.
17 Just to clarify, Carnap's book was called *Der logische Syntax der Sprache* and this title is most accurately translated as *The Logical Syntax of Language*. However, the standard English translation that was published in 1937 was given the title *The Logical Structure of Language*, and it is this version of Carnap's title that Chomsky is clearly echoing.
18 For more information about Montague's work, see Davis and Mithun 1979, and, for a useful collection of Montague's own papers, see Montague 1974.

Transforming generative grammar: 1955–1957

1 For details, see the discussion in Chomsky 1957b: 72–105.
2 Shannon was responsible for the first part of the book (pp. 1–91), while Weaver was responsible for the remainder, hence the rather specific reference below to the individual authors of what appears to be a co-authored book.
3 Chomsky's review of Hockett's *A Manual of Phonology* appeared in 1957 and drew heavily upon 'TMDL' and *SS*, hence the focus of the following discussion. For Chomsky's explicit discussion of Hockett, though, see Chomsky 1957a.
4 For some scene-setting, see Barsky 1997: 87–88.
5 For instance, see Matthews 1993: 134–142 and Newmeyer 1980: 19–36.
6 Although the introduction to *LSLT* is dated 1973, it was not published until 1975.
7 For a stimulating discussion of the associations between logical positivism and behaviourism see Smith 1986. For a primarily philosophical perspective on the type of epistemology Chomsky came to advocate in his later work, see 'Chomsky: Linguistics and Epistemology' in Nagel 1995. It should be noted, just for clarity, that while the conspicuous, mind-based philosophy that has been associated with generative grammar since the early 1960s is usually assumed to be a crucial part of Chomskyan syntax, it is (in theory) entirely separable from the formal procedures and theoretical constructs that constitute the machinery of generative grammar.

8 It is worth mentioning that in his (now usually ignored) 1954 review of Rieger's *Modern Hebrew*, which had been published in 1953, Chomsky commented favourably upon the type of data collection techniques that Rieger advocates, remarking that they constitute 'a method that a linguist might be tempted to use in constructing a linguistic corpus' (Chomsky 1954: 180). This brief observation may indicate that, in 1954, Chomsky was still primarily concerned with the sort of post-Bloomfieldian corpus-based discovery procedures that he would later reject, or, at least, it may reveal that he was not yet willing to question the validity of these methods in public.

9 For example, see the discussion in Katz 1981, chapter 1. Katz's assessment of the topic is a good example of the sort of opportunities for explication that have been missed in the past. His approach is philosophical rather than historiographical, and therefore he is too swift to project some of Chomsky's later ideas (especially his later 'rationalism') onto his earlier work. The title of Katz's chapter, 'From Harris's Nominalism to Chomsky's Conceptualism', indicates the nature of the deficiency. Also, inexplicably, Katz does not mention Carnap in the chapter, despite his obvious awareness of the influence of Carnap's work on linguistics in the 1950s.

10 See Chomsky 1975[1955]: 294–306 for full details concerning various problems with phrase structure grammar.

11 For example, see the succinct and (comparatively) non-technical discussion in Chomsky 1957b: 61–84.

12 For details, see Matthews, 1993: 133ff.

13 It should be noted that, although it appeared in the 1975 publication of *LSLT*, the introduction (part of which is quoted here) is dated 1973.

14 For this particular example, see Chomsky 1975[1955]: 175.

Conclusion

1 Feyerabend is here quoting Lovis Rosenfeld, and he has added the italics himself.
2 i.e., Bloomfield 1926, Sapir 1929, Lees 1957, Hockett 1967, Chomsky 2000b.
3 For similar diatribes, see Postal 2004.

Bibliography

Aarsleff, H. (1970), 'The History of Linguistics and Professor Chomsky', *Language* 44: 570–585.
Ajdukiewicz, K. (1965), *Pragmatic Logic*, Holland and the United States: D. Reidel Publishing Co.
Ajdukiewicz, K. (1978a[1934]), 'Language and Meaning', reprinted in English translation in Ajdukiewicz 1978c: 35–66.
Ajdukiewicz, K. (1978b[1931]), 'On the Meaning of Expressions', reprinted in English translation in Ajdukiewicz 1978c: 1–34.
Ajdukiewicz, K. (1978c), *The Scientific World-Perspective and Other Essays: 1931–1963*, ed. J. Giedymin, Holland and the United States: D. Reidel Publishing Co.
Ajdukiewicz, K. (1978a[1936]), 'Syntactic Connexion', reprinted in English translation in Ajdukiewicz 1978c: 118–139.
Ayer, A. J. (1936), *Language, Truth and Logic*, London: Gollancz.
Ayer, A. J. (1959), *Logical Positivism*, New York: Free Press.
Bach, E. (1964), *An Introduction to Transformational Grammars*, New York: Holt, Rinehart & Winston, Inc.
Baker, G. P. (1984), *Frege: Logical Excavations*, New York and Oxford: Oxford University Press.
Bar-Hillel, Y. (1953a), 'On Recursive Definitions in Empirical Science', 11th International Congress of Philosophy 5: 160–165.
Bar-Hillel, Y. (1953b), 'A Quasi-Arithmetical Notation for Syntactic Description', *Language* 29: 47–58.
Bar-Hillel, Y. (1954), 'Logical Syntax and Semantics', *Language* 30: 230–237.
Bar-Hillel, Y. (1963), 'Remarks on Carnap's Logical Syntax of Language', in Schilpp 1963: 519–543.
Bar-Hillel, Y. (1964), *Language and Information: Selected Essays on their Theory and Application*, Reading, Massachusetts: Addison-Wesley Publishing Co.
Barsky, R. F. (1997), *Noam Chomsky: A Life of Dissent*, Cambridge, Massachusetts: MIT Press.
Belyi, V. V. (1967), 'Some Facts about Weiss' Influence on Bloomfield', in Fought 1999, II: 115–118.
Berkeley, G. (1992[1734]), *The Analyst*, reprinted in Jesseph, D. M. (1992), *De Motu and The Analyst: A Modern Edition, with Introductions and Commentary*, Boston, and London: Kluwer Academic Publishers Dordrecht.

Birkhoff, G. (ed.) (1973), *A Source Book in Classical Analysis*, Cambridge, Massachusetts: Harvard University Press.
Bloch, B. (1948), 'A Set of Postulates for Phonemic Analysis', *Language* 24: 3–46.
Bloomfield, L. (1926), 'A Set of Postulates for the Science of Language', *Language* 2: 153–164.
Bloomfield, L. (1933), *Language*, New York: Henry Holt & Co.
Bloomfield, L. (1935), 'Linguistic Aspects of Science', *Philosophy of Science* 2: 499–517.
Bloomfield, L. (1936), 'Language or Ideas?', *Language* 12: 89–95.
Bloomfield, L. (1955[1939]), 'Linguistics Aspects of Science', in Neurath, O. Carnap, R. and Morris, C. (eds.), reprinted in 1955, *The International Encyclopedia of Unified Science*, Vol. I, Chicago: University of Chicago Press.
Bloomfield, L. (1970a[1937]), *The Language of Science*, unpublished manuscript fragments collected in Bloomfield 1970b: 333–338.
Bloomfield, L. (1970b), *A Leonard Bloomfield Anthology*, ed. C. F. Hockett, Bloomington: Indiana University Press.
Borgström, C. H. J. (1949), 'The Technique of Linguistic Descriptions', *Acta Linguistica* 5: 1–14.
Boyer, C. B. (1949), *The History of the Calculus and its Conceptual Development*, New York: Dover Publications Inc.
Bradley, F. H. (1883), *The Principles of Logic*, Oxford: Oxford University Press.
Brody, M. (2002), 'On the Status of Representations and Derivations', in Epstein and Seely 2002: 19–41.
Brouwer, L. E. J. (1912), 'Intuitionisme en formalisme: inaugurale rede', Amsterdam: Clausen.
Brouwer, L. E. J. (1979[1907]), *Over de grondslagen derwiskunde*, reprinted in English translation in van Stigt, W. P. (1979), 'The Rejected Parts of Brouwer's Dissertation on the Foundations of Mathematics', *Historia Mathematica* 6: 385–404.
Cantor, G. F. L. P. (1883), *Grundlagen einer allgemeinen Mannigfaltigkeitslehre*, Leipzig: Teubner.
Cantor, G. F. L. P. (1895), 'Beiträge zur Begründung der transfiniten Mengelehre', in Zermelo, E. (ed.) (1932), *Gesammelte Abhandlung mathematischen und philosophischen Inhalts*, Berlin: Springer, 282–311.
Cantor, G. F. L. P. (1937[1899]), letter in Noether, E., and Cavaillès, J. (1937), *Briefweschel Cantor-Dedekind*, Paris: Hermann, pp. 405–411.
Carnap, R. (1928), *Der logische Aufbau der Welt: Versuch einer Konstitutionstherorie der Begriffe*, Berlin: Welt-Kreis.
Carnap, R. (1937[1934]), *Logische Syntax der Sprache*, Vienna, reprinted in English translation in 1937 as *The Logical Structure of Language*, London and New York: Routledge.
Carnap, R. (1942), *Introduction to Semantics*, Cambridge, Massachusetts: Harvard University Press.
Carnap, R. (1944), *Formalization of Logic*, Cambridge, Massachusetts: Harvard University Press.
Carnap, R. (1952), 'Meaning Postulates', *Philosophical Studies* 3: 65–73.

Carnap, R. (1963), 'Intellectual Autobiography', in Schilpp 1963: 1–84.
Carnap, R. (1967[1928]), *The Logical Structure of the World: Pseudoproblems in Philosophy*, translated by R. A. George, London: Routledge & Kegan Paul.
Cauchy, A. L. (1821), *Analyse Algébrique*, Paris: Debure Frères.
Cauchy, A. L. (1823), *Leçon sur le calcul infinitésimal*, Paris: Debure Frères.
Cherry C. E., Halle M., and Jakobson R. (1953), 'Toward the Logical Description of Languages in their Phonemic Aspect', *Language* 29: 34–46.
Chomsky, N. (1953), 'Systems of Syntactic Analysis', *Journal of Symbolic Logic* 18: 242–256.
Chomsky, N. (1954), review of Rieger, E., *Modern Hebrew*, *Language* 30: 180–181.
Chomsky, N. (1955a), 'Logical Syntax and Semantics: Their Linguistic Relevance', *Language* 31: 36–45.
Chomsky, N. (1955b), 'Semantic Considerations in Grammar', *Monograph Series in Language and Linguistics*: 141–153.
Chomsky, N. (1956), 'Three Models for the Description of Language', *IRE Transactions of Information Theory, IT-2*: 113–124.
Chomsky, N. (1957a), review of Hockett's *A Manual of Phonology*, *International Journal of American Linguistics* 23: 223–234.
Chomsky, N. (1957b), *Syntactic Structures*, The Hague: Mouton Publishers.
Chomsky, N. (1959a), 'On Certain Formal Properties of Grammars', *Information and Control 2*, no. 2: 137–167.
Chomsky, N. (1959b), review of Skinner's *Verbal Behaviour*, *Language* 35: 26–58.
Chomsky, N. (1966), *Cartesian Linguistics: A Chapter in the History of Rationalist Thought*, New York and London: Harper & Row.
Chomsky, N. (1975[1955]), *The Logical Structure of Linguistic Theory*, Cambridge, Massachusetts: MIT Press.
Chomsky, N. (1979a), *Language and Responsibility*, New York: Pantheon.
Chomsky, N. (1979b[1951]), *Morphophonemics of Modern Hebrew*, New York: Garland.
Chomsky, N. (1988), *The Chomsky Reader*, London: Serpent's Tail.
Chomsky, N. (1995), *The Minimalist Program*, Cambridge, Massachusetts: MIT Press.
Chomsky, N. (2000a), 'Minimalist Inquiries: The Framework', in Michaels, D., Uriagereka, J., and Martin, R. (eds.), *Step by Step: Essays on Minimalist Syntax in Honor of Howard Lasnik*, Cambridge, Massachusetts: MIT Press.
Chomsky, N. (2000b), *New Horizons in the Study of Language and Mind*, Cambridge: Cambridge University Press.
Chomsky, N. (2004), 'Beyond Explanatory Adequacy', in Belletti, A. (ed.), *Structures and Beyond: The Cartography of Syntactic Structures*, Oxford Studies in Comparative Syntax, New York and Oxford: Oxford University Press, III: 104–131.
Chomsky, N., and Miller G. A. (1958), 'Finite State Languages', *Information and Control 2*, no. 2: 91–112.
Church, A. (1944), *Introduction to Mathematical Logic: Part 1*, Annals of Mathematics Studies, Princeton: Princeton University Press.
Church, A. (1956), *Introduction to Mathematical Logic: Volume 1*, Princeton: Princeton University Press.

Clark, R. W. (1975), *The Life of Bertrand Russell*, London: Jonathan Cape and Weidenfeld & Nicolson.
Collins, C. (2002), 'Eliminating Labels', in Epstein and Seely 2002: 42–64.
Copi, I. (1971), *The Theory of Logical Types*, London: Routledge & Kegan Paul.
Creath, R. (ed.), (1990), *Dear Carnap, . . . , Dear Van: the Quine–Carnap Correspondence and Related Work*, Berkeley: University of California Press.
Crossley, J. N., and Dummett, M. A. E. (1965), *Formal Systems and Recursive Functions*, Amsterdam: North-Holland.
Dauben, J. W. (1979), *Georg Cantor: His Mathematics and Philosophy of the Infinite*, Cambridge, Massachusetts: Harvard University Press.
Dauben, J. W. (1995), *Abraham Robinson: The Creation of Nonstandard Analysis: A Personal and Mathematical Odyssey*, Princeton: Princeton University Press.
Davis, S., and Mithun, M. (1979), *Linguistics, Philosophy and Montague Grammar*, Austin: University of Texas Press.
Dedekind, R. J. W. (1932[1872]), *Stetigkeit und irrationale Zahlen*, reprinted in Fricke, R., Noether, E., and Ore, O. (eds.), (1930–1932), *Gesammelte mathematische Werke*, Vieweg: Braunschweig; III: 315–334.
Dedekind, R. J. W. (1932[1888]), 'Was sind und was sollen die Zahlen?', reprinted in Fricke, R., Noether, E., and Ore, O. (eds.), (1930–1932), *Gesammelte mathematische Werke*, Vieweg: Braunschweig; III: 335–391.
Detlefsen, M. (1993), 'Hilbert's Formalism', *Revue Internationale de Philosophie* 47: 285–304.
Dugac, P. (1973), 'Eléments d'analyse de Karl Weierstrass', *Archive for the History of Exact Science* 10: 41–176.
Dummett, M. A. A. (1977), *Elements of Intuitionism*, Oxford: Clarendon Press.
Dummett, M. E. (1991), *Frege: Philosophy of Mathematics*, London: Duckworth/Cambridge, Massachusetts: Harvard University Press.
Embleton, S., Joseph, J. E., and Niederehe H.-J. (eds.) (1999), *The Emergence of Modern Language Science*, 2 vols., Amsterdam: John Benjamins.
Epstein, S. D., and Hornstein, N. (eds.) (1999), *Working Minimalism*, Cambridge, Massachusetts: MIT Press.
Epstein, S. D., and Seely, T. D. (eds.) (2002), *Derivation and Explanation in the Minimalist Program*, New York and London: Blackwell.
Euler, L. (1912[1755]), *Institutiones Calculi Differentialis*, reprinted in *Opera Omnia*, series 1, vol. 10: 69–72.
Ewald, W. (1996), *From Kant to Hilbert: A Source Book in the Foundations of Mathematics*, vols. I and II, Oxford: Clarendon Press.
Feyerabend, P. (2001[1975]), *Against Method*, revised 3rd ed, London and New York: Verso.
Fitting, M. (1981), *Fundamentals of Generalised Recursive Function Theory*, Amsterdam: North-Holland.
Fought, J. (ed.) (1999), *Leonard Bloomfield: Critical Assessments of Leading Linguists*, London and New York: Routledge.
Frampton, J., and Gutmann, S. (2002), 'Crash-Proof Syntax', in Epstein and Seely 2002: 90–105.

Fraser, C. G. (1997), *Calculus and Analytical Mechanics in the Age of Enlightenment*, London: Ashgate.
Frege, F. L. G. (1879), *Begriffsschrift, eine der arithmetischen nachgebildete Formelsprache des reinen Denkens*, Halle, Saale: Niebert.
Frege, F. L. G. (1884), *Die Grundlagen der Arithmetik. Eine logisch-mathematische Untersuchung über den Begriff der Zahl*, Breslau: Köbner.
Frege, F. L. G. (1893), *Die Grundgesetze der Arithmetik, begriffsschriftlich abgeleitet 1*, Jena: Pohle.
Friedman, M. (1999), *Reconsidering Logical Positivism*, Cambridge: Cambridge University Press.
Fries, C. C. (1952), *The Structure of English: An Introduction to the Construction of English Sentences*, New York and London: Longmans, Green.
Fries, C. C. (1954), 'Meaning and Linguistic Analysis', reprinted in Fought 1999, II: 84–97.
Gazdar, G., Klein, E., Pullum G., and Sag, I. (1985), *Generalised Phrase Structure Grammar*, Oxford: Basil Blackwell.
Gödel, K. (1986a), *Kurt Gödel: Collected Works*, 2 vols, Oxford: Oxford University Press.
Gödel, K. (1986b[1934]), 'On Undecidable Propositions of Formal Mathematical Systems', reprinted in Gödel 1986a, I: 346–371.
Gödel, K. (1986c[1931]), 'Über formal unentscheidbare Sätze der *Principia Mathematica* und verwandter Systeme', reprinted in Gödel 1986a, I: 144–194.
Goodman, N. (1943), 'On the Simplicity of Ideas', *Journal of Symbolic Logic* 8: 107–121.
Goodman, N. (1949), 'The Logical Simplicity of Predicates', *Journal of Symbolic Logic* 14: 32–41.
Goodman, N. (1950), 'An Improvement in the Theory of Simplicity', *Journal of Symbolic Logic* 14: 228–229.
Goodman, N. (1951), *The Structure of Appearance*, Cambridge, Massachusetts: Harvard University Press.
Goodman, N. (1952), 'New Notes on Simplicity', *Journal of Symbolic Logic* 17: 189–191.
Goodman, N. (1954), *Fact, Fiction, and Forecast*, London: Athlone Press.
Goodman, N. (1955), 'Axiomatic Measurement of Simplicity', *Journal of Philosophy* 52: 709–722.
Goodman, N. (1963), 'The Significance of Die logische Aufbau der Welt', in Schilpp 1963: 545–558.
Goodman, N. (1990[1941]), *A Study of Qualities*, Harvard Dissertations in Philosophy Series, Cambridge, Massachusetts: Harvard University Press.
Goodman, N., and Leonard, H. S. (1940), 'The Calculus of Individuals and its Uses', *Journal of Symbolic Logic* 5: 45–55.
Goodman, N., and Quine, W. V. O. (1940), 'Elimination of Extra-Logical Postulates', *Journal of Symbolic Logic* 5: 104–109.
Goodman, N., and Quine, W. V. O. (1947), 'Steps Towards a Constructive Nominalism', *Journal of Symbolic Logic* 12: 105–122.

Grabiner, J. V. (1981), *The Origins of Cauchy's Rigorous Calculus*, Cambridge, Massachusetts: MIT Press.
Graffi, G. (2001), *200 Years of Syntax: A Critical Survey*, Amsterdam: John Benjamins.
Grattan-Guinness, I. (2000), *The Search for Mathematical Roots, 1870–1940: Logics, Set Theories and the Foundations of Mathematics from Cantor through Russell to Gödel*, Princeton: Princeton University Press.
Grelling K. (1936), 'The Logical Paradoxes', *Mind* 45: 481–486.
Guicciardini, N. (1989), *The Development of Newtonian Calculus in Britain, 1700–1800*, Cambridge: Cambridge University Press.
Hallett, M. (1984), *Cantorian Set Theory and Limitation of Size*, Oxford: Oxford University Press.
Hanfling, O. (ed.) (1981), *Essential Reading in Logical Positivism*, Oxford: Basil Blackwell.
Harris, R. A. (1993), *The Linguistic Wars*, Oxford: Oxford University Press.
Harris, Z. S. (1946), 'From Morpheme to Utterance', *Language* 27: 161–183.
Harris, Z. S. (1951), *Methods in Structural Linguistics*, Chicago: University of Chicago Press.
Harris, Z. S. (1952), 'Discourse Analysis', *Language* 28: 1–30.
Harris, Z. S. (1957), 'Co-occurrence and Transformation in Linguistic Structure', *Language* 33: 283–340.
Harris, Z. S. (1991), *The Theory of Language and Information*, Oxford: Clarendon Press.
Harwood, F. W. (1955), 'Axiomatic Syntax: The Construction and Evaluation of a Syntactic Calculus', *Language* 31: 409–413.
Haugen, E. (1951), 'Directions in Modern Linguistics', *Language* 25: 211–222.
Hauser, M., Chomsky, N., and Fitch, T. (2002), 'The Faculty of Language: What is it, Who has it, and How did it evolve', *Science* 298: 1569–1579.
Heine, E. H. (1870), 'Über trigonometrische Reihen', *Journal für reine angewandte Mathematische* 71: 353–365.
Hilbert, D. (1899), *Grundlagen der Geometrie*, Leipzig: Teubner.
Hilbert, D. (1900), 'Über den Zahlbegriff', *Jahresbericht der Deutschen Mathematiker-Vereinigung* 8: 180–184.
Hilbert, D. (1932[1918]), 'Axiomatisches Denken', reprinted in *Gesammelte Abhandlungen*, Berlin: Springer-Verlag, vol. III, 146–156.
Hilbert, D. (1967a[1927]), 'Die Grundlagen der Mathematik', Abhandlungen aus dem mathematischen Seminar der Hamburgische Universität, 6, 65–85, reprinted in English translation in van Heijenoort 1967: 464–479.
Hilbert, D. (1967b[1904]), 'Über die Grundlagen der Logik und der Arithmetik', Verhandlungen des Dritten Internationalen Mathematiker-Kongress in Heidelberg vom 8 bis 13. August 1904, 174–185, Leipzig: Teubner, reprinted in English translation in van Heijenoort 1967: 130–138.
Hilbert, D. (1998[1922]), 'Neubegründung der Mathematik', Erste Mitteilung, Abhandlungen aus dem mathematischen Seminar der Hamburgische Universität, reprinted in English translation in Mancosu 1998: 198–214.

Hilbert, D., and Bernays, P. (1934–1939), *Grundlagen der Mathematik*, vols. I and II, Berlin: Verlag von Julius Springer.
Hintikka, J. (1995), *From Dedekind to Gödel: Essays on the Development of the Foundations of Mathematics*, London and New York: Kluwer.
Hiorth, F. (1974), *Noam Chomsky: Linguistics and Philosophy*, Oslo, Bergen, Tromsø: Universitetsforlaget.
Hjelmslev, L. (1961[1943]), *Omkring sprogteoriens grundlaeggelse*, reprinted in English translation as *Prolegomena to a Theory of Language* by F. J. Whitfield, Madison: University of Wisconsin Press.
Hockett, C. F. (1953), review of Shannon and Weaver's *The Mathematical Theory of Communication*, *Language* 29: 69–93.
Hockett, C. F. (1955), *A Manual of Phonology*, Chicago: University of Chicago Press.
Hockett, C. F. (1967), *Language, Mathematics and Linguistics*, The Hague: Mouton de Gruyter.
Hockett, C. F. (1968), *The State of the Art*, Janua Linguarum Series, Minor, 73, New York: Cornell University Press.
Hrbacek, K., and Jech, T. (1984), *Introduction to Set Theory*, 2nd edn, New York and Basel: Marcel Dekker, Inc.
Huck, G. J., and Goldsmith, J. A. (1995), *Ideology and Linguistic Theory: Noam Chomsky and the Deep Structure Debates*, New York and London: Routledge.
Huybregts, R., and Riemsdijk, H. V. (1982), *Noam Chomsky on the Generative Enterprise*, New Jersey: Foris Publishers.
Hylton, P. (1990), *Russell, Idealism, and the Emergence of Analytic Philosophy*, Oxford: Oxford University Press.
Hymes, D., and Fought, J. (1981[1975]), *American Structuralism*, The Hague, Paris, and New York: Mouton.
Jech, T. (1991), *Set Theory*, 2nd edn, Berlin and New York: Springer.
Johnson, P. E. (1972), *A History of Set Theory*, Boston: Prindle, Weber, & Schmidt.
Kasher, A. (ed.), (1991), *The Chomskyan Turn*, Oxford: Basil Blackwell.
Katz, J. (1981), *Language and Other Abstract Objects*, Oxford: Basil Blackwood.
Kino, A., Myhill, J., and Vesley, R. E. (eds.) (1970), *Intuitionism and Proof-Theory: Proceedings of the Summer Conference at Buffalo, N.Y., 1968*, Amsterdam: North-Holland.
Kleene, S. (1952), *Introduction to Metamathematics*, Amsterdam: North-Holland.
Kneale, W., and Kneale, M. (1962), *The Development of Logic*, Oxford: Clarendon Press.
Koerner, E. K. (1999), *Linguistic Historiography: Projects and Prospects*, Amsterdam: John Benjamins.
Kreisel, G. (1958), 'Hilbert's Programme', *Dialectica* 12: 346–372.
Kuhn, T. (1962), *The Structure of Scientific Revolutions*, Chicago: University of Chicago Press.
Lagrange, J. L. (1867[1760]), 'Essai d'une nouvelle méthode pour déterminer les maxima et les minima des formules intégrales indéfinies', *Miscellanea Taurinensia* 2: 173–195, reprinted in *Oeuvres*, I (1867), 355–362.

Lakoff, G. (1989), 'Philosophical Speculation and Cognitive Science', *Philosophical Psychology* 2: 55–76.
Lees, R. (1957), review of *Syntactic Structures*, *Language* 33: 375–408.
Leibniz, G. W. (1863a[1686]), 'De geometria recondita et analysi indivisibilum atque infinitorum', *Acta Eruditorum* 5, reprinted in Gerhardt, C. I. (ed.) (1863), *Mathematische Schriften*, Abth. 2, Band III, 226–235.
Leibniz, G. W. (1863b[1695]), Letter to Nieuwentijdt, in Gerhardt, C. I. (ed.) (1863), *Mathematische Schriften*, Abth. 2, Band V, 332–336.
Leibniz, G. W. (1863c[1684]), 'Nova Methodus pro maximis et minimis, itemque tangentibus, quae nec fractas nec irrationales quantitates moratur, et singulare pro illi calculi genus', *Acta Eruditorum* 3: 467–473, reprinted in Gerhardt, C. I. (ed.) (1863), *Mathematische Schriften*, Abth. 2, Band III.
Leibniz, G. W. (1978[1666]), *Dissertatio de Arte Combinatoria*, in Gerhardt, C. I. (ed.) (1875–1890; reprinted 1978), *Die philosophischen Schriften*, vol. IV, Berlin: Weidmannsche Buchhandlung.
Leśniewski, S. (1992a), *Collected Works*, 2 vols., ed. Surma, S. J., et al., Dordrecht, Bristol, and London: Kluwer.
Leśniewski, S. (1992b[1914]), 'Is a Class of Classes not Subordinated to Themselves, Subordinate to Itself?', reprinted in Leśniewski 1992a: 115–128.
Leśniewski, S. (1992c[1927]), 'On the Foundations of Mathematics', reprinted in Leśniewski 1992a: 174–382.
Linsky, L. (1952), *Semantics and the Philosophy of Language*, Urbana: University of Illinois Press.
Luschei, E. C. (1962), *The Logical Systems of Léśniewski*, Amsterdam: North-Holland.
Lyons, J. (1970), *Chomsky*, London: Fontana/Collins.
McCall, S. (ed.), (1967), *Polish Logic: 1920–1939*, Oxford: Oxford University Press.
Mancosu, P. (1998), *From Brouwer to Hilbert*, Oxford: Oxford University Press.
Mandelbrot, B. (1954), 'Structure formelle des textes et communication: deux études', *Word* 10: 1–27.
Manning, K. R. (1975), 'The Emergence of the Weierstrassian Approach to Complex Analysis', *Archive for History of Exact Science* 14: 297–383.
Martin, R. (1999), 'Case, the Extended Projection Principle, and Minimalism', in Epstein and Hornstein 1999: 1–26.
Matthews, P. H. (1993), *Grammatical Theory in the United States from Bloomfield to Chomsky*, Cambridge: Cambridge University Press.
Matthews, P. H. (2001), *A Short History of Structuralist Linguistics*, Cambridge: Cambridge University Press.
Miller, G. A. (1951), *Language and Communication*, New York: McGraw-Hill.
Montague, R. (1970), 'English as a Formal Language', reprinted in Montague 1974: 188–221.
Montague, R. (1974), *Formal Philosophy: Selected Papers of Richard Montague*, ed. R. H. Thomason, New Haven: Yale University Press.
Murray, O. S. (1980), 'Gatekeepers and the "Chomskian Revolution"', *Journal of the History of the Behavioural Sciences* 16: 73–88.

Murray, O. S. (1994), *Theory Groups and the Study of Language in North America: A Social History*, Amsterdam: John Benjamins.

Nagel, T. (1995) *Other Minds: Critical Essays, 1969–1994*, Oxford: Oxford University Press.

Newmeyer, F. J. (1980), *Linguistic Theory in America: The First Quarter-Century of Transformational Grammar*, New York and London: Academic Press.

Newmeyer, F. J. (1986), *Linguistic Theory in America*, 2nd edn, Orlando, Florida: Academic Press.

Newmeyer, F. J. (1996), *Generative Linguistics: A Historical Perspective*, London: Routledge.

Newton, I. (1967[1665]), 'A Method for Finding Theorems Concerning Quaestiones de Maximis et Minimis', in Whiteside, D. T. (ed.), *The Mathematical Papers of Isaac Newton 1664–1666*, Cambridge: Cambridge University Press, vol. I, 272–297.

Newton, I. (1969[1670]), 'De methodis serierum et fluxionum', in Whiteside, D. T. (ed.), *The Mathematical Papers of Isaac Newton 1664–1666*, Cambridge: Cambridge University Press, vol. III, 32–353.

Newton, I. (1972[1687/1726]), *Philosophiae Naturalis Principia Mathematica*, 3rd edn, ed. A. Koyré and B. Cohen; 2 vols., Cambridge: Cambridge University Press.

Orenstein, A. (2002), *W. V. Quine*, Boston, Massachusetts: Acumen Press.

Nunes, J. (1999), 'Linearization of Chains and Phonetic Realization of Chain Links', in Epstein and Hornstein 1999: 217–250.

Otero, C. P. (1994a), 'The Emergence of Transformational Generative Grammar', in Otero 1994b, 1–36.

Otero, C. P. (ed.), (1994b), *Noam Chomsky: Critical Assessments*, 4 vols., New York and London: Routledge.

Peano, G. (1959a[1889]), *Arithmetices Principia Nova Methodo Exposita*, reprinted in Unione Matematica Italiana (eds.), *Opera scelte* 2: 20–55.

Peano, G. (1959b[1891]), 'Principii di Logica Matematica', reprinted in Unione Matematica Italiana (eds.), *Opera scelte* 2: 92–101.

Post, E. (1944), 'Recursively Enumerable Sets of Positive Integers and their Decision Problems', *Bulletin of the American Mathematical Society* 50: 284–316.

Postal, P. M. (2004), *Skeptical Linguistic Essays*, Oxford: Oxford University Press.

Priest, Graham (2001), *An Introduction to Non-Classical Logic*, Cambridge: Cambridge University Press.

Quine, W. V. O. (1940), *Mathematical Logic*, Cambridge, Massachusetts: Harvard University Press.

Quine, W. V. O. (1946), 'Concatenation as a Basis for Arithmetic', *Journal of Symbolic Logic* 11: 105–114.

Quine, W. V. O. (1951), *Mathematical Logic*, revised 2nd edn, Cambridge, Massachusetts: Harvard University Press.

Quine, W. V. O. (1953), *From a Logical Point of View*, Cambridge, Massachusetts: Harvard University Press.

Quine, W. V. O. (1985), *The Time of My Life: An Autobiography*, Cambridge, Massachusetts: MIT Press.

Reichenbach, H. (1947), *Elements of Symbolic Logic*, New York: Macmillan.

Reid, C. (1996), *Hilbert*, New York: Springer-Verlag.
Richardson, A. (1998), *Carnap's Construction of the World: The Aufbau and the Emergence of Logical Positivism*, Cambridge: Cambridge University Press.
Riemann, G. F. B. (1990[1867]), 'Über die Darstellbarkeit einer Function durch eine trigonometrische Reihe', reprinted in *Gesammelte mathematische Werke*, Berlin: Springer, 227–271.
Robinson, A. (1996), *Non-Standard Analysis*, revised edn, Princeton: Princeton University Press.
Rosenbloom, P. C. (1950), *Elements of Mathematical Logic*, New York: Dover.
Russell, B. A. W. (1914), *Our Knowledge of the External World as a Field for Scientific Method in Philosophy*, La Salle: Open Court.
Russell, B. A. W. (1938[1903]), *Principles of Mathematics*, New York: W. W. Norton.
Sapir, E. (1929), 'The Status of Linguistics as a Science', *Language* 5: 207–214.
Schaffer, S. (1997), 'What is Science?', in J. Krige and P. Dominique (eds.), *Science in the Twentieth Century*, London: Harwood Academic Publishers.
Schilpp, P. A. (ed.), (1963), *The Philosophy of Rudolf Carnap*, La Salle: Open Court.
Shannon, C., and Weaver, W. (1949), *The Mathematical Theory of Communication*, Urbana: University of Illinois Press.
Sheynin, O. B. (1988), 'A. A. Markov's Work on Probability', *Archive for the History of Exact Science* 39: 337–377.
Simon, H. A. (1955), 'On a Class of Skew Distribution Functions', *Biometrika* 42: 425–440.
Smith, L. (1986), *Behaviorism and Logical Positivism: A Reassessment of The Alliance*, Stanford: Stanford University Press.
Smith, N. V. (2004), *Chomsky: Ideas and Ideals*, 2nd edn, Cambridge: Cambridge University Press.
Soare, R. I. (1996), 'Computability and Recursion', *Bulletin of Symbolic Logic* 2: 284–321.
Steinberg, D. (1999), 'How the Anti-Mentalist Skeletons in Chomsky's Closet Make Psychological Fiction of his Grammars', in Embleton et al. 1999: 267–282.
Struik, D. J. (ed.), (1969), *A Source Book in Mathematics, 1200–1800*, Cambridge, Massachusetts: Harvard University Press.
Suppe, F. (2000), 'Axiomatization', in Newton-Smith, W. H. (ed.), *A Companion to the Philosophy of Science*, Oxford: Blackwell, 9–12.
Tarski, A. (1944), 'The Semantic Conception of Truth and the Foundation of Semantics', *Philosophy and Phenomenological Research* 4: 341–375.
Tarski, A. (1956a[1931]), 'The Concept of Truth in Formalized Languages', reprinted in English translation in Tarski 1956c: 152–278.
Tarski, A. (1956b[1936]), 'The Establishment of Scientific Semantics', reprinted in English translation in Tarski 1956c: 401–408.
Tarski, A. (1956c), *Logic, Semantics and Metamathematics*, English translation by J. H. Woodger, Oxford: Clarendon Press.
Tomalin, M. (2002), 'The Formal Origins of Syntactic Theory', *Lingua* 112(10): 827–848.

Tomalin, M. (2003), 'Goodman, Quine, and Chomsky: from a Grammatical Point of View', *Linġua* 113(2): 1223–1253.
Tomalin, M. (2004), 'Leonard Bloomfield: Linguistics and Mathematics', *Historiographia Linguistica* 31(1): 105–136.
Turing, A. (1936), 'On Computable Numbers, With an Application to the Entscheidungsproblem', *Proceedings of the London Mathematical Society* 42: 230–265.
Uriagereka, J. (1998), *Rhyme and Reason*, Cambridge, Massachusetts: MIT Press.
Uriagereka, J. (1999), 'Multiple Spell-Out', in Epstein and Hornstein 1999: 251–282.
Van Heijenoort, J. (1967), *From Frege to Gödel: A Source Book in Mathematical Logic, 1879–1931*, Cambridge, Massachusetts: Harvard University Press.
Van Stigt, W. P. (1990), *Brouwer's Intuitionism*, Amsterdam: North-Holland.
Weinberg, J. R. (1936), *An Examination of Logical Positivism*, London: Kegan Paul.
Weiss, A. P. (1925), 'One Set of Postulates for a Behaviourist Psychology', *Psychology Review* 32: 83–87.
Wells, R. (1947), 'Immediate Constituents', *Language* 23: 81–117.
White, M. (1952), 'The Analytic and the Synthetic: An Untenable Divide', in Linsky 1952: 272–286.
Whitehead, A. N. (1898), *A Treatise on Universal Algebra with Applications*, Cambridge: Cambridge University Press.
Whitehead, A. N., and Russell, B. A. W. (1925[1910]), *Principia Mathematica*, 3 vols., Cambridge: Cambridge University Press.
Wilder, R. L. (1952), *Introduction to the Foundations of Mathematics*, New York: John Wiley.
Westfall, R. S. (1980), *Never at Rest: A Biography of Isaac Newton*, Cambridge: Cambridge University Press.
Woléski, J. (1989), *Logic and Philosophy in the Lvov–Warsaw School*, Dordrecht: Kluwer Academic Press.
Young, J. W. (1917), *Foundational Concepts of Algebra and Geometry*, New York: Macmillan Co.
Zipf, G. (1935), *The Psycho-Biology of Language: An Introduction to Dynamic Philology*, Cambridge, Massachusetts: MIT Press.
Zipf, G. (1949), *Human Behavior and the Principle of Least Effort: An Introduction To Human Ecology*, New York: Hafner Publishing Co.

Index

λ-calculus, 61
λ-definability, 61

Aarsleff, H., 201
abstraction, 49, 76, 163
active–passive constructions, 121, 134, 161, 163, 164, 166
Ajdukiewicz, K., 67–72, 88, 103, 105, 126, 129, 130, 184, 204
algebra, 26, 33, 34, 38, 48, 51, 56, 73, 97
algebraic topology, 46
alphabet, 49, 147, 178
America, 11, 33, 44, 77, 78, 101, 102
analysis, 25–28, 31, 38, 39, 201, 202
analysis of language, 106
analytic philosophy, 186
analytic truth, 88, 205
anthropology, 6
anti-mentalism, 17
antinomies, 69
apparent economy, 118
applied mathematics, 2
Aristotle, 46
arithmetic, 21, 28, 31–34, 38, 39, 42, 44, 45, 47, 55, 78, 86, 158
automata theory, 104
automatic speech recognition, 187
auxiliary predicates, 86
axiomatic geometry, 38, 48
axiomatic number theory, 39
axiomatic-deductive method, 125
   and Bloch, 58
   and Bloomfield, 55–57, 93, 177, 184
   and geometry, 38, 39
   and Harwood, 59, 186
   and Hilbert, 203
   and linguistic theory, 54, 60, 64, 73, 106
   and Logicism, 60
   and nineteenth-century mathematics, 27, 28
   and pre-TGG linguistic theories, 19
   and proof theory, 60
   and syntactic theory, 50
   and TGG, 2, 5, 19, 60, 177–179, 186, 188, 203
   and the formal sciences, 3
   and the foundations of mathematics, 51
axioms, 2, 3, 5, 27, 28, 31, 34–36, 39, 41–43, 49, 50, 55–57, 59, 68, 69, 73, 83, 101, 123, 124, 176–178, 188
Ayer, A. J., 204

Bach, E., 4, 5, 7
Baker, G. P., 202
Bar-Hillel, Y.
   and Bloomfield, 105, 106
   and Carnap, 8, 105, 126, 127, 135, 138, 204, 207
   and Categorial Grammar, 71, 72, 203
   and Chomsky, 8, 18, 132, 135, 138, 140
   and discovery procedures, 71
   and distributional procedures, 126
   and formal consequence, 133
   and formal languages, 127
   and Harwood, 58
   and logical syntax, 131
   and logical systems, 54, 88
   and recursion, 54, 65, 66, 168, 184, 191, 193
   and semantics, 127, 128, 135, 136
   and synonymy, 127
   and TGG, 73, 170, 184, 203, 204
   and the axiomatic-deductive method, 184
   and transformations, 127, 161–163, 167, 207
   and truth conditions, 128

on the relationship between logic and
linguistics, 109, 125, 126, 131, 133,
138, 184
Barrow, I., 22
Barsky, R. F., 110–112, 206, 207
behaviourism, 154, 201, 207
Bernoulli, J., 24
biological theory, 1
biology, 6
Birkhoff, G., 26
Bloch, B., 12, 54, 57–59, 67, 102, 175, 178,
184, 203
Bloomfield, L.
and Carnap, 130, 131
and distributional linguistics, 103, 104
and formal languages, 59
and formal syntax, 54, 93, 105
and Formalism, 13, 14, 94, 95, 180
and mathematics, 58
and meaning in linguistic theory, 95, 141,
149
and precision in linguistics, 67
and the axiomatic-deductive method, 54–57,
178, 184, 203
and the foundations of mathematics, 96–101
and the Vienna Circle, 93
influence on Bar-Hillel, 105, 130
influence on Bloch, 58
on linguistics as a science, 57, 198, 208
on the relationship between logic and
linguistics, 88
on the relationship between mathematics
and linguistics, 93, 94, 205
on the relationship between mathematics
and natural language, 56, 57
the influence of Weiss, 56
Bloomfieldians, 7
Bohr, N., 196
Boole, G., 33
Borgström, C. H. J., 106, 107
Bradley, F. H., 33
Brouwer, L. E. J., 44–48, 103
Burali-Forti, C., 32, 34
Burali-Forti Paradox, 32

calculus, 18, 21–28, 55, 202
calculus of individuals, 79, 122, 123, 150, 197,
198
calculus of relations, 37
calculus of variations, 26, 201

Cambridge, 9, 34, 175
Cambridge (Mass.), 78
Cantor, 28–32, 34, 46, 47, 205
Carnap, R., 89
and Bar-Hillel, 138
and Bloomfield, 130, 131
and constructional system theory, 73–77,
79, 151, 204
and formal languages, 89–91, 102, 134
and formal linguistics, 102
and formal syntax, 54, 93, 105
and Formalism, 176, 181
and formation rules, 126, 161, 167, 168, 207
and logical empiricism, 9, 11, 12, 150, 151,
153, 154
and logical epistemology, 78, 79, 87
and logical syntax, 106, 126, 168, 176
and meaning in linguistic theory, 91, 180
and meaning postulates, 129, 130
and metalanguage, 89
and natural languages, 90, 181
and proof theory, 49
and semantics, 128–130
and transformation rules, 127, 133, 134,
162–164, 167, 186, 207
and transformations, 92, 93
criticism of Chomsky, 138
influence on Bar-Hillel, 8, 105, 106, 127,
128, 130, 204, 207
influence on Bloomfield, 93, 94
influence on Chomsky, 111
influence on Goodman, 54
influence on Goodman and Quine, 78, 84
influence on Harris, 104, 132
influence on Hjelmslev, 102
influence on linguistics, 208
influence on Quine, 48, 77, 205
on formation and transformation rules,
90–92, 162, 164
on the relationship between formal and
natural language, 128
on the relationship between linguistics and
logic, 138
on the relationship between syntax and
logic, 126
case, 196
categorial analysis, 72
Categorial Grammar, 70, 72, 103, 126, 184,
203
Cauchy, A. L., 26–28, 55, 177

Cavalieri, 22
Cherry, C. E., 143
Chomsky, N.
   'LSS', 109, 126, 133–137
   'SSA', 121–124, 135, 136, 150, 151, 153, 206
   'TMDL', 145, 147, 148, 178, 207
   and anti-mentalism, 17
   and Bar-Hillel, 18, 138
   and Carnap, 137, 138
   and constructional system theory, 12, 73, 74, 125, 144, 155
   and constructive nominalism, 8, 122, 156, 186, 198, 201
   and discovery procedures, 125, 132, 140, 149, 151, 154, 208
   and empiricism, 185, 207
   and epistemology, 207
   and evaluation procedures, 150, 154, 155
   and finite-state grammars, 145–148
   and formal consequence, 133, 134
   and formal languages, 124, 136
   and formal linguistic theories, 8, 133, 176, 177, 182
   and formal syntax, 53
   and Formalism, 13, 14, 174, 176, 178, 179, 188
   and grammaticality, 148
   and linguistic levels, 156, 157
   and logic, 133, 134, 137, 158, 159
   and logical empiricism, 11, 154, 185
   and logical semantics, 134–136, 141
   and logical syntax and semantics, 8
   and logical systems, 135
   and mathematical linguistics, 15
   and meaning, 132–136, 181
   and P-markers, 164
   and politics, 187
   and predictive grammars, 169
   and rationalism, 207
   and recursion, 137, 171–173, 189–193
   and recursively enumerable sets, 169, 170
   and simplicity, 18, 84, 109, 112–120, 166, 167, 172, 195
   and 'SSA', 8
   and statistical models of language, 141, 145, 148, 149, 207
   and syntactic theory, 206
   and syntax and semantics, 179
   and the autonomy of syntax, 141, 149, 180, 181
   and the axiomatic-deductive method, 177, 178, 188, 203
   and the calculus of individuals, 123, 125, 135
   and the development of TGG, 3, 4, 12, 108, 140
   and the formal sciences, 6, 18, 111, 198, 208
   and the foundations of mathematics, 135
   and the history of linguistics, 7
   and the innateness hypothesis, 185
   and the post-Bloomfieldians, 18, 149, 175
   and the Spec–Head relation, 197
   and transformations, 133, 159–168, 181
   as an aging dictator, 16
   at Harvard, 11, 110
   at MIT, 110, 175
   biographical information, 109, 206
   influence of analytic philosophy, 88
   influence of Bar-Hillel, 12, 67, 140, 170, 184, 204
   influence of Carnap, 111
   influence of Goodman, 9, 14, 109, 112, 113, 117, 118, 121, 152, 156
   influence of Goodman and Quine, 7, 17, 18, 121–123, 150, 153, 159, 185
   influence of Harris, 110, 112, 114, 121, 122, 136
   influence of his mother, 109
   influence of Quine, 9, 112, 118, 133, 135, 153, 158
   influence of White, 133, 136
   influence on contemporary culture, 15
   LSLT, 3, 111, 115, 117, 118, 124, 137, 150, 155–158, 164–166, 170, 172, 173, 176, 177, 181, 184, 195, 206–208
   MMH, 17, 110, 112, 114, 160, 162
   MP, 188–190, 194, 197, 198, 206
   on linguistics as a science, 198
   on the origins of TGG, 1, 5, 6, 8–10
   on the relationship between logic and linguistics, 109, 126, 133, 162
   relationship with Bar-Hillel, 8
   relationship with Goodman, 111
   relationship with Harris, 110, 111
   relationship with Quine, 110, 205
   SS, 4, 149, 178, 203, 207
Chomsky, W. Z., 109
Christianity, 25

Church, A., 15, 49–51, 55, 61, 64
classical sets, 69
cognitive function, 190
competing grammars, 115, 116, 119, 120, 149, 154–156, 185, 194, 195
computability theory, 61, 130, 190–195
computer science, 15, 199
Conant, J. B., 110
concatenation, 78, 86, 117, 157–159
conjectures, 177
conjunction, 34, 36, 41, 42, 65, 86, 92
consistency of axioms, 43
consolidated grammar, 118, 119
constant function, 64
constructional system theory, 114
   and Carnap, 74, 75, 79, 151, 204
   and constructional levels, 204
   and discovery procedures, 124, 144
   and extralogical bases, 77, 80, 112, 117, 118, 158
   and extralogical primitives, 82
   and formal languages, 14
   and Formalism, 122
   and Goodman and Quine, 85
   and linguistic levels, 140, 158
   and logical analysis, 106
   and multigrade relations, 80
   and nominalism, 85, 87, 121
   and simplicity, 80–84, 113, 118, 121, 155, 185, 193
   and syntactic analysis, 121–123
   and syntactic theory, 123, 124, 158, 159
   influence on syntactic theory, 73, 122
   influence on TGG, 9, 12, 14, 17, 19, 117, 125, 131, 140, 151, 154–156, 185, 197, 206
   neglect of in historiographical studies of TGG, 14
   the development of, 19, 54
constructive nominalism, 7, 8, 12, 19, 85, 87, 89, 109, 122, 156, 185, 186, 197, 198
continuity, 47
continuous number line, 28
continuum, 46, 47
contradictions, 32, 43, 69, 102
conversations, 85
conversions, 117–120, 160, 170–173, 181, 196

Copenhagen Circle, 101, 107
copy theory of movement, 196
corpora, 71, 114–116, 118, 120, 121, 124, 132, 150, 154, 155, 168, 169
counterargument, 83
Curry, A., 96

D'Alembert, 26, 27
data, 2, 103, 154, 177
Dauben, J. W., 202
Davis, S., 207
De Morgan, A., 33
declarative, 52
Dedekind, R. J. W., 28, 29, 31, 46, 61
deduction, 3, 27, 35, 36, 55, 91, 102, 130, 132, 152, 179, 186
deep-structure, 199
definienda, 122
definiendum, 37
definition, 27, 41, 55, 63, 77, 91, 102, 117, 128, 129, 140, 156, 176–178
dependence, 39
derivation, 41, 43, 75, 83, 171, 174, 179, 189. 196
derivatives, 23, 25
Descartes, 22
descriptive adequacy, 193
descriptivism, 17
desideratum, 131
differential equations, 201
differentiation, 22–24, 27, 28, 202
discourse analysis, 161
discourse structure, 162
discovery procedures, 19, 71, 104, 124, 140, 149–151, 155, 169, 185, 208
discrete expression, 193
disjunction, 36, 41, 42, 76
distributional linguistics, 103, 127, 128, 176, 183, 204
Dugac, P., 202
Dummett, M. A. A., 202

economy, 14, 80–84, 113, 114, 116, 120, 167, 195, 196, 198
electromagnetism, 34
elegance, 196
Elegant Syntax, 196
elementary syntax, 49
elements, 3, 30, 31, 69, 75–77, 80, 92, 115, 119, 123, 127, 157, 160, 178, 190

empiricism, 7–9, 15, 17–19, 65–67, 84, 87, 123–125, 132, 151–153, 155, 156, 185, 207
epistemology, 74, 75, 89, 153, 207
EPP feature, 197
EST, 188, 199
ethics, 74
Euler, L., 24, 25, 27
Europe, 44, 78, 102
evaluation procedures, 12, 19, 115, 117, 125, 140, 149, 150, 155, 156, 185, 195, 206
Ewald, W., 203
existential operator, 41
explanatory adequacy, 193, 194
explanatory theory, 150
extralogical bases, 118, 124, 158
extralogical postulate, 81
extralogical primitives, 80–82, 153

faculty of language, 190, 191, 194
fallacy, 98, 100
Fermat, P. de, 22
Feyerabend, P., 196
Fine, N., 110
finite alphabets, 178
finite arithmetic, 30, 38
finite classes, 165
finite formulae, 100
finite grammars, 168–171, 193
finite lexicon, 58, 59, 178
finite mathematics, 50, 60, 63, 169, 190, 193
finite proofs, 63, 168, 179
finite sequences, 52, 64, 69
finite sets, 30, 31, 85, 142, 158, 169, 178, 190, 193
finite state grammars, 143, 145–148
finite state machines, 141, 144, 148
finite strings, 123
Fitch, T., 190–193
FLN hypothesis, 190–192
fluxional calculus, 23, 201
formal consequence, 134, 162
formal deduction, 89
formal discourse, 94
formal features, 188, 197
formal grammars, 119–121, 125, 169, 179, 190, 193, 195
formal inference, 43
formal languages
  and concatenation, 78, 158
  and Formalism, 39, 44, 89–91, 102, 128, 203
  and Intuitionism, 45
  and Leibniz, 32
  and logic, 60, 69, 73, 78, 84, 88–90, 153
  and logical syntax, 49
  and Logicism, 33, 68
  and mathematics, 97
  and meaning, 128–129, 207
  and natural languages, 49, 52, 53, 58, 69, 70, 73, 90, 123, 127, 130, 139, 182, 184
  and nominalism, 69, 85, 86, 123
  and science, 90
  and simplicity, 119
  and syntactic theory, 56, 70, 73, 123, 124, 128, 131, 133, 135, 178, 187
  and the axiomatic-deductive method, 56, 59
formal linguistics, 102, 106, 121, 158, 175–177, 193
formal notation, 160, 161
formal proofs, 42
formal relations, 134
formal rules, 90
formal sciences
  and Formalism, 95
  and linguistic theory, 1, 4, 7, 16, 18, 66, 71, 73, 95, 104, 109, 183
  and recursion, 64, 65, 191, 192
  and TGG, 1, 2, 4, 5, 15, 18–19, 140, 159, 174, 187, 188
  and the axiomatic-deductive method, 56
  and the post-Bloomfieldians, 10, 183
  definition of, 2, 3
  in the twentieth century, 21, 54
formal symbols, 41, 43, 50
formal syntax, 49, 53, 54, 86, 89, 91, 93–94, 96, 105, 117, 128, 166, 180
formal systems, 14, 40, 43–45, 49, 50, 52, 58, 65, 73, 80, 89, 91, 95, 102, 128, 137, 178, 179, 186
  and TGG, 5
formal theories, 5, 8, 53, 106, 107, 121, 155, 160, 162, 176, 177, 208
Formalism
  and Bloomfield, 94–96, 101, 104, 183
  and Carnap, 90, 91, 181
  and Chomsky, 122
  and Church, 49, 50
  and formal languages, 52
  and Gödel, 45

and Harris, 103
and Hjelmslev, 102
and Intuitionism, 45
and Logicism, 39, 42
and mathematics, 48
and meaning, 44, 50, 51, 91, 95, 130, 180
and Quine, 49
and recursion, 60, 61, 63, 168
and textbooks, 18
and TGG, 13, 17, 123, 140, 174–177, 180, 181, 186
and the foundations crisis, 18, 21, 32, 38, 40, 45, 183
and the post-Bloomfieldians, 102
and well-formedness, 70
and Wilder, 51
in the twentieth century, 183
formation rules, 92, 126, 163
formula, 40, 41, 43, 82, 100, 101
formulae, 23, 40, 41, 43, 87, 91, 178
Fought, 10, 11, 205
foundations crisis, 21, 29, 47, 51, 54, 94, 96–100, 183
foundations of algebra, 48
foundations of analysis, 21, 22, 25, 28, 177
foundations of arithmetic, 28, 33
foundations of geometry, 34, 38, 39, 44
foundations of logic, 39
foundations of mathematics, 8, 15, 18, 32, 39–40, 45–48, 51, 55, 85, 99, 103, 135, 136, 151
foundations of number theory, 28, 31
foundations of science, 97
Fraenkel, 31
Frank, 74
Frege, 33, 34, 73, 111, 202
French, 65, 66
Friedman, 204
Fries, 71, 126, 205
function, 37, 42, 43, 52, 61–65, 68, 147, 156, 158, 169, 170, 175
function-theoretic grammar, 52
functional categories, 197
fundamental theorem of the calculus, 22

Gassendi, P., 25
general recursive functions, 64
general theory of series, 38
Generalised Phrase Structure Grammar, 12, 206

generative grammar, 1, 6, 11, 16–20, 139, 150, 154, 169, 182, 187–191, 193, 194, 197–200, 206–208
generative procedures, 31, 140
Generative Semantics, 13, 14
geometric intuition, 38
geometry, 34, 39, 48, 55, 56, 58, 97
German, 77, 89, 90
Germany, 33
Gestalt psychology, 76
Gödel, K., 15, 45, 54, 61, 63, 64, 74, 104, 191–193, 203
Gödel's incompleteness theorem, 45, 61
Goldsmith, J. A., 14, 17, 199
Goodman, N.
    and analytic and synthetic truths, 87
    and constructional system theory, 14, 112, 121, 123, 124, 140, 197
    and constructive nominalism, 7, 54, 85–88, 122, 185
    and induction, 9, 87, 152, 155
    and Leonard, 79, 80
    and logical empiricism, 17, 18, 84, 150, 151, 153
    and logical epistemology, 87
    and Quine, 9, 78–80, 84
    and simplicity, 80–84, 116–118, 120, 193, 197
    and the calculus of individuals, 123, 125, 198
    influence of Carnap, 74, 78, 79, 85, 89, 205
    influence on Chomsky, 7, 8, 11, 12, 14, 18, 88, 109–112, 116–118, 121, 122, 150, 154, 159, 185, 186
    influence on Harris, 104
    neglect of in historiographical studies, 8
    rejection of Chomsky, 111
Grabiner, J. V., 26, 202
Graffi, G., 18
grammar, 2, 5, 7, 52, 112, 113, 115, 117, 118, 121, 141, 144, 145, 147, 150, 154, 156, 160, 165, 167–171, 173, 174, 178, 181, 191, 196, 206
grammar construction, 113–116, 127, 142, 150, 154, 156, 159, 169, 197
grammar evaluation, 12, 19, 115, 117, 125, 140, 149, 150, 154–156, 181, 185, 195, 206
grammatical levels, 206

grammatical transformations, 140, 162, 165, 167, 181
grammaticality, 59, 60, 66, 70, 72, 106, 114, 115, 120–122, 145, 147–149, 152, 157, 160, 164, 169, 178–180, 186, 197
Grassmann, H., 33
Grattan-Guinness, I., 44, 202, 203
Grelling, K., 205
Grelling's paradox, 98, 205

Hahn, H., 73, 74
Halle, 143
Hallett, M., 202
Hanfling, O., 204
Harris, R., 14
Harris, Z. S.
  and discovery procedures, 71, 117, 121, 124, 149, 204
  and distributional procedures, 104, 114, 126–127, 146
  and distributional techniques, 121
  and formal languages, 105
  and formal syntax, 54, 103, 105, 107
  and Formalism, 103
  and grammar construction, 113, 114
  and grammatical transformations, 126, 159–164, 166–168, 207
  and linguistic theory, 110
  and mathematics, 6, 104, 107, 175
  and meaning in linguistic theory, 141, 149
  as a structural linguist, 71
  defended by Chomsky, 138
  his 'theoretical nihilism', 110, 113
  influence of Carnap, 104, 105, 162
  influence on Bar-Hillel, 106
  influence on Chomsky, 7, 9, 18, 110, 112, 122, 136, 185
  influence on post-Bloomfieldians, 71
  intellectual development of, 103
  negative attitude towards simplicity, 113, 114
  on logic and linguistics, 131, 159, 162
  relationship with Chomsky, 110, 111
Harvard, 8, 11, 77, 78, 84, 85, 110–112, 151
Harwood, F. W., 54, 58, 59, 67, 88, 163, 164, 167, 184, 186
Haugen, E., 107
Hauser, M., 190–193
Hebrew, 109
Heine, E. H., 29

heterological paradox, 98
heuristic procedure, 83, 120
Heyting, A., 47
hierarchies, 68, 70, 158, 189, 190, 197
hierarchy of types, 122
Hilbert, D., 14, 15, 32, 38–44, 47–50, 61, 63, 89, 91, 98, 102, 160, 203
Hiorth, F., 7, 8, 124
historiography, 7, 16, 17, 183
Hjelmslev, L., 54, 101, 102, 105, 107, 181
Hockett, C. F., 6, 7, 11, 13, 101, 102, 110, 143–145, 148, 169, 175, 198, 207, 208
homonymity, 122, 123, 206
Hrbacek, K., 202
Huck, G. J., 14, 15, 17, 199
Humboldt, 5
Hylton, P., 202
Hymes, D., 10, 11, 205
hypothesis, 97, 187, 191

I-language, 195, 206
illogicality, 28, 34
immediate constituent analysis, 103
immediate dependent, 64
Immediate-Successor, 65
imperfections, 68
implication, 2, 36, 37, 41, 42, 88, 92, 113, 120, 130, 132, 152, 160, 162, 181
incompleteness, 45
induction, 9, 18, 61–64, 151–153, 155, 193
inference, 41, 43, 44, 63, 92, 93, 127, 134, 135, 152, 162, 163, 168
infinite classes, 96, 100, 101
infinite regress, 21
infinite sequence, 31
infinite series, 27
infinite sets, 29–31, 100, 169, 190
infinite structures, 147, 168–171, 173, 174, 190, 193
infinitesimals, 22–26, 202
infinity, 29, 31, 63
informal discourse, 94
information theory, 141, 145
initial function, 64
innateness hypothesis, 187, 194
inscriptional nominalism, 86, 122
integrals, 25
integration, 22, 27, 28, 201, 202
interpretable features, 196
intuition, 42, 43, 45, 85, 117, 169, 176

Intuitionism, 18, 21, 32, 45, 46, 51
irrational numbers, 100
iteration, 171

Jakobson, R., 143
Jech, T., 202
Jena, 73
Joos, M., 102

Kasher, A., 204
Katz, J., 208
kernel, 165, 173, 174
Kleene, S., 15, 50, 51, 54, 55, 61, 63, 65, 203
Kneale, W., 202
Koerner, E., 17, 201
Köhler, 76
Kuhn, T., 16, 110

labels, 190, 196
Lagrange, J. L., 26
Landen, J., 24
language faculty, 194
language of science, 97
Latin, 90
Lees, R., 1–3, 5, 188, 198, 208
Leibniz, 22, 24, 32, 201
Lenneberg, E., 187
Leonard, 80
Leśniewski, S., 67–70, 85, 103
lexical features, 188
lexical items, 189, 190
lexical properties, 189, 197
Lexical-Functional Grammar, 12
lexicalist theory, 197
lexicon, 197
limits, 23, 26, 28, 100, 147
linear grammar, 120, 171
linguistic levels, 115, 117, 140, 156, 157
linguistic theory
    and constructional system theory, 14, 151, 155, 158
    and discovery procedures, 150, 154, 185
    and distribution procedures, 128
    and evaluation procedures, 154
    and explanatory adequacy, 193
    and Formalism, 102, 104, 121, 177
    and linguistic levels, 157, 158
    and logic, 12, 19, 51, 52, 73, 94, 109, 121, 124, 131, 133, 135–137, 158, 162, 176, 184
    and logical empiricism, 9, 151
    and mathematics, 101
    and meaning, 13, 95, 132, 136, 138, 180
    and recursion, 65, 66, 170
    and simplicity, 113, 115, 116, 119, 196
    and stochastic processes, 141, 143, 144
    and syntax and semantics, 18, 179
    and TGG, 1–3, 7, 9, 11, 19, 108, 110, 156
    and the axiomatic-deductive method, 2, 57, 178
    and the formal sciences, 1, 4–7, 54, 183, 200
    and the foundations crisis, 96
    and the post-Bloomfieldians, 6, 10, 110, 176
    and transformations, 127
linguistics, 183–186
    and constructional system theory, 19, 122
    and empirical science, 67
    and Formalism, 5, 60, 89, 101, 102, 107, 176
    and historiography, 13
    and logic, 5, 89, 94, 105–107, 125, 130–134, 136–138, 159, 208
    and mathematics, 5, 6, 19, 54, 57, 93, 94, 96, 103, 175
    and nominalism, 122, 155
    and philosophy, 8
    and psychology, 95
    and recursion, 65
    and semiotics, 102
    and simplicity criteria, 115
    and statistics, 143, 148
    and structuralism, 102
    and the axiomatic-deductive method, 27, 55–57, 60, 177
    and the formal sciences, 16, 21, 32, 48, 73, 95, 105, 106, 198
    and the foundations crisis, 97, 98
    and the post-Bloomfieldians, 151, 176
    at MIT, 16
    Chomsky's introduction to, 110
    distributional linguistics, 104, 110, 127
    structural linguistics, 127
Linsky, L., 133
logic
    and algebra, 33
    and analysis, 26, 27
    and arithmetic, 39
    and constructional system theory, 79
    and Formalism, 39, 49–51, 89, 175, 182
    and inference, 162
    and Intuitionism, 46, 203

228 *Index*

logic (*cont.*)
  and linguistics, 5, 11, 12, 19, 51, 52, 58, 71, 91, 93, 94, 105, 106, 109, 125, 126, 130–132, 136–138, 148, 158, 159, 162, 175, 176, 184, 199
  and Logicism, 33, 35, 36, 38, 39, 42
  and mathematics, 35, 48, 73, 74, 94
  and nominalism, 85
  and operators, 33
  and recursion, 10, 19
  and relations, 33
  and set theory, 33, 122
  and TGG, 5, 6, 8, 60, 148, 151, 159
  and the formal sciences, 2, 7, 18
  and the foundations crisis, 33, 103
  and the Lvov-Warsaw school, 67, 68, 103
  Boolean logic, 33
  classical logic, 2, 33, 46
  conditional logic, 38
  constructional system theory, 84
  fuzzy logic, 38
  in the nineteenth century, 33, 202
  non-classical logic, 38
  origins of, 32, 202
  symbolic logic, 2, 32–35, 38, 48–51, 58, 67, 73, 74, 76, 89, 95, 98, 107, 122, 123, 130, 131, 137, 158, 163, 175, 206
logical analysis, 74, 90, 104, 106, 107, 161
logical arguments, 89
logical axioms, 42, 153
logical constants, 76
logical empiricism, 2, 9, 11, 84, 88, 150, 151, 153, 155, 156, 159, 185
logical epistemology, 74, 75, 78, 79, 87
logical form, 188
logical implication, 134
logical inference, 41, 159, 162
logical operators, 86
logical positivism, 74, 204, 207
logical relations, 93
logical semantics, 8, 69, 126, 129, 132, 135, 141, 184
logical syntax, 3, 8, 12, 18, 19, 48, 49, 52, 69, 73, 77, 78, 88–90, 92, 93, 96, 98, 104–106, 126, 128, 130–132, 134–136, 138, 162, 168, 176, 186, 207
logical systems, 35, 49, 52, 133, 135
Logicism, 18, 21, 32, 33, 38, 42, 45, 51, 60, 94, 186
logistic theory, 102

Lukasiewicz, J., 67, 103
Luschei, E. C., 204, 205
Lvov, 67
Lvov-Warsaw school, 54, 67, 102, 103, 128, 129, 184, 204

machine translation, 187
Maclaurin, C., 24
Mancosu, P., 203
Mandelbrot, 149
Markov, A., 141, 142
Markov process, 142, 144, 146, 148
mathematics
  and algebra, 48
  and analysis, 21, 22, 25
  and Bar-Hillel, 105
  and Bloomfield, 55, 56, 94, 96, 99, 184
  and Chomsky, 6, 9, 110, 151, 175, 182, 199
  and deduction, 35
  and Formalism, 40, 41, 43, 44, 48, 50, 89, 91, 95, 106
  and inference, 43
  and Intuitionism, 45, 46, 203
  and linguistics, 5–7, 10, 11, 54, 56, 93, 94, 96, 97, 101, 102, 175, 183
  and Logicism, 33–36, 38, 39, 68, 94
  and natural language, 56–58, 94, 97, 101
  and philosophy, 34
  and proofs, 27, 41, 42, 62
  and set theory, 31, 40, 96, 100
  and symbols, 102
  and TGG, 5, 8, 18, 123, 135
  and the axiomatic-deductive method, 5, 50, 55, 93
  and the formal sciences, 2, 74
  and the foundations crisis, 18, 29, 32, 33, 40, 47
Matthews, P. H., 13, 14, 16–18, 201, 204, 205, 207, 208
meaning, 2, 3, 13, 44, 50, 68–70, 80, 87, 88, 91, 95, 96, 98, 102, 126–136, 138, 149, 176, 179–181
meaning postulates, 130
mechanical grammars, 155
mechanical procedures, 71, 72, 83, 95, 117, 154
mentalism, 130
mereology, 68, 79, 80
Merge, 189, 190, 195
metalanguage, 65, 89, 128, 129, 178

metamathematics, 10, 13–15, 43, 44, 48–51, 65, 89, 102, 106, 175, 176, 178, 179, 181, 182
metaphysics, 74, 78
Miller, G. A., 143, 187
minimal search, 197
Minsky, M., 110
MIT, 16, 145, 175, 206
models, 142, 145
modern science, 199
Montague, R., 138, 139, 207
Montague Semantics, 138
morphemes, 103, 112, 123, 127, 144, 157, 204
MP, 194, 195, 197, 198
multivariate calculus, 21
Murray, O. S., 12, 16, 17, 205, 206

Nagel, T., 207
natural languages
 adequacy criteria for, 112, 130, 193
 and and constructional system theory, 123
 and Categorial Grammar, 70, 72
 and cognition, 56
 and competing grammars, 154
 and constructional system theory, 14, 121, 122
 and constructive nominalism, 89
 and Esperanto, 53
 and finite-state grammars, 145, 147
 and formal consequence, 134
 and formal languages, 52, 53, 58, 70, 90, 95, 123, 134–136, 139, 147, 178, 182
 and Formalism, 183
 and grammaticality, 60, 120
 and induction, 152, 153
 and inference, 134
 and infinity, 168, 169
 and knowledge, 175
 and linguistic data, 154
 and linguistic levels, 157
 and linguistic theory, 2
 and linguists, 127, 133
 and logic, 38, 51, 52, 58, 59, 73, 89, 94, 97, 126, 130, 131, 137, 158, 159, 175, 176, 184
 and logical epistemology, 74
 and logical syntax, 90, 92, 93, 104
 and mathematics, 45, 56, 94, 97, 101, 104, 105, 142, 183
 and meaning, 69, 87, 132, 134, 141, 181, 182
 and Montague Grammar, 139
 and pragmatics, 69
 and recursion, 67, 169, 170, 174
 and simplicity, 113, 195, 206
 and statistical modelling, 11, 141–149
 and structuralism, 143
 and synonyms, 133
 and TGG, 1, 141, 177
 and the axiomatic-deductive method, 2, 5, 55, 57, 58, 184
 and the foundations crisis, 98, 135, 136
 and the foundations of mathematics, 103
 and the real world, 2
 and transformations, 161–164
 and Zipfian distributions, 141
 complexity of, 134, 156
 English, 52, 53, 139
 French, 65
 German, 90, 207
 interdisciplinary approaches to the study of, 9, 10, 175
 Latin, 90
 Polish, 207
 properties of, 194
natural numbers, 64
natural philosophy, 23
natural science, 199
negation, 36, 37, 41, 42, 76
neologisms, 181
network, 83, 116
Neurath, O., 73, 93
Newmeyer, F. J., 11–13, 16, 207
Newton, 22–24, 201
nominalism, 7, 8, 54, 68, 69, 79, 82, 85–89, 121–124, 155, 158, 201, 208
non-standard analysis, 202
North America, 16
noun phrase, 65, 117
number theory, 21, 26–32, 38, 39, 43, 48, 51, 202
number-theoretic functions, 61–63
numeration, 189

object language, 86
ontology, 68, 75
optimality conditions, 120
ordinal numbers, 31
ordinary language, 175

Orenstein, A., 205
Otero, C. P., 15, 206
Oxford, 9, 175

paradigm, 150
paradoxes, 21, 32, 35, 69, 85, 99, 100, 205
Pascal, 22
passive transformation, 166
passives, 166
Peano, G., 28, 33, 34, 61, 62, 65
Peirce, C., 33
permutation, 165, 166
philosophy, 2, 6, 8, 15, 33, 34, 45, 46, 67, 68, 73, 74, 84, 87, 88, 105, 110, 136, 151–155, 175, 207
philosophy of language, 133
philosophy of mathematics, 104
phonemes, 57, 119, 127, 141, 143, 164, 204
phonemic analysis, 57, 58, 143, 157, 171
phonetic analysis, 143, 158
phonetic features, 98, 99
phonological analysis, 143, 194
phonological form, 188
phrasal projections, 194, 197
phrase, 98
phrase structure grammar, 120, 145, 157, 164, 166, 167, 170, 172–174, 178, 181, 197, 203, 208
phrase structure level, 172
physics, 199
Piattelli-Palmarini, M., 199
Platonism, 85, 86, 197
poetry, 141
Polish logicians, 67, 71, 102
Post, 15, 54, 61, 64, 104, 169, 170
post-Bloomfieldians, 6, 7, 9, 10, 12, 13, 15, 16, 18, 71, 102–104, 107, 136, 141, 143, 146, 149–152, 154, 168, 169, 175, 176, 183, 205, 208
Postal, P., 198, 199
postulates, 55–58, 116, 130, 133, 184
Prague, 77
Prall, D., 78
predicate calculus, 36, 37, 49, 50
predicates, 62, 80, 82, 83, 86, 118, 123
predictive grammars, 169
primitive recursion, 63
primitive recursive functions, 63, 64, 203
primitives, 75, 80, 81, 83, 91, 116, 122, 133, 188, 190, 197

principles, 5, 9, 14, 22, 33, 35, 40, 42, 46, 47, 151, 158, 193, 199
Principles and Parameters, 12, 188, 195, 199, 206
probability, 33, 142, 144, 149
proof theory, 40–45, 48–51, 60, 62, 65, 89, 102, 128, 160, 168, 174, 178–180, 184
proofs, 27, 41–43, 45, 49, 179, 183, 186
propositional calculus, 33, 36, 49
propositional functions, 37, 52
psychology, 6, 7, 11, 56, 58, 67, 76, 92, 95, 112, 130
pure mathematics, 2

qualities, 78, 113, 153
quantification, 33, 48, 87, 118
quantifiers, 49
quantum logic, 38
quantum mechanics, 15
quasi-analysis, 76
Quine, W. V. O.
  and analytic and synthetic truths, 87, 88, 133
  and concatenation, 78, 86, 158
  and constructional system theory, 121, 140, 197
  and constructive nominalism, 85–88, 122
  and Goodman, 78, 80, 84
  and logic, 48, 49, 55
  and logical empiricism, 9, 18, 135, 151, 153
  and logical epistemology, 87
  and logical syntax, 78
  and meaning, 135
  and simplicity, 80, 81, 116–118, 197
  and the Vienna Circle, 77
  his autobiography, 205
  his Ph.D., 77
  influence of Carnap, 74, 77–79, 85, 89
  influence on Chomsky, 7, 8, 12, 14, 18, 88, 110, 112, 118, 150, 153, 154, 159, 185, 186
  influence on Harris, 105
  neglect of in historiographical studies, 8
  relationship with Chomsky, 110, 111

rational numbers, 28
rationalism, 7, 9, 17, 88, 154, 195, 207
real economy, 118
real numbers, 39, 47
recursion, 19, 43, 61–63, 65, 66, 96, 167, 168, 171–173, 188, 190–193

Recursion Convention, 192
recursive components, 60, 64, 169–174, 190, 197
recursive definitions, 19, 62–67, 106, 131, 137, 140, 168, 170, 184, 186, 191, 193
recursive function theory, 10, 43, 50, 54, 60–65, 67, 73, 96, 104, 168, 169, 174, 175, 191–193
recursive rules, 12, 19, 170–174
recursive steps, 169, 189
recursively enumerable languages, 174
recursively enumerable sets, 61, 64, 168–170
reductionism, 157
Reichenbach, H., 51, 52, 105
relativity theory, 15
Richardson, A., 204
Rieger, 208
Riemann, G. F. B., 29
rigorisation, 18, 29, 55, 67
rigour, 2, 7, 26–28, 55, 64, 107, 137
Rosenbloom, P. C., 52
Rosenfield, 208
Russell, B., 34–39, 42, 48, 49, 60, 67, 69, 70, 76, 98, 111, 122, 205
Russell's paradox, 68, 98
Russia, 109

Sapir, E., 103, 104, 198, 208
Saussure, 102
Schaffer, S., 201
schemata, 64, 203
scheme, 71, 85, 153
Schlick, M., 74, 77, 93
Schröder, E., 33
Schnitt, 28
Schützenberger, M., 187
science, 6, 40, 57, 65, 74, 89, 90, 94, 97, 104, 130, 153, 185, 192, 198–200
science of language, 55
scientific language, 97
scientific method, 3, 186
scientific theory, 2, 9, 16, 90, 116, 151, 158
self-reference, 35, 41, 62, 96, 98, 99, 190, 193, 205
semantic, 70
semantics, 3, 18, 19, 68, 70, 95, 96, 102, 106, 121, 126, 128–130, 134–136, 138, 141, 149, 179–181, 183, 186, 194, 205
semiotics, 102
sense data, 76, 153

sentence, 52, 53, 58, 60, 65, 66, 70–72, 87, 88, 91–94, 117, 128, 129, 145–148, 159, 160, 164, 166, 173, 178, 180, 186
sentence generation, 179
sentential calculus, 68, 103
set theory, 18, 21, 29–37, 39, 40, 46–48, 50, 51, 60, 68–70, 86, 96, 98, 100, 101, 122, 202, 203, 205
sets, 30–32, 34, 47, 64, 69, 100, 123, 134, 157, 165, 168, 169, 197
Shannon, C., 141–146, 148
Sheynin, O. B., 141
similarity relations, 76, 124
simplicity, 185
  and constructional system theory, 9, 12, 80–84, 116, 118, 193
  and linguistic theory, 9, 12, 113, 115–117, 130, 196
  and recursion, 197
  and TGG, 109, 113–120, 151, 155, 156, 166, 171, 193–195
  simplicity criteria, 2, 14, 18, 19, 59, 81, 82, 87, 106, 112–121, 125, 149, 155, 156, 166, 167, 171, 172, 185, 193–195, 197, 198, 206
  theory-external, 195
  theory-internal, 81, 84, 113, 121, 132, 195–197, 206
Skolem, 103
Smith, L., 207
Smith, N. V., 206
Soare, R. I., 192
sociology, 130
solipsism, 46
spatial intuition, 38
Spec–Head, 197
speech forms, 97, 100
spell-out, 196
statistical modelling, 3, 11, 141, 143–145, 148, 149
statisticians, 141
Steinberg, D., 17
Stevenson, C., 78
stochastic grammars, 140, 141, 143–145, 143, 149
stochastic processes, 19, 141–143, 145, 148
structural linguistics, 11, 18, 71, 72, 95, 111, 125, 127, 130, 138, 143
structuralism, 10
Struik, D. J., 201

subject-predicate analysis, 33, 52
subsets, 30, 32, 58–60, 90, 165, 176
substrings, 181
successor function, 64
Suppe, F., 201
surface-structure, 199
syllables, 141
symbols, 45, 49, 50, 56, 72, 91, 92, 95, 103, 106, 123, 142, 145, 160, 164, 165, 176, 179
synonymy, 88, 127, 133, 134, 136
syntactic categories, 164
syntactic classes, 124
syntactic objects, 189, 190, 196
syntactic theory, 197
  and constructional system theory, 73, 112–114, 121, 123–125, 140
  and constructive nominalism, 122, 123, 186
  and discovery procedures, 154
  and empiricism, 17, 156
  and explanatory adequacy, 193
  and Formalism, 44, 122, 136, 175, 177, 179–182, 184, 186
  and induction, 13
  and logic, 8, 69, 70, 73, 89, 91, 109, 114, 184
  and logical empiricism, 77
  and logical epistemology, 74
  and mathematics, 10, 11, 14, 21, 22, 58, 105
  and nominalism, 19, 86
  and philosophy, 15
  and recursion, 12, 60, 61, 64, 66, 67, 168, 169, 184
  and simplicity, 117, 132
  and stochastic processes, 142
  and TGG, 4, 6, 10, 11, 16, 108, 111, 114, 140, 149
  and the axiomatic-deductive method, 58, 60, 184, 188
  and the formal sciences, 1, 4, 16, 19, 109, 199
  and the post-Bloomfieldians, 10, 12
  and transformations, 92, 140, 164
  categorial grammar, 70, 72, 126
  generative grammar, 188
syntacticians, 131, 141, 168
syntax, 70, 90, 91, 95, 126, 129, 132, 138, 140, 141, 143–145, 149, 161, 163, 169, 179, 180, 186, 191, 207, 208
synthetic truth, 205

Tarski, A., 67, 78, 85, 105, 129, 130, 204, 207
tautology, 36, 88, 129
Tawardowski, K., 67, 68
Taylor, B., 24, 27
terminal symbols, 164
TGG
  and Bar-Hillel, 184, 203
  and constructional system theory, 14, 73, 125
  and constructive nominalism, 8, 12, 197
  and discovery procedures, 71, 124
  and Goodman, 185
  and induction, 152
  and logical empiricism, 155, 159
  and logical syntax, 73, 105
  and meaning, 91, 181
  and Montague Grammar, 139
  and previous syntactic theories, 5
  and recursion, 60, 64, 67, 140, 168–170, 172–175, 190
  and simplicity, 14, 59, 84, 117, 120, 121, 185, 193–195, 206
  and the axiomatic-deductive method, 5, 60, 125, 177, 178, 203
  and the formal sciences, 2, 15, 19, 96, 174, 176, 186, 187
  and the history of ideas, 6
  and the post-Bloomfieldians, 7, 10–13, 16, 18, 169
  and transformations, 91, 93, 140, 159, 163–168
  as a scientific theory, 1, 4, 16, 198, 199
  as an explanatory theory, 150
  Chomsky on the origins of, 8, 10, 151
  definition of, 3
  Goodman's knowledge of, 111
  Harris' attitude towards, 111
  Hockett on the origins of, 6
  in the 1960s, 13, 14
  influence of analytic philosophy, 88
  influence of Carnap, 104, 186
  influence of Formalism, 50, 140, 174, 179, 180, 186, 188
  influence of logic, 8
  influence of Logicism, 60
  influence of Quine, 78, 88
  influence of the formal sciences, 4, 5, 18, 19, 21
  influence of White, 186

other histories of, 2, 4–8, 12–17, 186, 187
reception of, 2
the definition of, 4, 108
the development of, 1, 4, 17, 21, 54, 102, 107, 108, 140, 183, 186–188, 195, 198
the reception of, 1
theorems, 2, 3, 5, 26, 27, 31, 32, 45, 50, 63, 81, 103, 123, 124, 178
theoretical syntax, 49, 50
theory construction, 1
theory of descriptions, 163
theory of functions, 25, 27
theory of logical types, 35, 36, 68, 70, 122, 202, 205
theory of meaning, 135, 180
theory of reference, 135
theory of relations, 76
theory of simplicity, 84
theory-internal economy, 113, 114, 195
theory-internal simplicity, 19, 81, 84, 121, 132, 193–197, 206
thought and language, 45
traditional grammars, 107
transfinite arithmetic, 31, 32, 38, 42
transfinite set theory, 29
transformational level, 157, 164
transformations, 12, 19, 90–93, 102, 119–121, 126, 127, 133, 140, 145, 159–168, 173, 174, 181, 186, 207
translation, 89, 126, 137, 168, 176, 204, 207
trigonometric functions, 29
truth-conditional semantics, 2, 128, 129, 139, 207
Turing, A., 61, 104, 191, 192
Turing computable functions, 192
Turing machine, 191, 192
Turing Thesis, 192

UG, 4, 195, 206
ungrammaticality, 59, 60, 66, 148
universal operator, 41

Van Stigt, W. P., 46, 203
verb phrase, 117
verbs, 56, 65, 143
verifiability, 49, 180
Vienna, 67, 73, 74, 77, 205
Vienna Circle, 67, 73, 74, 77, 89, 93, 94, 98, 204

Warsaw, 68, 207
Warsaw-Lvov school, 130
Weaver, 141–144, 148, 207
Weierstrass, K., 28, 46, 202
Weiss, A. P., 56, 203
well-formedness, 70, 179, 180
well-ordering, 100
Wells, R., 102–105, 175
Wertheimer, 76
Weyl, H., 46
wh-questions, 166
White, M., 87, 88, 110, 133, 135
Whitehead, A. N., 15, 34–39, 42, 60, 67–69, 76, 77, 111, 122, 202, 205
Wilder, R. L., 51, 55
Wittgenstein, 111
Woleński, J., 204
word formation, 53

X-bar theory, 194, 197, 199

yes-or-no questions, 166
Young, J. W., 48, 51, 55

Zermelo, E., 31
Zipf, G., 141

For EU product safety concerns, contact us at Calle de José Abascal, 56–1°, 28003 Madrid, Spain or eugpsr@cambridge.org.

www.ingramcontent.com/pod-product-compliance
Ingram Content Group UK Ltd.
Pitfield, Milton Keynes, MK11 3LW, UK
UKHW012212030426
469672UK00010B/224